VISIT US AT

www.syngress.com

Syngress is committed to publishing high-quality books for IT Professionals and delivering those books in media and formats that fit the demands of our customers. We are also committed to extending the utility of the book you purchase via additional materials available from our Web site.

SOLUTIONS WEB SITE

To register your book, visit www.syngress.com/solutions. Once registered, you can access our solutions@syngress.com Web pages. There you may find an assortment of value-added features such as free e-books related to the topic of this book, URLs of related Web sites, FAQs from the book, corrections, and any updates from the author(s).

ULTIMATE CDs

Our Ultimate CD product line offers our readers budget-conscious compilations of some of our best-selling backlist titles in Adobe PDF form. These CDs are the perfect way to extend your reference library on key topics pertaining to your area of expertise, including Cisco Engineering, Microsoft Windows System Administration, CyberCrime Investigation, Open Source Security, and Firewall Configuration, to name a few.

DOWNLOADABLE E-BOOKS

For readers who can't wait for hard copy, we offer most of our titles in downloadable Adobe PDF form. These e-books are often available weeks before hard copies, and are priced affordably.

SYNGRESS OUTLET

Our outlet store at syngress.com features overstocked, out-of-print, or slightly hurt books at significant savings.

SITE LICENSING

Syngress has a well-established program for site licensing our e-books onto servers in corporations, educational institutions, and large organizations. Contact us at sales @syngress.com for more information.

CUSTOM PUBLISHING

Many organizations welcome the ability to combine parts of multiple Syngress books, as well as their own content, into a single volume for their own internal use. Contact us at sales@syngress.com for more information.

SYNGRESS®

SYNGRESS®

VIRTUALIZATION WITH XEN™
INCLUDING

XenEnterprise,™
XenServer,™ and
XenExpress™

David E. Williams   Technical Editor

Juan Garcia

Foreword by Simon Crosby
CTO and Founder, XenSource

SYNGRESS®

CONTAINS
XENEXPRESS™

Syngress Media®, Syngress®, "Career Advancement Through Skill Enhancement®," "Ask the Author UPDATE®," and "Hack Proofing®," are registered trademarks of Elsevier, Inc. "Syngress: The Definition of a Serious Security Library"™, "Mission Critical™," and "The Only Way to Stop a Hacker is to Think Like One™" are trademarks of Elsevier, Inc. Brands and product names mentioned in this book are trademarks or service marks of their respective companies.

KEY	SERIAL NUMBER
001	HJIRTCV764
002	PO9873D5FG
003	829KM8NJH2
004	BPOQ48722D
005	CVPLQ6WQ23
006	VBP965T5T5
007	HJJJ863WD3E
008	2987GVTWMK
009	629MP5SDJT
010	IMWQ295T6T

PUBLISHED BY
Syngress Publishing, Inc.
Elsevier, Inc.
30 Corporate Drive
Burlington, MA 01803

Virtualization with Xen™: Including XenEnterprise™, XenServer™, and XenExpress™

Printed in the United States of America
1 2 3 4 5 6 7 8 9 0
ISBN: 978-1-59749-167-9

Publisher: Amorette Pedersen
Acquisitions Editor: Andrew Williams
Technical Editor: David E. Williams
Cover Designer: Michael Kavish

Project Manager: Gary Byrne
Page Layout and Art: Patricia Lupien
Copy Editors: Audrey Doyle, Mike McGee
Indexer: Julie Kawabata

For information on rights, translations, and bulk sales, contact Matt Pedersen, Commercial Sales Director and Rights, at Elsevier; email m.pedersen@elsevier.com.

Acknowledgments

Syngress would like to thank Simon Crosby, Ian Pratt, Roger Klorese, Aimee Francioni, Leo Zarkhin, and the rest of the team at XenSource for your support and guidance throughout the development of this project. We could not have done it without you.

Lead Author

David E. Williams is a principal at Williams & Garcia, LLC, a consulting practice based in Atlanta, GA, specializing in effective enterprise infrastructure solutions. He specializes in the delivery of advanced solutions for x86 and x64 environments. Because David focuses on cost containment and reduction of complexity, virtualization technologies have played a key role in his recommended solutions and infrastructure designs. David has held several IT leadership positions in various organizations, and his responsibilities have included the operations and strategy of Windows, open systems, mainframe, storage, database, and data center technologies and services. He has also served as a senior architect and an advisory engineer for Fortune 1000 organizations, providing strategic direction on technology infrastructures for new enterprise-level projects.

David studied Music Engineering Technology at the University of Miami, and he holds MCSE+I, MCDBA, VCP, and CCNA certifications. When not obsessed with corporate infrastructures, he spends his time with his wife and three children.

Contributors

Kris Buytaert is Founder and CTO of X-Tend. He is a longtime Linux, Security, and Open Source consultant. He has consulting and development experience with multiple enterprise-level clients and government agencies. In addition to his high-level technical experience, he is also a team leader who likes to deliver his projects on time. He is a contributor to the Linux Documentation Project and author of various technical publications. Kris is a Red Hat Certified Engineer and is currently the maintainer of the openMosix HOWTO Web site. Kris is also a frequent speaker at Linux and OpenSource conferences. He is currently focusing on Linux clustering (both HA and HPC), virtualization, and large infrastructure management.

Juan R. Garcia is a Principal Consultant at Williams & Garcia, LLC. He provides strategic and technical consulting in legacy systems migrations, enterprise architecture, disaster recover planning, and enterprise IT resource consolidation to Williams & Garcia's customers. He specializes in open systems (UNIX/Linux), virtualization technologies (VMware, Xen, and AIX 5L), storage solutions, and RDMBS technologies. Juan's previous positions include Solutions Architect for Bellsouth, Senior Enterprise Architect for John H. Harland Co., and Technical Manager for Sun Professional Services.

Rami Rosen (B.Sc, Computer Science, Technion—Israel High Institute of Technology) is working as a Linux and Open Solaris kernel programmer accompanying advanced networking and security projects. His background includes positions in Ethernet switching and Avionic operating system start-ups. His specialities include virtualization technologies and kernel networking internals. His articles are occasionally published in the *Linux Journal* and the lwn.net Web site.

Foreword Contributor

Simon Crosby is an industry evangelist for the Xen™ open source hypervisor and CTO of XenSource Inc. In this position, he is responsible for XenEnterprise R&D, technology leadership, and product management. He also maintains a close affiliation to the Xen project run by Ian Pratt, the founder of XenSource. Prior to XenSource, Simon was a principal engineer at Intel, where he led strategic research in distributed autonomic computing, platform security, and trust. Before joining Intel, Simon founded CPlane Inc., a network optimization software vendor, and held a variety of executive roles while there, including president & CEO, chairman, and CTO. Prior to his position at CPlane, Simon was a tenured faculty member at the University of Cambridge, U.K., where he led research on network performance and control, and multimedia operating systems. He is an author of more than 35 research papers and patents on a number of data center and networking topics, including security, network and server virtualization, and resource optimization and performance. Simon is a frequent speaker on the topic of enterprise-grade virtualization with open source technologies, and he has most recently been a presenter at such well-known industry events as LinuxWorld, Interop, and the Server Blade Summit.

Contents

Foreword

The open source Xen project, led by Ian Pratt of the University of Cambridge and XenSource Inc., will arguably have a greater impact on the enterprise software industry than Linux has had. The Xen hypervisor is a lightweight, high-performance, secure virtualization platform that is now collaboratively developed by more than 20 of the industry's largest enterprise IT vendors as an open industry standard for virtualization. Its architecture has tremendous advantages over existing virtualization technologies: It has broad hardware support through its reuse of existing operating systems such as Linux to safely virtualize I/O for other guests; it offers superb resource partitioning for performance isolation and security; and it can be implemented either as a virtualization platform or as an integrated component within an operating system. Xen has been ported to a wide range of hardware architectures, including x86, x86_64, the Intel Itanium, IBM's PowerPC, the SGI Altix, and the ARM 9. It also is ideally suited to hardware-accelerated virtualization. For these reasons, and because Xen is freely available in source code form, every major OS vendor has either adopted Xen or the Xen architecture as a core component of the next major OS release for the x86 platform.

As a catalyst of change in the IT industry, the Xen project needs to scale its knowledge and skill base so that a competent IT pro can easily get a handle on the technology and how to deploy and use it. Cool technology can be adopted only as fast as human users can acquire the understanding and skills to use it. Perhaps more important, however, is the fact that the Xen project relies on the innovation of the community to continue the development of its feature set. It is therefore a great pleasure and also a great relief to introduce this timely, thorough, and highly accessible guide to the art of Xen virtualization. This book demystifies Xen by placing it in a practical context that any IT pro who wants to get something working will immediately understand, while also providing a thorough grounding in the architecture and implementation of the hypervisor. It also takes an important step beyond the basics of Xen by offering a detailed tutorial on how to use the definitive platform implementation of Xen, XenEnterprise from XenSource. Although enthusiasts may want to dig into Xen by building it from source, most readers will be delighted to find included with this book a CD containing the powerful free XenExpress bare-metal hypervisor from XenSource ready to install for production virtualization of Linux and Windows guests.

It is my hope that this book will achieve two aims: encourage a new generation of contributors to the Xen project and foster broad adoption of the Xen hypervisor as a ubiquitous open standard for virtualization.

—Simon Crosby
CTO and Founder
XenSource Inc.

About the CDs

This book includes two CDs to help you consolidate Windows, Linux, or mixed deployment with XenExpress 3.2. This free, production-ready virtualization platform enables you to quickly get started with Xen virtualization. With XenExpress you can host up to four virtual servers running Linux or Windows (Intel VT or AMD-V hardware-assist virtualization technology is required for Windows) on a broad range of standard server hardware. XenExpress supports dual-socket servers with up to 4 GB of RAM, offering you all of the base performance, tools, and easy-to-use features of XenEnterprise. Easily installed and seamlessly upgradable to XenEnterprise or XenServer, XenExpress is the ideal on-ramp to Xen.

## Chapter 1

An Introduction to Virtualization

Solutions in this chapter:

- **What Is Virtualization?**
- **Why Virtualize?**
- **How Does Virtualization Work?**
- **Types of Virtualization**
- **Common Use Cases for Virtualization**

☑ **Summary**

☑ **Solutions Fast Track**

☑ **Frequently Asked Questions**

Introduction

Virtualization is one of those buzz words that has been gaining immense popularity with IT professionals and executives alike. Promising to reduce the ever-growing infrastructure inside current data center implementations, virtualization technologies have cropped up from dozens of software and hardware companies. But what exactly is it? Is it right for everyone? And how can it benefit your organization?

Virtualization has actually been around more than three decades. Once only accessible by the large, rich, and prosperous enterprise, virtualization technologies are now available in every aspect of computing, including hardware, software, and communications, for a nominal cost. In many cases, the technology is freely available (thanks to open-source initiatives) or included for the price of products such as operating system software or storage hardware.

Well suited for most inline business applications, virtualization technologies have gained in popularity and are in widespread use for all but the most demanding workloads. Understanding the technology and the workloads to be run in a virtualized environment is key to every administrator and systems architect who wishes to deliver the benefits of virtualization to their organization or customers.

This chapter will introduce you to the core concepts of server, storage, and network virtualization as a foundation for learning more about Xen. This chapter will also illustrate the potential benefits of virtualization to any organization.

What Is Virtualization?

So what exactly is virtualization? Today, that question has many answers. Different manufacturers and independent software vendors coined that phrase to categorize their products as tools to help companies establish virtualized infrastructures. Those claims are not false, as long as their products accomplish some of the following key points (which are the objectives of any virtualization technology):

- Add a layer of abstraction between the applications and the hardware
- Enable a reduction in costs and complexity
- Provide the isolation of computer resources for improved reliability and security
- Improve service levels and the quality of service

- Better align IT processes with business goals
- Eliminate redundancy in, and maximize the utilization of, IT infrastructures

While the most common form of virtualization is focused on server hardware platforms, these goals and supporting technologies have also found their way into other critical—and expensive—components of modern data centers, including storage and network infrastructures.

But to answer the question "What is virtualization?" we must first discuss the history and origins of virtualization, as clearly as we understand it.

The History of Virtualization

In its conceived form, virtualization was better known in the 1960s as time sharing. Christopher Strachey, the first Professor of Computation at Oxford University and leader of the Programming Research Group, brought this term to life in his paper *Time Sharing in Large Fast Computers*. Strachey, who was a staunch advocate of maintaining a balance between practical and theoretical work in computing, was referring to what he called multiprogramming. This technique would allow one programmer to develop a program on his console while another programmer was debugging his, thus avoiding the usual wait for peripherals. Multiprogramming, as well as several other groundbreaking ideas, began to drive innovation, resulting in a series of computers that burst onto the scene. Two are considered part of the evolutionary lineage of virtualization as we currently know it—the Atlas and IBM's M44/44X.

The Atlas Computer

The first of the supercomputers of the early 1960s took advantage of concepts such as time sharing, multiprogramming, and shared peripheral control, and was dubbed the Atlas computer. A project run by the Department of Electrical Engineering at Manchester University and funded by Ferranti Limited, the Atlas was the fastest computer of its time. The speed it enjoyed was partially due to a separation of operating system processes in a component called the supervisor and the component responsible for executing user programs. The supervisor managed key resources, such as the computer's processing time, and was passed special instructions, or extracodes, to help it provision and manage the computing environment for the user program's instructions. In essence, this was the birth of the hypervisor, or virtual machine monitor.

In addition, Atlas introduced the concept of virtual memory, called one-level store, and paging techniques for the system memory. This core store was also logically separated from the store used by user programs, although the two were integrated. In many ways, this was the first step towards creating a layer of abstraction that all virtualization technologies have in common.

The M44/44X Project

Determined to maintain its title as the supreme innovator of computers, and motivated by the competitive atmosphere that existed, IBM answered back with the M44/44X Project. Nested at the IBM Thomas J. Watson Research Center in Yorktown, New York, the project created a similar architecture to that of the Atlas computer. This architecture was first to coin the term *virtual machines* and became IBM's contribution to the emerging time-sharing system concepts. The main machine was an IBM 7044 (M44) scientific computer and several simulated 7044 virtual machines, or 44Xs, using both hardware and software, virtual memory, and multiprogramming, respectively.

Unlike later implementations of time-sharing systems, M44/44X virtual machines did not implement a complete simulation of the underlying hardware. Instead, it fostered the notion that virtual machines were as efficient as more conventional approaches. To nail that notion, IBM successfully released successors of the M44/44X project that showed this idea was not only true, but could lead to a successful approach to computing.

CP/CMS

A later design, the IBM 7094, was finalized by MIT researchers and IBM engineers and introduced Compatible Time Sharing System (CTSS). The term "compatible" refers to the compatibility with the standard batch processing operating system used on the machine, the Fortran Monitor System (FMS). CTSS not only ran FMS in the main 7094 as the primary facility for the standard batch stream, but also ran an unmodified copy of FMS in each virtual machine in a background facility. The background jobs could access all peripherals, such as tapes, printers, punch card readers, and graphic displays, in the same fashion as the foreground FMS jobs as long as they did not interfere with foreground time-sharing processors or any supporting resources.

MIT continued to value the prospects of time sharing, and developed Project MAC as an effort to develop the next generation of advances in time-sharing technology, pressuring hardware manufacturers to deliver improved platforms for their work. IBM's response was a modified and customized version of its System/360

(S/360) that would include virtual memory and time-sharing concepts not previously released by IBM. This proposal to Project MAC was rejected by MIT, a crushing blow to the team at the Cambridge Scientific Center (CSC), whose only purpose was to support the MIT/IBM relationship through technical guidance and lab activities.

The fallout between the two, however, led to one of the most pivotal points in IBM's history. The CSC team, lead by Norm Rassmussen and Bob Creasy, a defect from Project MAC, contributed to the development of CP/CMS. In the late 1960s, the CSC developed the first successful virtual machine operating system based on fully virtualized hardware, the CP-40. The CP-67 was released as a reimplementation of the CP-40, as was later converted and implemented as the S/360-67 and later as the S/370. The success of this platform won back IBM's credibility at MIT as well as several of IBM's largest customers. It also led to the evolution of the platform and the virtual machine operating systems that ran on them, the most popular being VM/370. The VM/370 was capable of running many virtual machines, with larger virtual memory running on virtual copies of the hardware, all managed by a component called the virtual machine monitor (VMM) running on the real hardware. Each virtual machine was able to run a unique installation of IBM's operating system stably and with great performance.

Other Time-Sharing Projects

IBM's CTSS and CP/CMS efforts were not alone, although they were the most influential in the history of virtualization. As time sharing became widely accepted and recognized as an effective way to make early mainframes more affordable, other companies joined the time-sharing fray. Like IBM, those companies needed plenty of capital to fund the research and hardware investment needed to aggressively pursue time-sharing operating systems as the platform for running their programs and computations. Some other projects that jumped onto the bandwagon included:

- **Livermore Time-Sharing System (LTSS)** Developed by the Lawrence Livermore Laboratory in the late 1960s as the operating system for the Control Data CDC 7600 supercomputers. The CDC 7600 running LTSS took over the title of the world's fastest computer, trumping on the Atlas computer, which suffered from a form of trashing due to inefficiencies in its implementation of virtual memory.

- **Cray Time-Sharing System (CTSS)** (This is a different CTSS; it should not be confused with IBM's CTSS.) Developed for the early lines of Cray supercomputers in the early 1970s. The project was engineered by the Los Alamos Scientific Laboratory in conjunction with the Lawrence Livermore Laboratory, and stemmed from the research that Livermore had already done with the successful LTSS operating system. Cray X-MP computers running CTSS were used heavily by the United States Department of Energy for nuclear research.

- **New Livermore Time-Sharing System** (NLTSS) The last iteration of CTSS, this was developed to incorporate recent advances and concepts in computers, such as new communication protocols like TCP/IP and LINCS. However, it was not widely accepted by users of the Cray systems and was discontinued in the late 1980s.

Virtualization Explosion of the 1990s and Early 2000s

While we have discussed a summarized list of early virtualization efforts, the projects that have launched since those days are too numerous to reference in their entirety. Some have failed while others have gone on to be popular and accepted technologies throughout the technical community. Also, while efforts have been pushed in server virtualization, we have also seen attempts to virtualize and simplify the data center, whether through true virtualization as defined by the earlier set of goals or through infrastructure sharing and consolidation.

Many companies, such as Sun, Microsoft, and VMware, have released enterprise-class products that have wide acceptance, due in part to their existing customer bases. However, Xen threatens to challenge them all with its approach to virtualization. Being adopted by the Linux community and now being integrated as a built-in feature to most popular distributions, Xen will continue to enjoy a strong and steady increase in market share. Why? We'll discuss that later in the chapter. But first, back to the question: What is virtualization?

Configuring & Implementing...

Evolution of the IBM LPAR— More than Just Mainframe Technology

IBM has had a long history of Logical Partitions, or LPARs, on its mainframe product offerings, from System390 through present-day System z9 offerings. However, IBM has extended the LPAR technology beyond the mainframe, introducing it to its UNIX platform with the release of AIX 5L. Beginning with AIX 5L Version 5.1, administrators could use the familiar Hardware Management Console (HMC) or the Integrated Virtualization Manager to create LPARs with virtual hardware resources (dedicated or shared). With the latest release, AIX 5L Version 5.3, combined with the newest generation of System p with POWER5 processors, additional mainframe-derived virtualization features, such as micro-partitioning CPU resources for LPARs, became possible.

IBM's LPAR virtualization offerings include some unique virtualization approaches and virtual resource provisioning. A key component of what IBM terms the Advanced POWER Virtualization feature is the Virtual I/O Server. Virtual I/O servers satisfy part of the VMM, called the POWER Hypervisor, role. Though not responsible for CPU or memory virtualization, the Virtual I/O server handles all I/O operations for all LPARs. When deployed in redundant LPARs of their own, Virtual I/O servers provide a good strategy to improve availability for sets of AIX 5L or Linux client partitions, offering redundant connections to external Ethernet or storage resources.

Among the I/O resources managed by the Virtual I/O servers are:

- **Virtual Ethernet** Virtual Ethernet enables inter-partition communication without the need for physical network adapters in each partition. It allows the administrator to define point-to-point connections between partitions. Virtual Ethernet requires a POWER5 system with either IBM AIX 5L Version 5.3 or the appropriate level of Linux and an HMC to define the Virtual Ethernet devices.

- **Virtual Serial Adapter (VSA)** POWER5 systems include Virtual Serial ports that are used for virtual terminal support.

- **Client and Server Virtual SCSI** The POWER5 server uses SCSI as the mechanism for virtual storage devices. This is accomplished using a pair of virtual adapters; a virtual SCSI server adapter and a virtual

Continued

SCSI client adapter. These adapters are used to transfer SCSI commands between partitions. The SCSI server adapter, or target adapter, is responsible for executing any SCSI command it receives. It is owned by the Virtual I/O server partition. The virtual SCSI client adapter allows the client partition to access standard SCSI devices and LUNs assigned to the client partition. You may configure virtual server SCSI devices for Virtual I/O Server partitions, and virtual client SCSI devices for Linux and AIX partitions.

The Answer: Virtualization Is...

So with all that history behind us, and with so many companies claiming to wear the virtualization hat, how do we define it? In an effort to be as all-encompassing as possible, we can define virtualization as:

> A framework or methodology of dividing the resources of a computer hardware into multiple execution environments, by applying one or more concepts or technologies such as hardware and software partitioning, time sharing, partial or complete machine simulation, emulation, quality of service, and many others.

Just as it did during the late 1960s and early 1970s with IBM's VM/370, modern virtualization allows multiple operating system instances to run concurrently on a single computer, albeit much less expensive than the mainframes of those days. Each OS instance shares the available resources available on the common physical hardware, as illustrated in Figure 1.1. Software, referred to as a virtual machine monitor (VMM), controls use and access to the CPU, memory, storage, and network resources underneath.

Figure 1.1 Virtual Machines Riding on Top of the Physical Hardware

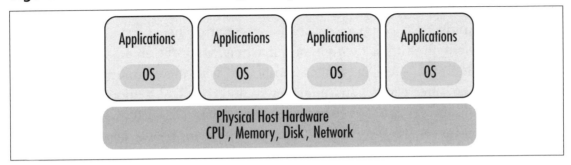

Why Virtualize?

From the mid–1990s until present day, the trend in the data center has been towards a decentralized paradigm, scaling the application and system infrastructure outward in a horizontal fashion. The trend has been commonly referred to as "server sprawl." As more applications and application environments are deployed, the number of servers implemented within the data center grows at exponential rates. Centralized servers were seen as too expensive to purchase and maintain for many companies not already established on such a computing platform. While big-frame, big-iron servers continued to survive, the midrange and entry-level server market bustled with new life and opportunities for all but the most intense use cases. It is important to understand why IT organizations favored decentralization, and why it was seen as necessary to shift from the original paradigm of a centralized computing platform to one of many.

Decentralization versus Centralization

Virtualization is a modified solution between two paradigms—centralized and decentralized systems. Instead of purchasing and maintaining an entire physical computer, and its necessary peripherals for every application, each application can be given its own operating environment, complete with I/O, processing power, and memory, all sharing their underlying physical hardware. This provides the benefits of decentralization, like security and stability, while making the most of a machine's resources and providing better returns on the investment in technology.

With the popularity of Windows and lighter-weight open systems distributed platforms, the promise that many hoped to achieve included better return on assets and a lower total cost of ownership (TCO). The commoditization of inexpensive hardware and software platforms added additional fuel to the evangelism of that promise, but enterprises quickly realized that the promise had turned into a nightmare due to the horizontal scaling required to provision new server instances.

On the positive side, companies were able to control their fixed asset costs as applications were given their own physical machine, using the abundant commodity hardware options available. Decentralization helped with the ongoing maintenance of each application, since patches and upgrades could be applied without interfering with other running systems. For the same reason, decentralization improves security since a compromised system is isolated from other systems on the network. As IT processes became more refined and established as a governance mechanism in many enterprises, the software development life cycle (SDLC) took advantage of the decentralization of n-tier applications. Serving as a model or process for software development, SDLC imposes a rigid structure on the development of a software product by defining not only development phases (such as requirements gathering, software architecture and design, testing, implementation, and maintenance), but rules that guide the development process through each phase. In many cases, the phases overlap, requiring them to have their own dedicated n-tier configuration.

However, the server sprawl intensified, as multiple iterations of the same application were needed to support the SDLC for development, quality assurance, load testing, and finally production environments. Each application's sandbox came at the expense of more power consumption, less physical space, and a greater management effort which, together, account for up to tens (if not hundreds) of thousands of dollars in annual maintenance costs per machine. In addition to this maintenance overhead, decentralization decreased the efficiency of each machine, leaving the average server idle 85 to 90 percent of the time. These inefficiencies further eroded any potential cost or labor savings promised by decentralization.

In Table 1.1, we evaluate three-year costs incurred by Foo Company to create a decentralized configuration composed of five two-way x86 servers with software licensed per physical CPU, as shown in Figure 1.2. These costs include the purchase of five new two-way servers, ten CPU licenses (two per server) of our application, and soft costs for infrastructure, power, and cooling. Storage is not factored in because we assume that in both the physical and virtual scenarios, the servers would be connected to external storage of the same capacity; hence, storage costs remain the same for both. The Physical Cost represents a three-year cost since most companies depreciate their capital fixed assets for 36 months. Overall, our costs are $74,950.

Table 1.1 A Simple Example of the Cost of Five Two-Way Application Servers

Component	Unit Cost	Physical Cost	Virtual Cost
Server hardware	$7,500.00	$37,500.00	$7,500.00
Software licenses/CPU	$2,000.00	$20,000.00	$4,000.00
Supporting infrastructure	$2,500.00	$12,500.00	$2,500.00
Power per server year	$180.00	$2,700.00	$540.00
Cooling per server year	$150.00	$2,250.00	$450.00
Total three-year costs:		$74,950.00	$ 16,490.00
Realized savings over three years:		**$ 58,460.00**	

Figure 1.2 A Decentralized Five-Server Configuration

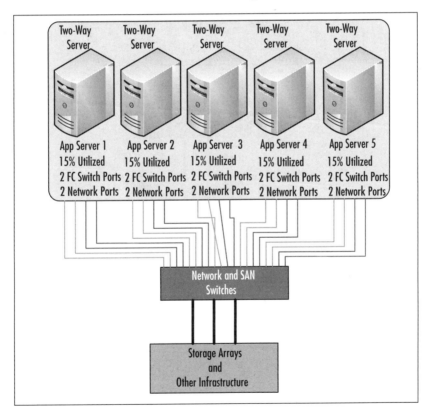

In contrast, the table also shows a similarly configured centralized setup of five OS/application instances hosted on a single two-way server with sufficient hardware

resources for the combined workload, as shown in Figure 1.3. Although savings are realized by the 5:1 reduction in server hardware, that savings is matched by the savings in software cost (5:1 reduction in physical CPUs to license), supporting infrastructure, power, and cooling.

Figure 1.3 A Centralized Five-Server Configuration

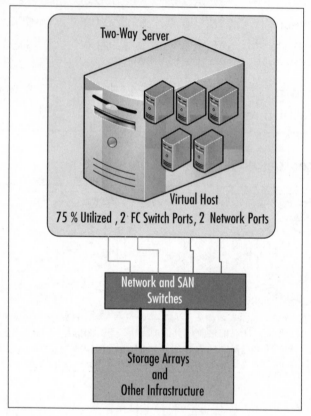

WARNING

When building the business case and assessing the financial impact of virtualization, be sure not to overcommit the hosts with a large number of virtual machines. Depending on the workload, physical hosts can manage as many as 20 to 30 virtualization machines, or as little as four to five. Spend time up front gathering performance information about your current workloads, especially during peak hours, to help properly plan and justify your virtualization strategy.

If we assume that each server would average 15-percent utilization if run on physical hardware, consolidation of the workloads into a centralized virtual is feasible. The hard and soft costs factored into the calculations more closely demonstrate the total cost of ownership in this simple model, labor excluded. It is important to note that *Supporting Infrastructure*, as denoted in the table, includes rack, cabling, and network/storage connectivity costs. This is often overlooked; however, it is critical to include this in your cost benefit analysis since each Fibre-Channel (FC) switch port consumed could cost as much as $1,500, and each network port as much as $300. As illustrated in the figures, there are ten FC and ten network connections in the decentralized example compared to two FC and two network connections. Port costs alone would save Foo a considerable amount. As the table shows, a savings of almost 80 percent could be realized by implementing the servers with virtualization technologies.

Designing & Planning…

A Virtualized Environment Requires a Reliable, High-Capacity Network

To successfully consolidate server workloads onto a virtualized environment, it is essential that all server subsystems (CPU, memory, network, and disk) can accommodate the additional workload. While most virtualization products require a single network connection to operate, careful attention to, and planning of, the networking infrastructure of a virtual environment can ensure both optimal performance and high availability.

Multiple virtual machines will increase network traffic. With multiple workloads, the network capacity needs to scale to match the requirements of the combined workloads expected on the host. In general, as long as the host's processor is not fully utilized, the consolidated network traffic will be the sum of the traffic generated by each virtual machine.

True Tangible Benefits

Virtualization is a critical part of system optimization efforts. While it could simply be a way to reduce and simplify your server infrastructure, it can also be a tool to transform the way you think about your data center as a whole. Figure 1.4 illustrates the model of system optimization. You will notice that virtualization, or physical consolidation, is the foundation for all other optimization steps, followed by logical consolidation and then an overall rationalization of systems and applications, identifying applications that are unneeded or redundant and can thus be eliminated.

Figure 1.4 Virtualization's Role in System Optimization

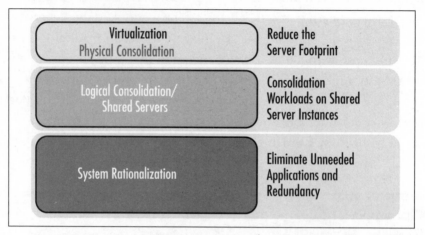

In Table 1.2 you will find a sample list of benefits that often help IT organization justify their movement toward a virtual infrastructure. Although each organization's circumstances are different, you only need a few of these points to apply to your situation to build a strong business case for virtualization.

Table 1.2 Benefits of Virtualization

Category	Benefit
Consolidation	Increase server utilization
	Simplify legacy software migration
	Host mixed operating systems per physical platform
	Streamline test and development environments
Reliability	Isolate software faults
	Reallocate existing partitions
	Create dedicated or as-needed failover partitions
Security	Contain digital attacks through fault isolation
	Apply different security settings to each partition

Consolidation

Three drivers have motivated, if not accelerated, the acceptance and adoption of virtualization technologies—consolidation, reliability, and security. The goal behind consolidation is to combine and unify. In the case of virtualization, workloads are combined on fewer physical platforms capable of sustaining their demand for computing resources, such as CPU, memory, and I/O. In modern data centers, many workloads are far from taxing the hardware they run on, resulting in infrastructure waste and lower returns. Through consolidation, virtualization allows you to combine server instances, or operating systems and their workloads, in a strategic manner and place them on shared hardware with sufficient resource availability to satisfy resource demands. The result is increased utilization. It is often thought that servers shouldn't be forced to run close to their full-capacity levels; however, the opposite is true. In order to maximize that investment, servers should run as close to capacity as possible, without impacting the running workloads or business process relying on their performance. With proper planning and understanding of those workloads, virtualization will help increase server utilization while decreasing the number of physical platforms needed.

Another benefit of consolidation virtualization focuses on legacy system migrations. Server hardware has developed to such levels that they are often incompatible with legacy operating systems and applications. Newer processor technologies, supporting chipsets, and the high-speed buses sought after can often cripple legacy systems, if not render them inoperable without the possibility of full recompilation. Virtualization helps ease and simplify legacy system migrations by providing a common and widely compatible platform upon which legacy system instances can run. This improves the chances that applications can be migrated for older, unsupported, and riskier platforms to newer hardware and supported hardware with minimal impact.

In the past, operating systems were bound to a specific hardware platform. This tied many organizations' hands, forcing them to make large investments in hardware in order to maintain their critical business applications. Due to the commoditization of hardware, though, many of the common operating systems currently available can run on a wide range of server architectures, the most popular of which is the x86 architecture. You can run Windows, UNIX, and your choice of Linux distributions on the x86 architecture. Virtualization technologies built on top of x86 architecture can, in turn, host heterogeneous environments. Multiple operating systems, including those previously mentioned, can be consolidated to the same physical hardware, further reducing acquisition and maintenance costs.

Finally, consolidation efforts help streamline development and test environments. Rather than having uncontrolled sprawl throughout your infrastructure as new projects and releases begin or existing applications are maintained, virtualization allows you to consolidate many of those workloads onto substantially fewer physical servers. Given that development and test loads are less demanding by nature than production, consolidation of those environments through virtualization can yield even greater savings than their production counterparts.

Designing & Planning...

More Cores Equal More Guests... Sometimes

When designing the physical platform for your virtualization and consolidation efforts, be sure to take advantage of the current offering of Intel and AMD multicore processors. Do keep in mind, though, that increasing your core count, and subsequently your total processing power, does not proportionally relate to how many virtual machines you can host. Many factors can contribute to reduced guest performance, including memory, bus congestion (especially true for slower Intel front-side bus architectures or NUMA-based four-way Opteron servers), I/O bus congestion, as well as external factors such as the network infrastructure and the SAN.

Carefully plan your hardware design with virtual machine placement in mind. Focus more on the combined workload than the virtual machine count when sizing your physical host servers. Also consider your virtualization product's features that you will use and how it may add overhead and consume resources needed by your virtual machines. Also consider the capability of your platform to scale as resource demands increase—too few memory slots, and you will quickly run out of RAM; too few PCI/PCI-X/PCI-e slots and you will not be able to scale your I/O by adding additional NICs or HBAs.

Finally, consider the level of redundancy and known reliability of the physical server hardware and supporting infrastructure. Remember that when your host fails, a host outage is much more than just one server down; all the virtual machines it was hosting will experience the outage as well.

Continued

Always keep in mind the key hardware traits required for any virtualization host:

- Performance
- Flexibility
- Reliability

Reliability

More than ever before, reliability has become a mandate and concern for many IT organizations. It has a direct relationship to system availability, application uptime, and, consequently, revenue generation. Companies are willing to, and often do, invest heavily into their server infrastructure to ensure that their critical line-of-business applications remain online and their business operation goes uninterrupted. By investing in additional hardware and software to account for software faults, infrastructures are fortified to tolerate failures and unplanned downtime with interruption. Doing so, though, has proven to be very costly.

Virtualization technologies are sensitive to this and address this area by providing high isolation between running virtual machines. A system fault in one virtual machine, or partition, will not affect the other partitions running on the same hardware platform. This isolation logically protects and shields virtual machines at the lowest level by causing them to be unaware, and thus not impacted, by conditions outside of their allocations. This layer of abstraction, a key component in virtualization, makes each partition just as if it was running on dedicated hardware.

Such isolation does not impede flexibility, as it would in a purely physical world. Partitions can be reallocated to serve other functions as needed. Imagine a server hosting a client/server application that is only used during the 8 A.M. to 5 P.M. hours Monday through Friday, another that runs batch processes to close out business operations nightly, and another that is responsible for data maintenance jobs over the weekend. In a purely physical world, they would exist as three dedicated servers that are highly utilized during their respective hours of operation, but sit idle when not performing their purpose. This accounts for much computing waste and an underutilization of expensive investments. Virtualization addresses this by allowing a single logical or physical partition to be reallocated to each function as needed. On weekdays, it would host the client/server application by day and run the batch processes at night. On the weekends, it would then be reallocated for the data maintenance tasks, only to return to hosting the client/server application the following Monday morning. This flexibility allows IT organizations to utilize "part-time" partitions to run core business processes in the same manner as they would physical servers, but achieve lower costs while maintaining high levels of reliability.

Another area that increases costs is the deployment of standby or failover servers to maintain system availability during times of planned or unplanned outages. While capable of hosting the targeted workloads, such equipment remains idle between those outages, and in some cases, never gets used at all. They are often reduced to expensive paperweights, providing little value to the business while costing it much. Virtualization helps solve this by allowing just-in-time or on-demand provisioning of additional partitions as needed. For example, a partition that has been built (OS and applications) and configured can be put into an inactive (powered-off or suspended) state, ready to be activated when a failure occurs. When needed, the partition becomes active without any concern about hardware procurement, installation, or configuration. Another example is an active/passive cluster. In these clusters, the failover node must be active and online, not inactive. However, the platform hosting the cluster node must be dedicated to that cluster. This has caused many organizations to make a large investment in multiple failover nodes, which sit in their data centers idle, waiting to be used in case of an outage. Using server virtualization, these nodes can be combined onto fewer hardware platforms, as partitions hosting failover nodes are collocated on fewer physical hosts.

Security

The same technology that provides application fault isolation can also provide security fault isolation. Should a particular partition be compromised, it is isolated from the other partitions, stopping the compromise from being extended to them. Solutions can also be implemented that further isolate compromised partitions and OS instances by denying them the very resources they rely on to exist. CPU cycles can be reduced, network and disk I/O access severed, or the system halted altogether. Such tasks would be difficult, if not impossible, to perform if the compromised instance was running directly on a physical host.

When you are consolidating workloads through virtualization, security configurations can remain specific to the partition rather than the server as a whole. An example of this would be super-user accounts. Applications consolidated to a single operating system running directly on top of a physical server would share various security settings—in particular, root or administrator access would be the same for all. However, when the same workloads are consolidated to virtual partitions, each partition can be configured with different credentials, thus maintaining the isolation of system access with administrative privileges often required to comply with federal or industry regulations.

Simply put, virtualization is an obvious move in just about any company, small or large. Just imagine that your manager calls you into the office and begins to explain his or her concerns about cost containment, data center space diminishing, timelines getting narrower, and corporate mandates doing more with less. It won't take too many attempts to explain how virtualization can help address all of those concerns. After realizing you had the answer all along, it will make your IT manager's day to learn this technology is the silver bullet that will satisfy the needs of the business while providing superior value in IT operations and infrastructure management and delivery.

NOTE

Most Virtual Machine Monitor (VMM) implementations are capable of interactive sessions with administrators through CLI or Web interfaces. Although secure, a compromised VMM will expose every virtual machine managed by that VMM. So exercise extreme caution when granting access or providing credentials for authentication to the VMM management interface.

How Does Virtualization Work?

While there are various ways to virtualize computing resources using a true VMM, they all have the same goal: to allow operating systems to run independently and in an isolated manner identical to when it is running directly on top of the hardware platform. But how exactly is this accomplished? While hardware virtualization still exists that fully virtualizes and abstracts hardware similar to how the System370 did, such hardware-based virtualization technologies tend to be less flexible and costly. As a result, a slew of software hypervisor and VMMs have cropped up to perform virtualization through software-based mechanisms. They ensure a level of isolation where the low-level, nucleus core of the CPU architecture is brought up closer to the software levels of the architecture to allow each virtual machine to have its own dedicated environment. In fact, the relationship between the CPU architecture and the virtualized operating systems is the key to how virtualization actually works successfully.

OS Relationships with the CPU Architecture

Ideal hardware architectures are those in which the operating system and CPU are designed and built for each other, and are tightly coupled. Proper use of complex system call requires careful coordination between the operating system and CPU. This symbiotic relationship in the OS and CPU architecture provides many advantages in security and stability. One such example was the MULTICS time-sharing system, which was designed for a special CPU architecture, which in turn was designed for it.

What made MULTICS so special in its day was its approach to segregating software operations to eliminate the risk or chance of a compromise or instability in a failed component from impacting other components. It placed formal mechanisms, called *protection rings*, in place to segregate the trusted operating system from the untrusted user programs. MULTICS included eight of these protection rings, a quite elaborate design, allowing different levels of isolation and abstraction from the core nucleus of the unrestricted interaction with the hardware. The hardware platform, designed in tandem by GE and MIT, was engineered specifically for the MULTICS operating system and incorporated hardware "hooks" enhancing the segregation even further. Unfortunately, this design approach proved to be too costly and proprietary for mainstream acceptance.

The most common CPU architecture used in modern computers is the IA-32, or x86-compatible, architecture. Beginning with the 80286 chipset, the x86 family provided two main methods of addressing memory: real mode and protected mode. In the 80386 chipset and later, a third mode was introduced called virtual 8086 mode, or VM86, that allowed for the execution of programs written for real mode but circumvented the real-mode rules without having to raise them into protected mode. Real mode, which is limited to a single megabyte of memory, quickly became obsolete; and virtual mode was locked in at 16-bit operation, becoming obsolete when 32-bit operating systems became widely available for the x86 architecture. Protected mode, the saving grace for x86, provided numerous new features to support multitasking. These included segmenting processes, so they could no longer write outside their address space, along with hardware support for virtual memory and task switching.

In the x86 family, protected mode uses four privilege levels, or rings, numbered 0 to 3. System memory is divided into segments, and each segment is assigned and dedicated to a particular ring. The processor uses the privilege level to determine what can and cannot be done with code or data within a segment. The term "rings" comes from the MULTICS system, where privilege levels were visualized as a set of concentric rings. Ring-0 is considered to be the innermost ring, with total control of the processor. Ring-3, the outermost ring, is provided only with restricted access, as illustrated in Figure 1.5.

Figure 1.5 Privilege Rings of the x86 Architecture

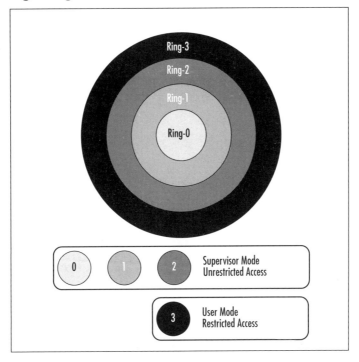

The same concept of protection rings exists in modern OS architecture. Windows, Linux, and most UNIX variants all use rings, although they have reduced the four-ring structure to a two-layer approach that uses only Rings 0 and 3. Ring-0 is commonly called *Supervisor Mode*, while Ring-3 is known as *User Mode*. Security mechanisms in the hardware enforce restrictions on Ring-3 by limiting code access to segments, paging, and input/output. If a user program running in Ring-3 tries to address memory outside of its segments, a hardware interrupt stops code execution. Some assembly language instructions are not even available for execution outside of Ring-0 due to their low-level nature.

The Virtual Machine Monitor and Ring-0 Presentation

The Supervisor Mode is the execution mode on an x86 processor that enables the execution of all instructions, including privileged instructions such as I/O and memory management operations. It is in Supervisor Mode (Ring 0) where the operating system would normally run. Since Ring-3 is based on Ring-0, any system compromise or instability directly impacts User Mode running in Ring-3. In order to isolate Ring-0 for each virtualized guest, it then becomes necessary to move Ring-0 closer to the guests. By doing so, a Ring-0 failure for one virtualized guest does not impact Ring-0, or consequently Ring-3, of any other guest. The perceived Ring-0 for guests can reside in either Ring-1, -2, or -3 for x86 architectures. Of course, the further the perceived Ring-0 is away from the true Ring-0, the more distant it is from executing direct hardware operations, leading to reduced performance and independence.

Virtualization moves Ring-0 up the privilege rings model by placing the Virtual Machine Monitor, or VMM, in one of the rings, which in turn presents the Ring-0 implementation to the hosted virtual machines. It is upon this presented Ring-0 that guest operating systems run, while the VMM handles the actual interaction with the underlying hardware platform for CPU, memory, and I/O resource access. There are two types of VMMs that address the presentation of Ring-0 as follows:

- **Type 1 VMM** Software that runs directly on top of a given hardware platform on the true Ring-0. Guest operating systems then run at a higher level above the hardware, allowing for true isolation of each virtual machine.

- **Type 2 VMM** Software that runs within an operating system, usually in Ring-3. Since there are no additional rings above Ring-3 in the x86 architecture, the presented Ring-0 that the virtual machines run on is as distant from the actual hardware platform as it can be. Although this offers some advantages, it is usually compounded by performance-impeding factors as calls to the hardware must traverse many diverse layers before the operations are returned to the guest operating system.

See Appendix B of this book for an overview of several virtualization products.

The VMM Role Explored

To create virtual partitions in a server, a thin software layer called the Virtual Machine Monitor (VMM) runs directly on the physical hardware platform. One or more guest operating systems and application stacks can then be run on top of the VMM. Figure 1.6 expands our original illustration of a virtualized environment presented in Figure 1.1.

Figure 1.6 The OS and Application Stack Managed by the VMM Software Layer

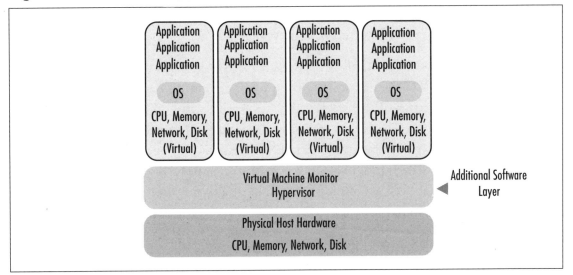

The VMM is the center of server virtualization. It manages hardware resources and arbitrates the requests of the multiple guest operating systems and application stacks. It presents a virtual set of CPU, memory, I/O, and Disk resources to each guest either based on the actual physical hardware or based on a standard and consistent selection of custom hardware. This section further discusses the role of the VMM and design considerations that are used when designing a VMM.

The Popek and Goldberg Requirements

Often referred to as the original reference source for VMM criteria, the Popek and Goldberg Virtualization Requirements define the conditions for a computer architecture to support virtualization. Written in 1974 for the third-generation computer systems of those days, they generalized the conditions that the software that provides the abstraction of a virtual machine, or VMM, must satisfy. These conditions, or properties, are

- **Equivalence** A program running under the VMM should exhibit a predictable behavior that is essentially identical to that demonstrated when running on the underlying hardware platform directly. This is sometimes referred to as *Fidelity*.

- **Resource control** The VMM must be in complete control of the actual hardware resources virtualized for the guest operating systems at all times. This is sometimes referred to as *Safety*.

- **Efficiency** An overwhelming number of machine instructions must be executed without VMM intervention or, in other words, by the hardware itself. This is sometimes referred to as *Performance*.

According to Popek and Goldberg, the problem that VMM developers must address is creating a VMM that satisfies the preceding conditions when operating within the characteristics of the Instruction Set Architecture (ISA) of the targeted hardware platform. The ISA can be classified into three groups of instructions: privileged, control sensitive, and behavior. Privileged instructions are those that trap if the processor is in User Mode and do not trap if it is in Supervisor Mode. Control-sensitive instructions are those that attempt to change the configuration of actual resources in the hardware platform. Behavior instructions are those whose behavior or result depends on the configuration of resources

VMMs must work with each group of instructions while maintaining the conditions of equivalence, resource control, and efficiency. Virtually all modern-day VMMs satisfy the first two: equivalence and resource control. They do so by effectively managing the guest operating system and hardware platform underneath through emulation, isolation, allocation, and encapsulation, as explained in Table 1.3.

Table 1.3 VMM Functions and Responsibilities

Function	Description
Emulation	Emulation is important for all guest operating systems. The VMM must present a complete hardware environment, or virtual machine, for each software stack, whether it is an operating system or application. Ideally, the OS and application are completely unaware they are sharing hardware resources with other applications. Emulation is key to satisfying the equivalence property.

Continued

Table 1.3 continued VMM Functions and Responsibilities

Function	Description
Isolation	Isolation, though not required, is important for a secure and reliable environment. Through hardware abstraction, each virtual machine should be sufficiently separated and independent from the operations and activities of other virtual machines. Faults that occur in a single virtual machine should not impact others, thus providing high levels of security and availability.
Allocation	The VMM must methodically allocate platform resources to the virtual machines that it manages. Resources for processing, memory, network I/O, and storage must be balanced to optimize performance and align service levels with business requirements. Through allocation, the VMM satisfies the resource control property and, to some extent, the efficiency property as well.
Encapsulation	Encapsulation, though not mandated in the Popek and Goldberg requirements, enables each software stack (OS and application) to be highly portable, able to be copied or moved from one platform running the VMM to another. In some cases, this level or portability even allows live, running virtual machines to be migrated. Encapsulation must include state information in order to maintain the integrity of the transferred virtual machine.

The Challenge: VMMs for the x86 Architecture

Referring back to the IA-32 (x86) architecture, we note that all software runs in one of the four privilege rings. The OS traditionally runs in Ring-0, which affords privileged access to the widest range of processor and platform resources. Individual applications usually run in Ring-3, which restricts certain functions (such as memory mapping) that might impact other applications. In this way, the OS retains control to ensure smooth operation.

Since the VMM must have privileged control of platform resources, the usual solution is to run the VMM in Ring-0, and guest operating systems in Ring-1 or Ring-3. However, modern operating systems have been specifically designed to run in

Ring-0. This creates certain challenges. In particular, there are 17 "privileged" instructions that control critical platform resources. These instructions are used occasionally in most existing OS versions. When an OS is not running in Ring-0, any one of these instructions can create a conflict, causing either a system fault or an incorrect response. The challenge faced by VMMs for the IA-32 (x86) architecture is maintaining the Popek and Goldberg requirements while working with the IA-32 ISA.

Types of Virtualization

Many forms of virtualization exist in modern information technology. The most common is server virtualization, which is what most people think of when the term "virtualization" is referenced. However, in addition to server virtualization, IT organizations use other types of virtualization, based on other connotations of the word. Many think of virtualization as meaning "partitioning" a computing resource into multiple entities. Virtualization can also mean just the opposite: presenting multiple entities as a single virtual entity, thus hiding or masking the true computing resources that are performing the work in the background. Many manufacturers and independent software vendors have developed products that utilize the latter approach to virtualization. Of the most common are virtualization products for storage, network, and applications.

Server Virtualization

Server virtualization is the more dominant form of virtualization in use today. Though the concepts we have discussed so far have been about virtualization in general, they are most exhibited in server virtualization products. Implementations of server virtualization exist on, and for all, CPU platforms and architectures, the most popular being the IA-32 or x86. The challenges posed by the x86 architecture's ISA and the Popek and Goldberg requirements have led to several approaches to VMM development. While there are many different implementations of a VMM for x86, they can be summarized into four distinct categories. Table 1.4 provides additional information about each category for server virtualization.

Table 1.4 Types of Server Virtualization

Type of Virtualization	Description	Pros	Cons
Full virtualization	A virtualization technique that provides complete simulation of the underlying hardware. The result is a system in which all software capable of execution on the raw hardware can be run in the virtual machine. Full virtualization has the widest range of support of guest operating systems.	Provides complete isolation of each virtual machine and the VMM; most operating systems can be installed without any modification. Provides near-native CPU and memory performance; uses sophisticated techniques to trap and emulate instructions in runtime via binary patching.	Requires the right combination of hardware and software elements; not quite possible on the x86 architecture in its pure form because of some of the privileged calls that cannot be trapped; performance can be impacted by trap-and-emulate techniques of x86 privileged instructions.
Paravirtualization	A virtualization technique that provides partial simulation of the underlying hardware. Most, but not all, of the hardware features are simulated. The key feature is address space virtualization, granting each virtual machine its own unique address space.	Easier to implement than full virtualization; when no hardware assistance is available, paravirtualized guests tend to be the highest performing virtual machines for network and disk I/O.	Operating systems running in paravirtualized virtual machines cannot be run without substantial modification; virtual machines suffer from lack of backward compatibility and are not very portable.

Continued

Table 1.4 continued Types of Server Virtualization

Type of Virtualization	Description	Pros	Cons
Operating system Virtualization	This concept is based on a single operating system instance.	Tends to be very lean and efficient; single OS installation for management and updates; runs at native speeds; supports all native hardware and OS features that the host is configured for.	Does not support hosting mixed OS families, such as Windows and Linux; virtual machines are not as isolated or secure as with the other virtualization types; Ring-0 is a full operating system rather than a stripped-down microkernel as the VMM, so it adds overhead and complexity; difficult to identify the source of high resource loads; also difficult to limit resource consumption per guest.
Native virtualization	This technique is the newest to the x86 group of virtualization technologies. Often referred to as hybrid virtualization, this type is a combination of full virtualization or paravirtualization combined with I/O acceleration techniques. Similar to full virtualization, guest operating systems can be installed without modification. It takes advantage of the latest CPU technology for x86, Intel VT, and AMD-V.	Handles non-virtualizable instructions by using trap-and-emulate in hardware versus software; selectively employs accelerations techniques for memory and I/O operations; supports x64 (64-bit x86 extensions) targeted operating systems; has the highest CPU, memory, and I/O performance of all types of x86 virtual machines.	Requires CPU architecture that supports hardware-assisted acceleration; still requires some OS modification for paravirtualized guests, although less than pure paravirtualization.

Designing & Planning...

Hardware-Assisting Processors Enhance Virtualization

To maximize the performance of your x86-based physical platform and the hosted virtual machines, be sure to select processors that support hardware-assisted virtualization. Both Intel, providing Intel Virtualization Technology (Intel VT), and AMD, providing "Pacifica" (AMD-V), offer such technologies in their latest generation of processors available for servers as well as desktops and notebooks.

Hardware-assisting processors give the guest OS the authority it needs to have direct access to platform resources without sharing control of the hardware. Previously, the VMM had to emulate the hardware to the guest OS while it retained control of the physical platform. These new processors give both the VMM and the guest OS the authority each needs to run without hardware emulation or OS modification.

They also help VMM developers design a more simplified VMM. Since hardware-assisted processors can now handle the compute-intensive calculations needed to manage the tasks of handing off platform control to a guest OS, the computational burden is reduced on the VMM. Also, key state information for the CPU and guest OS can now be stored in protected memory that only the VMM has access to, protecting the integrity of the handoff process.

Finally, hardware-assisted processors, all of which support 64-bit processing, now allow the benefits of 64-bit computing to filter up to the guest OS and its hosted applications. This provides virtual machines with greater capabilities, headroom, and scalability.

Storage Virtualization

Storage vendors have been offering high–performance storage solutions to their customers for quite some time now. In its most basic form, storage virtualization exists in the assembly of multiple physical disk drives, or spindles, into a single entity that is presented to the host server and operating system, such as with RAID implementations. This can be considered virtualization because all the drives are used and interacted with as a single logical drive, although composed of two or more drives in the background.

The true storage tier and its components were further masked by the introduction and adoption of storage area network (SAN) technologies. Without any change to the operating system code responsible for managing storage subsystems, IT organizations are now sharing storage components between multiple servers, even though each server thinks it has its own dedicated physical storage, in actuality storage administrators have simply carved out a virtual quantity of drive space and presented it to the hosts for use.

More advanced technologies that take storage virtualization to the next level have begun to hit the market. Products exist that are capable of migrating storage in real time from one storage platform to another in the background based on rules and policies (such as retention policies, age of data, or last-time accessed) without any interruption or impact to the host. Software products exist that trap and emulate native SCSI commands and translate them to other storage instructions in the background, making it possible for a disk array to look like a suite of tape drives and tape libraries to back up software and operating systems without any modification.

Network Virtualization

As with storage vendors, manufacturers of network hardware have been in the virtualization arena for some time, although not always recognized as virtualization. The most popular forms of network virtualization are:

- **Virtual LAN (VLAN)** Ratified in the IEEE 802.1Q standard, VLANs are a method of creating independent logical networks within a shared physical network. Network administrators incorporate VLANs into their network design to logically segment broadcast domains and control the interaction between devices on different network segments. VLAN technology has evolved and is a common feature in the application-specific integrated circuits (ASICs) of just about all modern-day Ethernet switches. Although multiple devices can be physically connected to the same network switch, VLANs allow network administrators to create multiple virtual networks that isolate each segment from the others. Each segment utilizes a portion of the available resources (CPU, memory, bandwidth, and so on) in the host switch.

- **Virtual IP (VIP)** An IP address that is not connected to a specific computer or network interface in a computer. VIPs are usually assigned to a network device that is in-path of the traversing network traffic. Incoming packets are sent to the VIP but are redirected to the actual interface of the receiving host(s). VIPs are mostly used for redundancy and load-balancing scenarios, where multiple systems are hosting a common application and are capable of receiving the traffic as redirected by the network device.

■ **Virtual private network (VPN)** A private communication network used to communicate confidentially over a public network. VPN traffic is often carried over highly insecure network mediums, such as the Internet, creating a secure channel for sensitive and confidential information to traverse from one site to another. It is also used as a means of extending remote employees home networks to the corporate network. Although special software is usually needed to establish the connection, once established, interaction with other resources on the network is handled the same way it would be on a true physical network, without requiring any modification of the network stack or operating system.

Application Virtualization

Application virtualization, or software virtualization, is the newest member of the ever-growing virtualization family. It is a new approach to software management. Breaking the paradigm and bond between applications, the operating system, and the hardware hosting the operating system, application virtualization uses virtual software packages to place applications and data rather than conventional installation procedures. Application packages can be instantly activated or deactivated, reset to their default configuration, and thus mitigate the risk of interference with other applications as they run in their own computing space.

Some of the benefits of application virtualization are:

■ **Eliminates application conflicts** Applications are guaranteed to use the correct-version files and property file/Registry settings without any modification to the operating systems and without interfering with other applications.

■ **Reduces roll-outs through instant provisioning** Administrators can create pre-packaged applications that can be deployed quickly locally or remotely over the network, even across slow links. Virtual software applications can even be streamed to systems on-demand without invoking a setup or installation procedure.

- **Runs multiple versions of an application** Multiple versions can run on the same operating system instance without any conflicts, improving the migration to newer versions of applications and speeding the testing and integration of new features into the environment.

Common Use Cases for Virtualization

Now that we have discussed the concept, history, and types of virtualization in depth, the last thing to review before diving into virtualization with Xen's hypervisor, or VMM, is the use cases for virtualization. As mentioned earlier, not every scenario can appropriately be implemented using virtualization technologies. Some workloads are large enough and consistent enough to warranty their own dedicated computing resources. Others are so large it takes a farm of resources just to be able to handle the workload, as is the case with high-performance clusters (HPCs). However, most workloads, regardless of the size of your company, are great candidates for virtualization; and by doing so, you can realize substantial benefits.

If you have not already adopted virtualization technologies as part of your infrastructure strategy, the following are some examples where you can put virtualization to work for you:

- Technology refresh

- Business continuity and disaster recovery

- Proof of concept (POC) deployments

- Virtual desktops

- Rapid development, test lab, and software configuration management

Technology Refresh

Asset life-cycle management is an area that gets many CFOs' and CIOs' attention because of the cost imposed to the business. As one phase of the life cycle, a technology refresh, or the replacement of older fixed assets with newer ones, can stand out on a department or corporate profit and loss statement, even with the lower prices of technology today. In many cases, it makes more sense to replace them than to pay to maintain aging and often obsolete equipment. But what if you could reduce the cost further?

During a technology refresh, the opportunity to virtualize and consolidate some of your existing workloads is great. There are some basic questions you should ask before undertaking any technology refresh, as represented in Table 1.5. If you could answer to one or more of these questions, then virtualization should be the answer you have been looking for.

Table 1.5 Factors to Consider When Choosing Virtualization for a Technology Refresh

Factor to Consider	How Virtualization Addresses It
Q: Is the server that is being refreshed hosting an application that is still valuable to the company rather than being deprecated or obsolete?	If the application still provides value to the company, then it is a good strategy to make sure the application and operating system are hosted on a reliable, supported hardware environment. Virtualization can help by reducing the costs, both hard and soft, of refreshing your infrastructure.
Q: Is current performance acceptable to the business?	New servers can be several times more powerful than the servers you are planning on refreshing. If you did a physical-to-physical refresh, that would lead to underutilized servers and considerable waste of processing power. If you deem current performance to be satisfactory, then a virtual machine is perfect for your application, especially since virtual machines can often perform at near-native levels.
Q: Is there a trend that shows that additional resources will be needed in the short term?	Upgrading server resources can be a costly and time-consuming effort with considerable downtime. A virtualized environment is flexible, and upgrade can often be performed dynamically on some platforms. For others, it is as simple as taking a few minutes to power down the virtual machine, reconfigure resource allocation, and then power the virtual machine up.

Continued

Table 1.5 continued Factors to Consider When Choosing Virtualization for a Technology Refresh

Factor to Consider	How Virtualization Addresses It
Q: Can legacy applications be migrated easily and cost-effectively to a newer operating system or hardware?	Many legacy operating systems and applications are difficult to migrate to new hardware platforms with substantial modification. The hardware environment presented by the VMM, on the other hand, often has simple hardware with drivers available for all operating systems supported, making migrations much simpler.
Q: Will there be issues or complications either restoring applications and data to a new server or reinstalling and configuring the applications and data from the ground up?	A process known as physical-to-virtual (P2V) allows you to make an image of your servers and convert them to virtual machines, eliminating the need to restore from backup or possibly reinstall the application from scratch. In some cases, this can happen without any downtime.
Q: Is the application one that requires higher availability and recoverability from failure or some other system compromise?	Features such as live migrations allow single-instance virtual machines to achieve higher availability than on a physical platform. Or if a clustered or load-balanced environment is desired but is not possible because of the hardware investment, making your failover node(s) virtual machines can incur minimal up-front costs that equate to substantial savings down the road.

Business Continuity and Disaster Recovery

Business continuity and disaster recovery initiatives have picked up over the past few years. Customer demand and federal regulations have helped accelerate those efforts and give them the attention they have needed for some time. However, business continuity plans (BCPs) can often require a large investment in standby technology in order to achieve the recovery point and time objectives. As a result, IT disaster recovery can be a slow moving, never-ending process.

Virtualization is an ideal platform for most cases since it eliminates the need to purchase an excessive amount of equipment "just in case." Most software vendors of backup/recovery products support the restoration of operation systems and applications of physical servers to virtual machines. And if you currently use a recovery service provider because hosting your own hot site was too costly, virtualization may make that option more achievable by substantially reducing the investment your company needs to make.

For example, if your company has identified 50 servers that comprise your mission-critical applications and must be brought back online within 72 hours of a disaster, you would need 50 servers available and all the supporting data center and network infrastructure to support them (space, HVAC, power, and so on) at your recovery site. However, establishing your recovery site with virtualization technologies, you could reduce that number to five physical servers, each targeted to host ten virtual machines, a modest quantity based on what most companies achieve currently. That is a 90 percent reduction in acquisition costs for the servers as well as the environment costs to support them. Just think of the space reduction going from 50 to 5 servers!

Proof of Concept Deployments

Business managers often get frustrated with IT's inability to provision an environment to host a proof of concept (POC) for a proposed application that is intended to add value to the business. Most IT organizations do not have spare assets (at least any that are viable) lying around, nor have the time to spend to provision an application that is not associated with an approved "move-forward" project. As a result, most POCs are either set up on inadequate equipment, such as desktops, or not established at all, presenting a risk of missed opportunity for the business.

Virtual machines find their strength in situations such as this. Rapid provisioning, no hardware investment needed, safe, secure, and reliable… all the qualities needed to quickly build a POC environment and keep it running during the time it is needed. Even better, if the POC is successful and you decide to go to production with the application, you can migrate your virtual machine from your test infrastructure to your production virtual infrastructure without having to rebuild the application, saving lots of time in the end.

Virtual Desktops

Companies often have huge investments in client PCs for their user base, many of which do not fall into the category of power users. Similar to server hardware, client PC hardware continues to improve and get more powerful, often being underutilized. If you have users that run a CRM application, e-mail, a Web browser, and some productivity applications such as spreadsheets and word processing, those users are well suited for a virtual desktop environment. Placing a thin client with keyboard, mouse, and monitor on their desk, the computing power can safely and securely be moved into the data center, hosted as a virtual machine on server hardware. In environments requiring desktop hardware encryption, PC firewalls, and other security devices, this can lead to a substantial reduction in complexity and software licensing as well.

If you are planning on rolling out a new wave of PCs for hundreds of call center agents or in a manufacturing environment (just think of how dirty those shiny new, underutilized PCs will get in just a few days on the shop floor), consider instead creating a virtualized desktop infrastructure in your data center and saving your company lots of money while you are at it.

Rapid Development, Test Lab, and Software Configuration Management

Development teams have always been good candidates for virtualization. Whether it's a desktop-based virtualization product or hosting some development servers as virtual machines in the data center, virtualization has proven to be effective in increasing the productivity of developers, the quality of their work, and the speed at which they complete their coding. In the same way, virtualization can speed up the testing cycles and also allow a higher density of automated testing, thus accelerating the time to release or to market.

Virtualization enables companies to streamline their software life cycle. From development and testing, through integration, staging, deployment, and management, virtualization offers a comprehensive framework for virtual software life-cycle automation that streamlines these adjacent yet often disconnected processes, and closes the loops between them. In addition to these obvious benefits, you can creatively design solutions around a virtual infrastructure to help your software development and test teams to:

- Provide remote lab access and desktop hosting for offsite or offshore development resources, minimizing duplication of lab equipment at each site.

- Close the loop between software development and quality assurance—capturing and moving defect state configurations.

- Reproduce and resolve defects on demand.

- Clone or image a production virtual machine and host it in your QA test infrastructure for security patch, service pack, or maintenance release testing.

- Push a staged configuration into production after successful testing is completed, minimizing errors associated with incorrect deployment and configuration of the production environment.

Summary

Virtualization is an abstraction layer that breaks the standard paradigm of computer architecture, decoupling the operating system from the physical hardware platform and the applications that run on it. As a result, IT organizations can achieve greater IT resource utilization and flexibility. Virtualization allows multiple virtual machines, often with heterogeneous operating systems, to run in isolation, side-by-side, on the same physical machine. Each virtual machine has its own set of virtual hardware (CPU, memory, network interfaces, and disk storage) upon which an operating system and applications are loaded. The operating system sees the set of hardware and is unaware of the sharing nature with other guest operating systems running on the same physical hardware platform. Virtualization technology and its core components, such as the Virtual Machine Monitor, manage the interaction with the operating system calls to the virtual hardware and the actual execution that takes place on the underlying physical hardware.

Virtualization was first introduced in the 1960s to allow partitioning of large, mainframe hardware, a scarce and expensive resource. Over time, minicomputers and PCs provided a more efficient, affordable way to distribute processing power. By the 1980s, virtualization was no longer widely employed. However, in the 1990s, researchers began to see how virtualization could solve some of the problems associated with the proliferation of less expensive hardware, including underutilization, escalating management costs, and vulnerability.

Today, virtualization is growing as a core technology in the forefront of data center management. The technology is helping businesses, both large and small, solve their problems with scalability, security, and management of their global IT infrastructure while effectively containing, if not reducing, costs.

Solutions Fast Track

What Is Virtualization?

☑ Virtualization technologies have been around since the 1960s. Beginning with the Atlas and M44/44X projects, the concept of time sharing and virtual memory was introduced to the computing world.

☑ Funded by large research centers and system manufacturers, early virtualization technology was only available to those with sufficient resources and clout to fund the purchase of the big-iron equipment.

☑ As time sharing evolved, IBM developed the roots and early architecture of the virtual machine monitor, or VMM. Many of the features and design elements of the System370 and its succeeding iterations are still found in modern-day virtualization technologies.

☑ After a short quiet period when the computing world took its eyes off of virtualization, a resurgent emphasis began again in the mid-1990s, putting virtualization back into the limelight as an effective means to gain high returns on a company's investment.

Why Virtualize?

☑ As virtualization technology transitioned from the mainframe world to midrange and entry-level hardware platforms and the operating systems that they ran, there was a shift from having either a decentralized or a centralized computing model to having a hybrid of the two. Large computers could now be partitioned into smaller units, giving all of the benefits of logical decentralization while taking advantage of a physical centralization.

☑ While there are many benefits that companies will realize as they adopt and implement virtualization solutions, the most prominent ones are consolidation of their proliferating sprawl of servers, increased reliability of computing platforms upon which their important business applications run, and greater security through isolation and fault containment.

How Does Virtualization Work?

☑ The operating system and the CPU architecture historically have been bound and mated one to the other. This inherent relationship is exemplified by secure and stable computing platforms that segregate various levels of privilege and priority through rings of isolation and access, the most critical being Ring-0.

☑ The most common CPU architecture, the IA-32 or x86 architecture, follows a similar privileged model containing four rings, 0 to 4. Operating systems that run on x86 platforms are installed in Ring-0, called Supervisor Mode, while applications execute in Ring-3, called User Mode.

☑ The Virtual Machine Monitor (VMM) presents the virtual or perceived Ring-0 for guest operating systems, enabling isolation from each platform. Each VMM meets a set of conditions referred to as the Popek and Goldberg Requirements, written in 1974. Though composed for third-generation computers of that time, the requirements are general enough to apply to modern VMM implementations.

☑ While striving to hold true to the Popek and Goldberg requirements, developers of VMMs for the x86 architecture face several challenges due in part to the non-virtualizable instructions in the IA-32 ISA. Because of those challenges, the x86 architecture cannot be virtualized in the purest form; however, x86 VMMs are close enough that they can be considered to be true to the requirements.

Types of Virtualization

☑ Server Virtualization is the most common form of virtualization, and the original. Managed by the VMM, physical server resources are used to provision multiple virtual machines, each presented with its own isolated and independent hardware set. Of the top three forms of virtualization are full virtualization, paravirtualization, and operating system virtualization. An additional form, called native virtualization, is gaining in popularity and blends the best of full virtualization and paravirtualization along with hardware acceleration logic.

☑ Other areas have and continue to experience benefits of virtualization, including storage, network, and application technologies.

Common Use Cases for Virtualization

☑ A technology refresh of older, aging equipment is an opportune time to consider implementing a virtual infrastructure, consolidating workloads and easing migrations through virtualization technologies.

☑ Business can reduce recovery facility costs by incorporating the benefits of virtualization into the BCP and DR architectures.

☑ Virtualization also gives greater levels of flexibility and allows IT organizations to achieve on-demand service levels. This is evident with easily deployed proof-of-concept, pilot, or mock environments with virtually no overhead to facilitate or manage it.

☑ The benefits of virtualization can be driven beyond the walls of the data center to the desktop. Desktop virtualization can help organizations reduce costs while maintaining control of their client environment and providing additional layers of security at no additional cost.

☑ Virtualization is, and has been, at home in the software development life cycle. Such technologies help streamline development, testing, and release management and processes while increasing productivity and shortening the window of time from design to market.

Frequently Asked Questions

The following Frequently Asked Questions, answered by the authors of this book, are designed to both measure your understanding of the concepts presented in this chapter and to assist you with real-life implementation of these concepts. To have your questions about this chapter answered by the author, browse to **www.syngress.com/solutions** and click on the **"Ask the Author"** form.

Q: What is virtual machine technology used for?

A: Virtual machine technology serves a variety of purposes. It enables hardware consolidation, simplified system recovery, and the re-hosting of earlier applications because multiple operating systems can run on one computer. One key application for virtual machine technology is cross-platform integration. Other key applications include server consolidation, the automation and consolidation of development and testing environments, the re-hosting of earlier versions of applications, simplifying system recovery environments, and software demonstrations.

Q: How does virtualization address a CIO's pain points?

A: IT organizations need to control costs, improve quality, reduce risks and increase business agility, all of which are critical to a business' success. With virtualization, lower costs and improved business agility are no longer trade-offs. By enabling IT resources to be pooled and shared, IT organizations are provided with the ability to reduce costs and improve overall IT performance.

Q: What is the status of virtualization standards?

A: True open standards for getting all the layers talking and working together aren't ready yet, let alone giving users interoperable choices between competitive vendors. Users are forced to rely on de facto standards at this time. For instance, users can deploy two different virtualization products within one environment, especially if each provides the ability to import virtual machines from the other. But that is about as far as interoperability currently extends.

Q: When is a product not really virtualization but something else?

A: Application vendors have been known to overuse the term and label their product "virtualization ready." But by definition, the application should not be to tell whether it is on a virtualized platform or not. Some vendors also label their isolation tools as virtualization. To isolate an application means files are installed but are redirected or shielded from the operating system. That is not the same as true virtualization, which lets you change any underlying component, even network and operating system settings, without having to tweak the application.

Q: What is the ideal way to deploy virtualization?

A: Although enterprises gain incremental benefits from applying virtualization in one area, they gain much more by using it across every tier of the IT infrastructure. For example, when server virtualization is deployed with network and storage virtualization, the entire infrastructure becomes more flexible, making it capable of dynamically adapting to various business needs and demands.

Q: What are some of the issues to watch out for?

A: Companies beginning to deploy virtualization technologies should be cautious of the following: software costs/licensing from proliferating virtual machines, capacity planning, training, high and unrealistic consolidation expectations, and upfront hardware investment, to name a few. Also, sufficient planning up front is important to avoid issues that can cause unplanned outages affecting a larger number of critical business applications and processes.

## Chapter 2

Introducing Xen

Solutions in this chapter:

- What Is Xen?
- Xen's Virtualization Model Explored
- CPU Virtualization
- Memory Virtualization
- I/O Virtualization
- The Xenstore

☑ Summary

☑ Solutions Fast Track

☑ Frequently Asked Questions

Introduction

In Chapter 1, we reviewed the origins and theory behind virtualization. Various systems have been developed to subdivide, or virtualize, resources of a single physical computer. These systems exist on a wide variety of platforms. Some are dedicated to a particular hardware platform and guest operating system, while others can be installed on a variety of architecture and support a diverse selection of guests. Their approach varies, but they all share one goal: to assist with high levels of consolidation, increase server utilization, and enable rapid provisioning of partitions to meet your business needs on demand. Xen has been proven to accomplish all that, and has been very successful in doing so.

With its root in open source, and with heavy development still coming from the open-source community, Xen is posed to be one of the most popular and widely used virtual machine monitors (VMMs) for its supported platforms. Many operating systems are integrating Xen's hypervisor into the operating system itself; soon it will not be necessary to even install Xen to begin achieving greater efficiency in your data center. However, Xen is much more than just another free VMM. XenSource, the company currently leading ongoing development efforts of the VMM, has brought Xen into the commercial limelight as a viable solution for the enterprise data center.

This chapter will discuss Xen in detail, including the open-source release as well as the commercial variants from XenSource—XenExpress, XenServer, and XenEnterprise. We will illustrate the underpinnings of the product as well to give you a solid understanding of how Xen works and what to expect. We also review some best practices and tips on how to extract the most benefit from the product as we discuss critical architectural components.

What Is Xen?

Xen is an open-source VMM, or hypervisor, for both 32- and 64-bit processor architectures. It runs as software directly on top of the bare-metal, physical hardware and enables you to run several virtual guest operating systems on the same host computer at the same time. The virtual machines are executed securely and efficiently with near-native performance.

The Xen project originated as a research project of the Systems Research Group at the University of Cambridge Computer Laboratory. The project was dubbed the XenoServers Project, and was funded by the UK's Engineering and Physical Sciences

Research Council (EPSRC). The goal of the project is to provide a public infrastructure that is globally reaching and accessible for purposes of wide-area distributed computing. With a special dedication to systems research, and led by senior researcher Ian Pratt, the project has produced the Xen hypervisor as its core technology.

Xen was released to the public in a two-step approach. First, Pratt and several other original contributors released a paper titled "Xen and the Art of Virtualization" at the bi-annual Symposium on Operating Systems Principles (SOSP) describing the hypervisor and its approach to bringing virtualization to the x86 CPU architecture in October 2003. At the same time, the first public release, version 1.0, was made available for download. Since then, Xen has grown and matured, playing a key role in many production implementations. Xen is also the base technology for a changing approach to hosting and software as a service (SaaS) models.

Xen development in the open-source community is now led by XenSource, founded by Pratt. Although a channel for commercial enterprise-class solutions based on Xen technology, XenSource is very much committed to the growth of the Xen community, fostering and inspiring developers to take the hypervisor beyond its current state, and dedicating its own resources to the development effort as well. Table 2.1 lists the top 15 contributors to the Xen code base. Note that the majority of the coding is done by XenSource engineering resources, followed by the open-source community. Of the technology partners working with XenSource, IBM and Intel have made the greatest contributions to the project since the release of version 3.0.

Table 2.1 Code Statistics Since the 3.0.0 Release of the Xen Hypervisor

Contributor	Aliases	Check-ins	Insertions	% Involved
xensource.com	16	1,281	363,449	64.2%
other	30	189	48,132	8.5%
ibm.com	30	271	40,928	7.2%
intel.com	26	290	29,545	5.2%
hp.com	8	126	19,275	3.4%
novell.com	8	78	17,108	3.0%
valinux.co.jp	3	156	12,143	2.1%
bull.net	1	145	11,926	2.1%
ncsc.mil	3	25	6,048	1.1%
fujitsu.com	13	119	6,442	1.1%

Continued

Table 2.1 continued Code Statistics Since the 3.0.0 Release of the Xen Hypervisor

Contributor	Aliases	Check-ins	Insertions	% Involved
redhat.com	7	68	4,822	< 1%
amd.com	5	61	2,671	< 1%
virtualiron.com	5	23	1,434	< 1%
cam.ac.uk	1	9	1,211	< 1%
unisys.com	3	7	857	< 1%
		Total:	565,991	

TIP

If you are interested in reviewing the source code for Xen, or obtaining the "under-development" version of Xen for the latest in upcoming features, visit http://xenbits.xensource.com.

It is interesting to observe the variety of contributors to the Xen project, ranging from XenSource themselves to technology leaders in the x86 arena for systems and CPU architecture (notably those with the largest budget for x86 research and development) to key Linux distributors. Xen is even contributed to by governmental and educational institutions. With such a wide selection of contributors of diverse backgrounds, Xen has great potential to meet the needs of your organization, regardless of size, budget, or whether it is private or public.

This section reviews the features and requirements of Xen's commercial and open-source versions.

Features of Xen

Xen offers a powerful set of enterprise-class functionality, making it as suitable for larger implementations running mission-critical applications as it is for small and medium-sized businesses. These features include:

- Virtual machines with near-native performance
- Full support on x86 (32-bit), x86 (32-bit) with Physical Address Extension (PAE), and x86 with 64-bit extensions

- Support for almost all hardware with Linux drivers available

- Multiple vCPUs supported in each guest machine (Windows and Linux), up to 32-way

- Dynamic resource allocation through hot-plug vCPUs (if the guest operating system supports it)

- Live, zero-downtime migration of running virtual machines between two physical hosts

- Support of hardware-assist processors from Intel (Intel-VT) and AMD (AMD-V), allowing unmodified guest operating systems

Xen supports two modes of virtualization: paravirtualization and full virtualization. For paravirtualization, guest operating systems must be modified and the kernel recompiled to support proper interaction with the Xen VMM. Although this limits the selection of operating systems that can be run in this mode, it offers performance benefits in return. Full virtualization was introduced in version 3.0 with the addition of support for hardware-assisted processor architectures. This mode is only available to physical hosts with Intel-VT or AMD-V processors. Full virtualization enables unmodified guest operating systems to be run, and is the only way to run Microsoft Windows guests, with a minor performance penalty.

The XenServer Product Family

As we discussed earlier, two flavors of Xen are available: open source and the commercial product. Both have roughly the same features, with the commercial product touting a new management tool and being a bit more refined overall. In particular, XenSource's commercial XenServer product family includes the open-source Xen hypervisor with lots of add-ons surrounding it. You can benefit from the following features offered by XenSource's products:

- **Ease of use** XenEnterprise, XenServer, and XenExpress are offered as packaged and supported virtualization. Comprised of three elements, it contains the Xen hypervisor, port of Linux and NetBSD, and management tools that are run in User Mode. XenServer is simple to install on bare metal from a boot CD or across the network. It leverages standard Linux drivers to support a wide and diverse range of network and storage hardware.

- **Robust virtualization** A highly scalable platform, XenEnterprise can run on up to 64-socket SMP systems and support up to 32 vCPUs in a guest virtual machine. Exceptional performance can be achieved, especially in configurations that can take advantage of hardware virtualization through the latest processors from Intel and AMD. This hardware virtualization also allows XenEnterprise to host Windows and Linux virtual machines, all managed through a single management tool.

- **Powerful management** Rapid provisioning, performance monitoring, and some trending via the XenServer Administrator Console, physical-to-virtual migrations, and command-line user space tools that can be run locally or remotely make XenEnterprise as efficient to manage and administer as it is to run virtual machines.

Table 2.2 shows a comparison of the XenServer product family, including the open-source release. These features are current as of the XenServer 3.2 and Xen open-source 3.0.4 release.

Table 2.2 The XenServer Product Family

	XenEnterprise Multi-OS Virtualization	XenServer Windows Virtualization	XenExpress On-Ramp to Xen
User Type	Enterprise IT, OEMs	Windows IT Pro	IT Enthusiast/Developer
Concurrent VMs	No software-imposed limit; limited only by available hardware resources	Eight concurrent VMs	Four concurrent VMs
Physical RAM	Unlimited RAM	8GB max	4GB max
Physical CPU	Up to 32 sockets (32-way)	Dual-socket (2-way)	Dual-socket (2-way)
Shared Storage	Yes, Fibre Channel and iSCSI-based SAN	No	No
Windows Guest Support	Windows Server 2003 Windows Server 2003 R2 Windows XP SP2 Windows 2000 SP4	Windows Server 2003 Windows Server 2003 R2 Windows XP SP2 Windows 2000 SP4	Windows Server 2003 Windows Server 2003 R2 Windows XP SP2 Windows 2000 SP4

Continued

Table 2.2 continued The XenServer Product Family

	XenEnterprise Multi-OS Virtualization	XenServer Windows Virtualization	XenExpress On-Ramp to Xen
Linux Guest Support	RHEL 3.6–5.0 SLES 9.2–10.1 Debian Sarge Others via HVM	Windows only	RHEL 3.6–5.0 SLES 9.2–10.1 Debian Sarge Others via HVM
Physical-to-Virtual Migrations (P2V)	Linux P2V included and via XenSource partners; Windows P2V available from XenSource partners	Windows P2V available from XenSource partners	Linux P2V included and via XenSource partners; Windows P2V available from XenSource partners
Live Migration	Yes	No	No
QoS Resource Controls for vCPU and VIFs	Yes	No	No
VLAN tagging in virtual bridges	Yes	No	No
64-bit guest support	No	No	No
Paravirtualized (PV) drivers included	Yes; signed for Windows	Yes, signed	Yes; signed for Windows
Administration Details	1 or more Xen hosts using Administrator Console	1 or more Xen hosts using Administrator Console	Only support a single Xen host using Administrator Console
Cost of Software License	< $1,000 USD per 2-CPU	< $100 USD per 2-CPU	Free

NOTE

You can learn more about each Xen product and download a free trial (or the full open-source product) at the following locations:

- **Xen 3.0 (open source)** www.xensource.com/xen/xen/
- **XenServer Express** www.xensource.com/products/xen_express/
- **XenServer** www.xensource.com/products/xen_server/
- **XenServer Enterprise** www.xensource.com/products/ xen_enterprise/index.html

Xen's Virtualization Model Explored

Although we have been speaking about server virtualization as it relates to the operating system running in a hardware environment (physical or virtual), the focus for any organization that is deploying virtualization technologies for their systems architecture should be on applications. The server platform merely hosts the applications, where the application and data themselves are the intellectual property that actually provides value to the business. Achieving consolidation, optimization, higher availability, and increased flexibility of a company's application portfolio is where virtualization's "sweet-spot" is found, helping customers realize the true business value and benefit of their IT investment.

Architecture Overview

There have been various ways to host multiple applications on a single server, in a shared-services fashion. The most basic method is to host the files and processes for multiple applications on a single instance of the operating system. While it is possible to achieve some level of protection among the different processes using conventional operating systems techniques, the processes are not as well isolated as with dedicated hardware. In fact, a fault experienced by a particular application can not only impact other processes executing on the same operating system, but it can impact the operating system itself, making recovery of all processes difficult if not impossible, as in how configuration requires a delicate balance of privileged mode software (device drivers, operating systems APIs, and so on) and all user mode software, especially those that share common libraries or binaries. More common than fault isolation, however, is the need for performance isolation.

A common issue with "stacked" applications that are co-located and executing on the same operating system instance is the competition for resources. Concurrent processing for CPU, memory, or I/O bound processes can cause the host machine to easily become oversubscribed. Each process believes that it has the cumulative amount of resources to use and will attempt to use them as needed. While it is possible to create containers within a particular operating system to help assure that the processes are getting all the correct resources they have been allocated and no more, this isolation technique has not been shown to provide consistent results or be reliable.

In most cases, enterprise-grade operating systems have, as a minimum process, schedulers that proxy the requests to the operating system for resources. However, when left to its own devices, an application process may be impervious to other processes in the system and "hog" any available resources. Operating systems augment these scheduling limitations by providing resource managers that allow for finer grain control over process resource utilization. These tools, however, are generally complicated to implement and manage, and impose greater administrative overhead when adding new applications.

While dedicating physical server hardware to a single operating system instance provides both the fault and performance isolation desired by most enterprises, it becomes inefficient in cost. The real solution to the issue is server virtualization. As explained in Chapter 1, various types of virtualization technologies are available, each with their own set of strengths and challenges. Xen has been developed as a viable and capable virtual machine monitor for the x86 architecture, taking advantage of paravirtualization (its primary virtualization technique) and full virtualization.

Processor Architecture

Xen currently supports a wide complement of hardware and operating systems. Part of its value proposition is being a commodity VMM for commodity hardware, allowing you to virtualize popular operating systems. Although Xen was originally developed as a VMM project for x86, experimental ports are being developed and tested for additional platforms, including Intel's Itanium and Itanium 2 (IA-64) and IBM's PowerPC. Table 2.3 lists the currently supported CPU architectures, as well as the Xen features available for each architecture.

Table 2.3 Xen Features by CPU Architecture

Feature	x86 (no PAE)	x86 (with PAE)	x64 (x86_64)	IA-64	POWERPC
Privileged Domains	X	X	X	X	X
Guest Domains	X	X	X	X	X
SMP Guests	X	X	X	X	
Save/Restore/Migrate	X	X	X	X	
More than 4GB RAM		X	X	X	X
Progressive PV	X	X	X	X	X
Driver Domains	X	X	X		

As of release 3.0.0, Xen also supports the hardware virtualization features provided by the latest processors for Intel and AMD, supporting Intel-VT and AMD-V, respectively. For Intel processors, the feature is called XVM, while AMD processors announce the feature as SVM. In Xen nomenclature, though, both are simply referred to as HVM since they are functionally equivalent and provide the same benefit to Xen. Hardware virtualization allows Xen to host operating systems that cannot be modified and run in a traditional paravirtualized manner. While Intel's and AMD's approaches are different, the net result is the ability to virtualize CPU and memory effectively and efficiently, allowing Xen to run virtually any operating system. Even with HVM, though, special paravirtualization device drivers are available to allow HVM guests to utilize Xen's virtual I/O architecture for maximum efficiency, performance, security, and isolation. For more information, please see Chapter 7.

Paravirtualization with Xen

Xen has an elegantly simple design for a complex architecture. Its architecture was derived from an attempt to account for the idiosyncrasies of the x86 CPU platform as it applies to virtual machine monitors, or hypervisors. One of the main goals of the design was to separate the "how," "when," and "what" (in other words, the policy and the mechanism) as much as possible. Other implementations of x86 VMMs placed the entire burden on the hypervisor; while offering a great degree of flexibility and success, these VMMs led to a sacrifice in performance. However, the developers of Xen believed that an optimal approach to hypervisor design was to let the hypervisor deal with low level complexities, such as CPU scheduling and access control, and not higher-level matters better suited for the guest operating system environments themselves.

As a result of this architecture methodology, the demarcation point, so to speak, in Xen's architecture became a question of control and management. The hypervisor's focus is on basic control operations (the mechanism, or the "how"), leaving the decision making (the policies, or "what" and "when") to the guest operating system. This fits well with the nature of the VMM, where the hypervisor only handles tasks that require direct privileged access. In essence, Xen presents a virtual machine abstraction that is very similar to the hardware platform beneath, without creating an exact copy of it. This technique is at the heart of what is called paravirtualization.

To accomplish this, paravirtualization does require some modification to the guest operating system to make it aware of the underlying virtualization layer, improving its interaction with both the virtual world it has been presented as well as the actual physical world it is running on top of. Although application binaries do not need to be modified as well, operating system modifications facilitate improved performance and support better handling of time-sensitive operations. Paravirtualization does have certain requirements for memory management, CPU, and device I/O, as shown in Table 2.4.

Table 2.4 Paravirtualization Requirements and Considerations

Item Type	Item	Requirements or Special Consideration
Memory Management	Segmentation	Cannot insert privileged segment descriptors and cannot overlap with the top end of the linear address space.
	Paging	Guest operating system has direct read access to hardware-level page tables, but updates are batched or performed individually and validated by the hypervisor.
CPU	Protection	The guest operating system must run at a more restricted privilege level than Xen—in other words, it cannot run in Ring-0.
	Exceptions	The guest operating system must register a table for exception trap handlers.
	System calls	The guest operating system may install a handler for system calls, allowing direct calls from an application or the operating system itself. Some of these calls do not need to be handled directly by Xen.
	Interrupts	Hardware interrupts are replaced with a notification event mechanism.
	Time	The guest operating system must be aware and account for both real, wall-clock time as well as virtual time.
Device I/O	Network and Disk	Virtual devices are simple to access. Data is transferred using asynchronous I/O rings, and interrupt-like communication to the guest operating system is handled through event notifications.

Xen Domains

Figure 2.1 illustrates the system structure of a typical full-virtualization VMM for the x86 architecture. While similar in function to other VMMs, Xen has a unique system structure that is broken down into the underlying hardware, VMM (or hypervisor), a control region, and the virtual machines themselves, as illustrated in Figure 2.2. The hypervisor exposes an abstraction layer that contains both Management and Virtual Hardware APIs, including a control interface that allows guests to interact directly and indirectly with the underlying hardware. Interacting with the Management API is a control region that has privileged access to hardware and contains user mode management code. Both the control region and the virtual machines are referred to as domains. At boot time, the system initiates a special domain that is allowed to use the control interface, referred to as Domain-0 (dom0). This initial domain hosts the user mode management software used to administer the Xen environment, whether through command-line tools or using the XenSource Administrator Console. It is also responsible for starting and stopping a less-privileged domain type, guest domains, referred to as Domain-U (domU), via the control interface, as well as control domU CPU scheduling, memory allocations, and access to devices such as physical disk storage and network interfaces. A domU is also referred to as a Xen Virtual Machine, or XenVM.

Figure 2.1 System Structure of the Typical Full-Virtualization VMM for x86

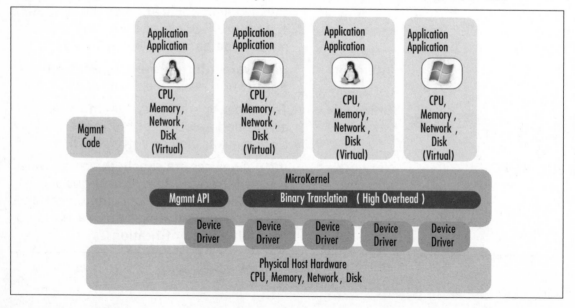

Figure 2.2 System Structure of the Xen VMM

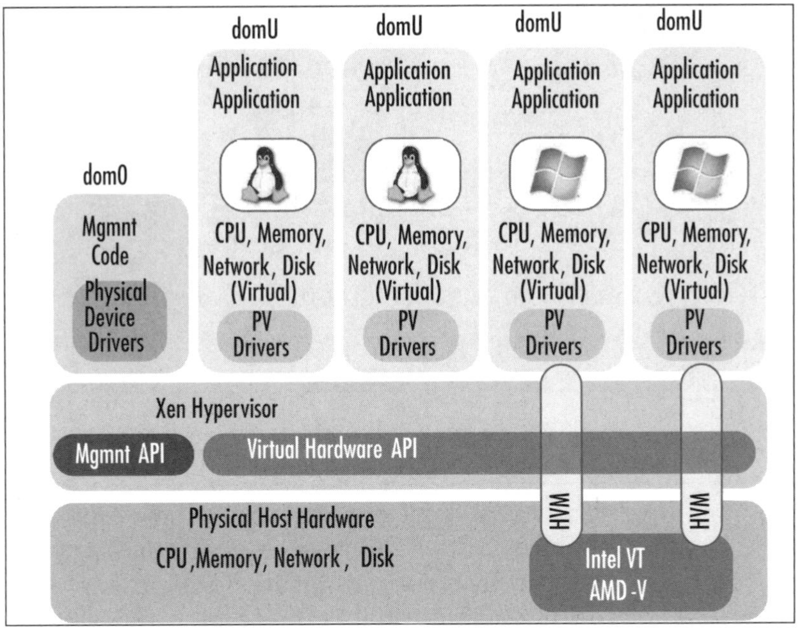

The control domain, dom0, functions like a standard Linux installation. You can run user mode applications, such as those used to manage the Xen environment, as well as install the device drivers needed to support your hardware platform. Because of the ability to compile and run practically any hardware device with available Linux drivers, Xen has a wide array of hardware that it supports. This gives IT organizations greater flexibility with their selection of physical network and storage devices and allows Xen to be implemented on just about any x86 environment.

Configuring & Implementing…

Hardware Compatibility for Domain-0

The following URLs offer a list of supported and tested hardware maintained by the user community. While this does not represent every configuration that will run Xen without issues, it will give you an idea of the type of hardware users have successfully implemented Xen with. For example, if you find an HP, Dell, or IBM server on the list, you can be sure the network interface cards and storage adapters used by the server will work in just about any other server

Continued

with the same hardware, even though other servers are not listed. You can find the hardware compatibility list at:

http://wiki.xensource.com/xenwiki/HardwareCompatibilityList
or
http://hcl.xensource.com/

If you would like to add your configuration to the list, XenSource offers a XenTest tool that will assess your hardware platform's compatibility and report the results. You can download this tool at the following sites:

HTTP www.xensource.com/xen/downloads/dl_x30tcd.html

BitTorrent www.xensource.com/xen/downloads/dl_x30tcd_bt.html

WARNING

You should minimize the number of processes running inside Domain-0, or dom0. This domain is a highly privileged domain. As such, any instability or system compromise induced by a running process will impact all guest domains as well. In addition, dom0 shares the same physical hardware that the guest domains are using. As dom0 consumes more resources, fewer will be available to domUs.

The Virtual Hardware API includes a control interface that manages the exposure of physical devices, both creation and deletion, through the following virtual I/O devices:

- Virtual Network Interfaces (VIFs)

- Virtual Firewall and Routers (VFRs)

- Virtual Block Devices (VBDs)

Each virtual I/O device has an Access Control List (ACL) associated with it. Similar to ACLs for a file system or network resource, this ACL contains the information about the domUs that have access to the devices, as well as restrictions and the type of access allowed—for instance, read-only, write, and so on.

The control interface as well as aggregated statistics that profile the state of the Xen system components, are exported to a suite of User Mode management tools run in dom0. These tools can be used to:

- Create and delete domUs

- Create and delete virtual I/O devices

- Monitor network activity

- Migrate live virtual machines from one Xen host to another

- Monitor performance on a systemwide or per-domain level

A complete list of management tools, both native as well as third-party, are discussed in greater detail in Chapters 4 and 5.

The Virtual Hardware API is also responsible for managing the transfer of control interactions between Xen and the overlying domUs. It does so through the use of hypercalls, synchronous calls from the domains to Xen, and events—an asynchronous mechanism to deliver notifications from Xen to the domains.

The hypercall interface allows the guest operating system to perform privileged operations by initiating a trap in the hypervisor. This is done in a manner similar to the system calls that the operating system would perform to underlying hardware, except that they occur from Ring-1 to Ring-0. These CPU- and memory-bound instructions are then carried out by the hypervisor against the physical hardware resources.

Comparatively, Xen communicates with the domains via an asynchronous event mechanism in the same manner the guest operating system would communicate through device interrupts. The control interface takes advantage of this event mechanism to send other important events, such as domain termination requests. Each event is sent as a flag to a particular type of occurrence. The occurrence can be an acknowledgement that a domain request has been completed or be used to notify the domain of a change of state in its operating environment. Though the hypervisor is responsible for updating each domain's queue of pending events, it is the responsibility of the domain itself to respond to event notifications, the deferral of event handling, and to reset the queue. This makes the event mechanism very lightweight from the hypervisor's perspective and accomplishes the objective we discussed earlier, to have the hypervisor share the burden with the guest operating systems themselves.

To better understand Xen's architecture, we will take a behind-the-scenes look at Xen, including the virtual machine abstraction and interfaces. We will reflect on how Xen virtualizes the following computing elements:

- CPU
- Memory management
- I/O

CPU Virtualization

On the x86 processor architecture, virtualization of the CPU presents several challenges, especially for guest operating systems that assume they are running directly on top of the hardware in Ring-0. While the x86 architecture provides four privileged rings or levels, the typical operating system only uses two: Ring-0 and Ring-3. In a typical VMM for x86, the operating system would coexist with applications in Ring-3. To protect itself, it would run in a completely different and unique address space, indirectly passing control to and from the application via the VMM. This can lead to several isolated inefficiencies that impact performance and flexibility.

An efficient approach to address this issue is to take advantage of the unused privileged levels, Ring-1 and Ring-2. These rings have not been used by an x86 operating system since IBM's OS/2. Any operating system that complies with this arrangement (the use of Ring-0 and Ring-3 only) can, technically, be ported to run on Xen. The operating system would be modified to execute in Ring-1, which still provides isolation and protection from other domUs and keeps it from executing high-privileged Ring-0 instructions, but offers improved isolation from User Mode applications.

Xen paravirtualizes a guest operating system running in a domU by mandating the validation and execution of instructions within Xen. If the domU attempts to execute a privileged instruction, it is trapped and failed by the hypervisor. However, an extended interface is presented to dom0, allowing it to create and boot other domains. This interface also allows dom0 access to high-level control operations such as CPU scheduling. CPU virtualization by Xen must account for exceptions, CPU scheduling, and time. Table 2.5 lists the common hypercalls used in Xen to manage CPU virtualization.

Table 2.5 Xen CPU Hypercalls

Category	Hypercall	Description
Virtual CPU Setup	set_callbacks	Register events callbacks for event processing.
	set_trap_table	Insert entries into the domain's unique trap handler table.
	vcpu_op	Provided for the management of virtual CPUs. Can be used to bring vCPUs up and down to test their current status.
CPU Scheduling and Timer	sched_op_new	Used to request the scheduling of a privileged operation with the hypervisor.
	set_timer_op	Used to request a timer event at a specific system time.
Context Switching	stack_switch	Used to request a kernel stack switch from the hypervisor.
	fpu_taskswitch	Used to facilitate, save, and restore a floating point state, enabling the guest to trap such activity and save/restore the state in a single call.
	switch_vm86	Allows guests to run in vm86 mode.

Exceptions

Xen takes a unique approach to dealing with exceptions. Using a special hypercall, *set_trap_table*, each domain maintains its own unique and dedicated table of trap handlers. Exceptions, such as memory faults and operating system traps, are addressed using trap handlers found in a specialized exception stack frame. This stack frame is identical to that found in the underlying x86 hardware platform, requiring very little modification of the exception process code in the guest operating system. Consequently, exceptions are handled two ways. The first is catered to system calls in the guest operating system and takes advantage of an accelerated exception handler that is registered by each guest and accessed directly by the processor. Although Xen still performs validation to trap privileged instructions, these system calls are carried out at near-native speeds without having to be executed in Ring-0. In other words,

Xen does not actually execute the system call on behalf of the guest. The second is for page faults, a difficult and rather impossible exception to address without the involvement of the hypervisor. The technique used for system calls cannot be performed for page faults since they must be carried out in Ring-0 by Xen. Such exceptions are carried out by Xen and the register values stored for retrieval by the guest in Ring-1.

CPU Scheduling

CPU scheduling is critical in server virtualization technology. It is the means in which virtual CPU (vCPU) are carried out by the hypervisor on the underlying CPU architecture. In order to optimize scheduling and allow near-native performance, the scheduling scheme must be efficient and not waste any processing cycles. These types of schemes are referred to as work-conserving; that is, they do not allow CPU resources to go unused. So long as there is capacity enough to execute instructions and there are instructions to be executed, work-conserving schemes will assign trapped guest instructions and assign them to physical CPUs to be carried out. If the workload in not congested, such schemes operate like simple first-in-first-out (FIFO) queuing schemes. However, should the processor queue become congested, the instructions will be queued and will be executed based on the priority and weight set in the scheduling scheme.

In comparison, non-work-conserving queue servicing may allow CPU capacity to go unused. In such cases, there is no advantage to executing instructions sooner than necessary, and downstream physical CPU resources may be spared by limiting instruction execution to the rate at which they can be carried out. It is possible to combine both work-conserving and non-work-conserving schemes in the same hypervisor.

One of the CPU schedulers available in Xen is based on the Borrowed Virtual Time (BVT) scheduling scheme. This is a hybrid algorithm that is both work-conserving and has mechanisms for low-latency dispatch, or domain wake-up, if a domain receives an event notification. The latter is important in a hypervisor to minimize the effect of virtualization on operating system subsystems designed to run in a timely manner. BVT accomplishes its low-latency characteristic by making use of virtual-time warping. This mechanism breaks the rules of "fair-share" and grants early, low-latency favor to domains woken up due to an event. Xen offers two scheduling schemes, Simple Earliest Deadline First (sEDF) and Credit schedulers, and makes it possible to implement a custom scheme of your own through a uniform

API for CPU schedulers. The Credit scheduler is optimized for SMP platforms and is the preferred choice. Credit-based scheduling will survive the retirement of sEDF when deprecated in future versions of Xen. BVT is a Credit scheduler.

Scheduling parameters are managed on a per-domain basis using the User Mode management tools running in dom0. While typical credit schedulers running on an SMP host will dynamically move across the physical CPUs in a work-conserving manner to maximize domain and system processor throughput, vCPUs can also be restricted to execute only on a subset of the host's physical CPUs, called pinning. For example, you may want an application server running in a particular domU to only run on CPU 2 and 3 of a four CPU server. Even if CPUs 0 and 1 have free cycles, they will not execute instructions for that domain—hence, the non-work-conserving ability of the hybrid scheduling model.

To view your current sEDF scheduling settings for all domains, run the following command without any parameters:

```
xm sched-sedf
```

To see the credit-based settings, you can execute the *xm sched-credit* with the –d option referencing the target domain ("1" in our example), as follows:

```
xm sched-credit -d 1
```

The output will indicate the cap as well as the relative weight (the default value is 256), as follows. Note that this command gives you the values for a single domain rather than an overall look at all domains, as with the *xm sched-sedf* command.

```
{'cap': 0, 'weight': 256}
```

TIP

Xen provides a command-line interface to manage schedulers. In the following, the first example references the syntax for customizing the sEDF scheduler for a specific domU, while the second is the syntax for customizing the Credit scheduler.
Example #1. sEDF Scheduler Customization:
```
xm sched-sedf <dom-id> <period> <slice> <latency-hint> <extra> <weight>
```
Example #2. Credit Scheduler Customization:
```
xm sched-credit -d <dom-id> -w <weight> -c <cap>
```
For more information on defining the sEDF scheduler, as well as others available with Xen, visit http://wiki.xensource.com/xenwiki/Scheduling. To learn more about Credit-based scheduling, visit http://wiki.xensource.com/xenwiki/CreditScheduler.

Time

Within a virtual infrastructure, timing becomes critical and can become confusing for guest operating systems. They need to know about both real and virtual time. Real time, referred to as wall-clock time, is managed by the hypervisor; however, virtual time becomes even more important to the guest operating system and for the scheduling of time-sensitive operations. There are several concepts to consider when discussing time in Xen. The following is a list of those concepts and a brief description:

- **System time** A 64-bit counter that holds the number of nanoseconds since system boot. At start-of-day, a guest's system time clock represents the time since that domain was created or started.

- **Wall-clock time** This is the time from dom0's perspective, and is maintained by dom0. The time is presented in seconds and microseconds since January 1, 1970, adjusting for leap years. As the key reference of time, it is important that this time be as accurate as possible. One way to do so is to utilize a Network Time Protocol (NTP) client within dom0.

- **Domain virtual time** This time is similar to the system time, but only progresses when the domain is scheduled. Time stops when the domain is de-scheduled. Virtual time is important (as noted in the previous section on CPU Scheduling), because the share of the CPU that a domain receives is based on the rate at which virtual time increases.

- **Cycle counter time** This timer is used to provide a fine-grained reference of time. Cycle counter time is used to extrapolate the other timers, or time references. It is important that the time is synchronized between each physical CPU.

Xen maintains timestamps for both system time and wall-clock time and exports those timestamps through a page of memory shared between Xen and each domain. Xen provides the cycle counter time when each timestamp is calculated, as well as the CPU frequency in hertz (Hz). This allows each guest to accurately extrapolate system and wall-clock times by factoring in the current cycle counter time. Without this extrapolation, the time references would often be inaccurate since the values in the shared page memory may be stale. In addition, the timestamps also have a version number associated with them. This version number is incremented twice for each update of each timestamp. First, it is incremented before updating timestamps, and then a second time after the update completes successfully. The version numbers are compared by the guest by checking to see if the two numbers match. If they do, the guest can assume that the time read is in a consistent state. If not, the guest knows that a timestamp update is in progress and returns to read the time values after the update has completed.

In addition to real and virtual time, Xen incorporate timers to help maintain accurate time in the guest operating system. Xen uses two types of timers. The first is a periodic timer that sends a timer event to the currently executing (awake) domain every 10ms. A timer event is also sent by the Xen scheduler to a domain when it is scheduled. The guest OS uses these events to make time adjustments while it is inactive. The second type is an intentionally scheduled timer requested by each domain using the *set_timer_op* hypercall. This timer can be used by a guest to implement the timeout concept. For example, if the guest schedules a timed event when making a hypercall to write to virtual memory and the corresponding notification of success has not been received when the scheduled timed event is received, the guest can timeout the original operation.

Memory Virtualization

Memory virtualization is probably the most difficult task that a VMM must perform. Xen is responsible for managing the allocation of physical memory to domains, and for ensuring the safe use of the paging and segmentation hardware. Since several domains share the same memory, care must be taken to maintain isolation. The hypervisor must ensure that no two unprivileged domains, or domUs, access the same memory area. Each page or directory table update must be validated by the hypervisor to ensure that domains only manipulate their own tables. Domains may batch these operations to be more efficient through sequential updates. Segmentation is virtualized in a similar manner, placing the hypervisor in a gate-keeper role to ensure that the domains' segments do not overlap or are invalid in some way or other.

Similar to CPU virtualization, the Xen guest must trap any privileged calls that would require Ring-0 access and pass them to the hypervisor using hypercalls. Table 2.6 highlights the main hypercalls used to manage memory virtualization. To better understand how Xen manages memory, we will discuss memory allocation, virtual address translation, and page tables types and segmentation.

Table 2.6 Xen Memory Hypercalls

Category	Hypercall	Description
Page Table Management	mmu_update	Updates the domain's page table, usually in batch.
	update_va_mapping	Used to update a single page table entry (PTE) for a specific virtual memory address rather than in batch.
	mmuext_op	Used to perform extended memory operations, such as cache flushing, or to reassign page ownership.
	vm_assist	Used to toggle various memory management modes.
Virtual Address Translation	set_gdt	Used to create a new global descriptor table (GDT) for a domain.
	update_descriptor	Used to update either global or local descriptor tables (GDT/LTD).

Memory Allocation

As we have been discussing, in addition to allocating a portion of the physical system RAM for its own private use, Xen also reserves a small portion of every virtual address space. This allocation is dependent on the underlying platform, as Figures 2.3 and 2.4 illustrate.

NOTE

While the x86 architecture can theoretically support up to 64GB in PAE mode and up to 8TB for x64 implementations, only XenEnterprise can utilize the full amount of RAM in such systems. XenServer and XenExpress are limited to 8GB and 4GB, respectively.

Figure 2.3 Memory Allocation for 32-bit x86 with and without PAE

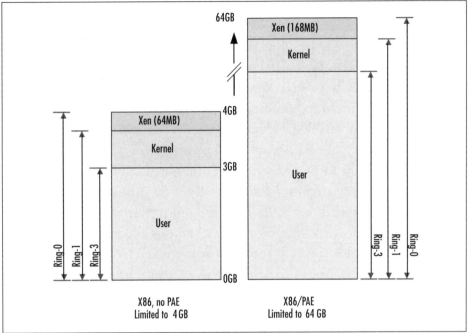

Figure 2.4 Memory Allocation for x64

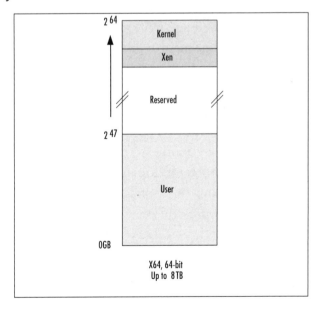

In 32-bit x86 architecture, with and without PAE, segmentation is used to protect the Xen hypervisor from the kernel. The reservation of the 64MB, or 168MB, respectively, region does not impact the speed at which system calls are serviced. In comparison, the x64 architecture is quite generous with the reservation allocation to Xen; however, there is no protection from segment limits as in the x86 architecture. This requires Xen to use page-level protection tactics to protect the hypervisor from kernel memory operations.

With regard to allocations of the domUs, each domain has a maximum and current consumed physical memory allocation. Xen has implemented a balloon driver concept for each domain, enabled independently, that allows the operating system to adjust its current memory allocation up to the maximum limit configured. This allows "unused" allocation to be consumed in other areas, potentially allowing for stable over-commitment of memory resources. Because of this constantly changing memory allocation, combined with the creation and termination of domains, memory is allocated and freed dynamically at a granularity of the page-level. Xen cannot guarantee that a domain will receive a contiguous allocation of physical memory to use. While this breaks the rules of most x86-compatible operating systems, Xen makes up for it with the use of pseudo-physical memory compared to machine, or true physical, memory. Machine memory refers to the total amount of RAM in the physical host, including any reservations made to Xen. Machine memory is made up of 4kB page frames, whether allocated to Xen or to a domU, and is counted in a linear fashion regardless of that allocation. Pseudo-physical memory is the abstraction of those page frames on a per-domain basis.

This is how Xen "fools" each domain into thinking it has a contiguous stretch of memory starting always with frame 0. As machine memory frames leap and skip frame numbers, the pseudo-physical memory continues to represent a consistently numbered, and hence contiguous, page space. This is achieved without any pixie dust, but rather through the use of two tables. The first is readable by the hypervisor and all domains and maps machine page frames to pseudo-physical ones (machine-to-physical). The second is supplied to each domain independently, and maps the inverse, pseudo-physical page frames to machine ones (physical-to-machine). Using both tables, the domain is able to provide the abstraction to facilitate even the pickiest of operating systems.

Page Tables and Segmentation

In the x86 architecture, the memory is divided into three kinds of addresses: logical, linear, and physical. A logical address is a storage location address that may or may not relate directly to a physical location. The *logical address* is usually used when requesting information from a controller. A *linear address* (or a flat address space) is memory that is addressed starting with 0. Each subsequent byte is referenced by the next sequential number (0, 1, 2, 3, and so on) all the way to the end of memory. This is how most non-x86 CPUs address memory. The x86 architecture uses a segmented address space in which memory is broken up into 64KB segments, and a segment register always points to the base of the segment currently being addressed. The 32-bit mode in this architecture is considered a flat address space, but it too uses segments. A *physical address* is an address represented by bits on a physical address bus. The physical address may be different from the logical address, in which case the memory management unit translates the logical address into a physical address.

The CPU uses two units to transform the logical address into physical addresses. The first is called the *segmented unit* and the other is called the *paging unit*, as illustrated in Figure 2.5.

Figure 2.5 Segmented and Paging Units Convert Address Spaces

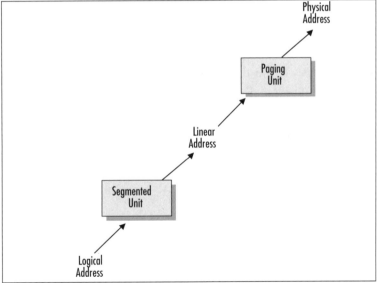

The basic idea behind the segmentation control unit model is that memory is managed using a set of segments. Essentially, each segment is its own address space. A segment consists of two components, the *base address* that contains the address of some physical memory location and the *length value* that specifies the length of the segment. Each segment is a 16-bit field called a *segment identifier* or *segment selector*. x86 hardware consists of a few programmable registers called *segment registers*, which hold these segment selectors. These registers are cs (code segment), ds (data segment), and ss (stack segment). Each segment identifier identifies a segment that is represented by a 64-bit (eight bytes) *segment descriptor*. These segment descriptors are stored in a global descriptor table (GDT) and can also be stored in a local descriptor table (LDT).

Each time a segment selector is loaded onto segment registers, the corresponding segment descriptor is loaded from memory into a matching CPU register. Each segment descriptor is eight bytes long and represents a single segment in memory. These are stored in LDTs or GDTs. The segment descriptor entry contains both a pointer to the first byte in the associated segment represented by the Base field and a 20-bit value (the *Limit* field), which represents the size of the segment in memory.

The paging unit, on the other hand, translates the linear addresses into physical ones as shown in Figure 2.5. A set of linear addresses are grouped together to form pages. These linear addresses are contiguous in nature—the paging unit maps these sets of contiguous memory to a corresponding set of contiguous physical addresses called *page frames*. Note that the paging unit visualizes RAM to be partitioned into a fixed size of page frames.

The data structure that maps these pages to page frames is called a *page table* (*PT*). These page tables are stored in the main memory and are properly initialized by the operating system kernel before enabling the paging control unit.

The translation of linear addresses into their corresponding physical location is a two-step process. The first step converts the address space from a translation table called *Page Directory* (*PD*) to a second table called the PT. The second step converts the address space from the PT to the required page frame.

So what does this all mean to Xen?

Xen uses the paging unit more than it does the segmentation unit. Each segment descriptor uses the same set of addresses for linear addressing, thus minimizing the need to use the segmentation unit to convert logical addresses to linear addresses. By using the paging unit more than the segmentation unit, Xen greatly facilitates efficient memory management for the hypervisor and the guest domains.

Returning to our discussion on memory virtualization, you will recall that the Xen hypervisor has only one role in this area, which is to validate the page table updates passed via hypercall to ensure safety and isolation. To aid in this validation effort, Xen associates a type and reference count with each physical machine page frame. A frame may have any one (and exactly one) of the following types at any point:

- Page Directory (PD)

- Page Table (PT)

- Local Descriptor Table (LDT)

- Global Descriptor Table (GDT)

- Writable (RW)

Since Xen's involvement is only to manage "write" operations, guests can map and access any of its own page frames without intervention from the hypervisor, regardless of the frame type. However, a frame cannot be reallocated to another use using the *mmu_update* hypercall until its reference count is zero. Frames can also be pinned to PD or PT after the hypervisor has completed the validation of an entry, allowing guests to control the allocation of frames for page-table use. Through this mechanism, Xen can give the guests the illusion of being able to write to memory pages directly. When a Xen-aware (or paravirtualized) guest wants to write to a memory page of type PD or PT, it can request that it be writable by using the *vm_assist* hypercall in conjunction with *mmu_update*. Xen then allows the write operation to succeed, but traps it. The page is temporarily removed from the page table until validated by Xen and reconnected. But again, pinned frames cannot be reallocated to another frame type until they are unpinned and the reference count zeroed.

While this level of interaction with the hypervisor may appear costly from a resource perspective, efficiency can be maintained by executing a series of hypervisor calls in batch rather than performing a single hypercall for each operation. This is done making use of the *multicall* hypercall. This technique can be used to highly optimize hypercall-intensive actions, such as context switches, which may require several calls to both CPU and memory virtualization components in the Xen hypervisor.

Virtual Address Translation

The management of memory is directly impacted by page tables and the Translation Lookaside Buffer (TLB). The page table is the data structure used by a computer system to store the mapping between virtual addresses and physical addresses. The TLB is a cache in a CPU that is used to improve the speed of virtual address translation. It has a fixed number of entries containing part of the page table that translate virtual memory addresses into physical machine addresses.

The TLB is typically content-addressable memory that uses the virtual addresses as a key that can be given as search input returns the physical address as a search result. If the search returns a match for the virtual memory address—in other words, the translation is successful—the physical address is used to access memory. If the virtual address cannot be found in the TLB, the translation takes an alternate route to identify the physical address via the page table, usually resulting in a longer operation that is costly from a resource perspective. The process can be even longer if the translation tables have been swapped out to secondary storage, such as a page or swap file on the hard drive. Some processor architectures provide a software-managed TLB, in particular RISC architecture such as SPARC, Alpha, and MIPS. However, the x86 CPU architecture does not have a software-managed TLB, relying on hardware to service TLB requests and handle misses. Refer to the sidebar for more information on TLB misses.

Therein lies the challenge for x86-targeted VMMs such as Xen. In order to achieve the highest memory performance possible, all valid translations must be present in the hardware-accessible page table. The x86 architecture does not tag the TLB (a process to indicate mappings that have been used); address space switches (between the hypervisor's and the domains' address spaces) require a complete TLB flush. Placing this burden on the hypervisor or control domains, typically dom0, would be costly. Instead, the developers of Xen opted to tackle this problem in two ways. First, in a manner consistent with other virtualization obstacles, the responsibility is placed on the guest operating systems to allocate and manage the hardware page tables, thus relieving and lightening the load of the hypervisor, whose role is reduced to validation of page table updates to ensure safety and isolation. Second, Xen utilizes a dedicated memory range for itself, avoiding the dreaded TLB flush that occurs when entering and leaving the hypervisor. More is discussed on this in the section titled "Memory Allocation" earlier in this chapter.

Architecture Concepts...

Translation Lookaside Buffer Miss

When a Translation Lookaside Buffer (TLB) miss occurs, two schemes are commonly found in modern architectures. With hardware TLB management, such as the type found in the x86 architecture, the CPU itself walks the page tables to see if there is a valid page table entry for the specified virtual address. If an entry exists, it is loaded into the TLB and the TLB access is retried. This time the

Continued

access will hit, and the program can proceed normally. If the CPU finds no valid entry for the virtual address in the page tables, it raises a page fault exception, which the operating system must handle. Handling page faults usually involves bringing the requested data into physical memory, setting up a page table entry to map the faulting virtual address to the correct physical address, and restarting the program.

With software-managed TLBs, a TLB miss generates a "TLB miss" exception, and the operating system must walk the page tables and perform the translation in software. The operating system then loads the translation into the TLB and restarts the program from the instruction that caused the TLB miss. Like with hardware-based TLB management, if the operating system finds no valid translation in the page tables, a page fault has occurred, and the operating system must handle it accordingly.

To illustrate the performance impact of a TLB miss in the x86 architecture, take into consideration the typical hit time of 0.5 to 1.0 clock cycles to find a virtual address in the TLB. If a TLB miss occurs and the CPU resorts to walking the page table to find the virtual address, the miss penalty can range from 10 to 30 additional clock cycles. If the TLB hit rate for a particular system took one clock cycle, a miss took 30 clock cycles, and the TLB miss rate was 10 percent, the effective memory cycle rate would average 3.9 clock cycles per memory access, or almost four times slower than its potential.

Correlating this to CPU selection, a CPU with larger cache can make a substantial performance improvement. Even with the multicore architectures available for x86 and x64 platforms, a larger cache shared by all the cores is better than an individual cache per core. For example, the dual-core Intel Xeon 5050 processor running at 3.0GHz with 2MB of L2 cache per core has lower performance than the Intel Xeon 5110 running at 1.6GHz with 4MB L2 cache shared between the cores. Though not the only reason for the performance increase, the cache model does contribute. Since both cores can be load-balanced to execute operations, they have a better chance of finding virtual addresses in the shared TLB and can reduce page table walks.

Page table creation is managed by each guest. When a new page table is created, the guest operating system allocates addresses from its own memory reservation and registers it with Xen after initialization. Though residing in its memory space, the guest gives us direct write privileges to the hypervisor, which validates any updates passed to it from the guest through hypercalls. Xen does not guarantee that the page table memory is contiguous, although the guest operating system believes it is; in fact, in most cases, it is not contiguous. In addition, the memory reserved by Xen is not able to be mapped as page-table memory for any guest.

Finally, Xen supports the use of shadow page tables. When using this technique, Xen creates an identical replica of the page tables allocated and initialized by the guest operating system. The guest reads and writes from its resident version of the page tables, while Xen copies all changes in real time to the shadow page table. If a domain commits a page table update that generates a fault, Xen will either send and event notification to the operating system to handle the page fault or, in more serious cases, it will terminate the domain. Either way, the safety and isolation of dom0 and the other domUs is maintained. This technique is useful for operating systems whose CPU and memory operations cannot be paravirtualized, such as Microsoft Windows, and to optimize live XenVM migrations of paravirtualized guests.

I/O Virtualization

Virtualizing I/O devices, such as network interfaces and hard drives, follows a school of thought similar to CPU and memory virtualization. That is, the virtual machine monitor can emulate the underlying hardware or it can work together with modified and highly customized software running in the guest virtual machines to optimize I/O operations for performance, reliability, and security. To be successful at fully virtualizing I/O devices, the VMM must not only look like the underlying hardware but must also be compatible with the software device drivers to be used, as well as emulate things like interrupts, data buses, and resource sharing of the actual physical hardware. This task can often lead to substantial overhead in the VMM and impacted performance.

Waiving any attempt at emulation, the Xen makes use of paravirtualization abstracts to present I/O devices to unprivileged domains containing supported guest operating systems. These abstracts are less complex than the ones for CPU and memory, and they often do not require modification of the guest operating system. Instead, paravirtualization can be accomplished by installing device drivers that are coded to be Xen-aware and interact with the hypervisor APIs (see Table 2.7 for a list of common hypercalls for I/O) that expose the communication to and from the actual physical I/O devices. So while Microsoft Windows and other "closed" operating systems must rely on HVM support to virtualize CPU and memory operations, they can take advantage of the benefits of paravirtualization for I/O. This design is both efficient and meets all requirements for protection and isolation.

Table 2.7 Xen I/O Hypercalls

Category	Hypercall	Description
Event Channels	event_channel_op	Used for all operations on event channels and ports.
Grant Tables	grant_table_op	Used to managed map/unmap, set, dump, or transfer commands against grant tables.
I/O Configuration	physdev_op	Used to set and query IRQ configuration details and other PCI BIOS operations.

I/O data is transferred to and from guest domains and Xen using shared-memory, asynchronous descriptor rings. We will discuss these rings shortly, but note that these rings are key to providing a high-performance mechanism to communicate with Xen when passing buffer information through the system while also providing a means for the hypervisor to perform its validation checks efficiently.

This section will triage the myriad components required to effectively paravirtualize I/O in addition to providing greater insight into the tricks-of-the-trade and up-and-coming techniques available through hardware innovation, including the following:

- Device I/O rings
- Event channels
- Virtual I/O devices and split device drivers
- Driver domains
- Software and hardware IOMMUs

Device I/O Rings

With the hypervisor's role of providing an abstraction layer that both protects and isolates guest operating systems from I/O devices, it is important that a means to transfer data be implemented that allows data to move quickly with little overhead. Two factors have led to the design of the mechanism used in Xen: resource management and event notification. The developers of Xen attempted to reduce the amount of work required when processing data in the event an interrupt is received by a device and to thus provide a level of resource accountability. This was accomplished by:

- Managing the asynchronous buffers at a level where the processing time can be correctly accounted for against the appropriate and benefiting domain.

- Reducing crosstalk in I/O buffers by requiring guest operating systems to commit a portion of their memory allocation for device I/O rather than using the shared buffer pool.

- Using the hypervisor to pin the underlying page frames, similar to memory management procedures discussed earlier, to protect data during transfer.

Within the structure of the I/O rings are inbound and outbound queues. These queues do not contain any actual data, but rather act as pointers to I/O buffers allocated by the guest operating systems referenced by I/O descriptors. Working with these queues are pairs of producers and consumers. Each domain has its own producer and consumer used to access the I/O rings, and the Xen hypervisor has a shared producer and consumer that communicates with the domains as well.

Let's step through the process to better understand how this mechanism works. This process is represented in Figure 2.6. As we walk through it, it may help to visualize a round table surface that spins around with the domains and the hypervisor at the outside edge of the perimeter of the ring. Although the table spins like a wheel in a set direction, the domains and hypervisor are static in location. When a domain wants to use an I/O device, it places a request in the requests queue (the spinning wheel) as the *request producer*. This request advances or updates a request pointer that is shared globally among the domains and the hypervisor. Xen then removes these requests for processing as the *request consumer*, advancing an associated request consumer pointer, which is private to Xen. Responses to the requests are also placed on this spinning wheel in the response queue. Xen places each response as the *response producer* on the ring and advances or updates a shared pointer for responses. The appropriate guest then picks up the response and advances or updates its private response pointer as the *response consumer*.

Figure 2.6 The Device I/O Ring

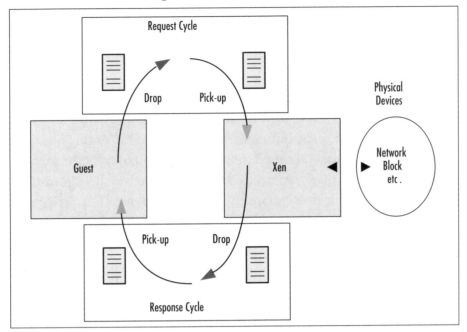

Since the I/O rings are asynchronous, order is not important or required. Each request has a unique identifier associated with it, which Xen uses to mark the corresponding response. There are advantages to the asynchronous nature of this mechanism. First, Xen can reorder the I/O operations efficiently in order to take advantage of scheduling and priority factors when interfacing with the physical devices. This can be particularly effective with block devices, such as mass storage drive arrays. Second, no formal notification or event is sent when a request is made. Xen does not pick up new requests from a domain until the guest sends a hypercall to do so. This allows guests to queue up a series of requests for a similar type of I/O transaction and then send a single hypercall, allowing Xen to pick and service the requests in a more efficient manner. This is particularly effective with network traffic. The same is true with responses. The "fast" transfer nature of BVT allows a domain to be awoken and to retrieve a batch of related responses in a single transaction rather than consuming cycles picking up each response individually. The process is efficient enough to satisfy time-sensitive operations such as certain TCP traffic inside the guest.

In some cases, however, the guest may not want reordering to occur. In such cases, the guest domain can explicitly pass down reorder barriers to prevent the hypervisor from reordering requests in batches. The barriers prevent the elevator scheduler managing the execution of I/O operations from performing its round-robin technique and to execute the operations in the domain's batch in sequence. This can be important in some block device operations, such as write-ahead logs, where the integrity of the data comes at the mercy of the sequence of data arrival.

Event Channels

We previously mentioned the event notification mechanism used by the Xen hypervisor to communicate with guest domains. At the foundation of this mechanism are event channels. Event channels are mediums through which events, the Xen equivalent of a hardware interrupt, are transmitted. The epitome of "the flip of the bit," events are simply a single bit that is transitioned to a value of "1" to trigger that the event has occurred.

Used in a reverse communication from hypervisor to guest, event notifications are received via an upcall (the reciprocal of the hypercall) from Xen. No mechanism exists to track multiple occurrences of the same event, so additional events are masked, or suppressed, until the bit is cleared again, and action must be taken by the guest operating system itself. However, event masking (setting the bit to "1" and leaving it at that value) can be done purposely by the guest to mimic the same functionality as disabling interrupts.

Event channels make use of a variety of commands available in the *event_channel_op* hypercall. These commands are used to set the even channel port to use for communication, to bind and unbind event sessions with domains, and to even bind and unbind event channel ports to specific IRQs. This makes capturing interrupts quite easy and flexible when modifying guest operating systems for paravirtualization in Xen.

Virtual I/O Devices and Split Device Drivers

Instead of providing access to physical devices, Xen offers virtualized views of them. This is not the same as presenting virtual emulation of devices, such as network interfaces or storage devices, but rather devices that guest domains can use to interface with the underlying physical I/O hardware.

When Xen boots and launches dom0, it exports a subset of the devices in the systems to the other domains, based on each domain's configuration. The devices are exported as *class devices*, either as block devices or network devices, but not as a specific hardware model. The interaction with these class devices is based on a translation between domains and the Xen hypervisor via a split device driver architecture.

As illustrated in Figure 2.7, this architecture comprises two cooperating drivers: the *frontend driver* which runs in an unprivileged domU, and the *backend driver*, which runs in a domain with real access to real hardware. While dom0 is usually the only domain that supports the backend drivers, it is possible to create additional privileged domains to fulfill this role.

Figure 2.7 The Split Device Driver Architecture

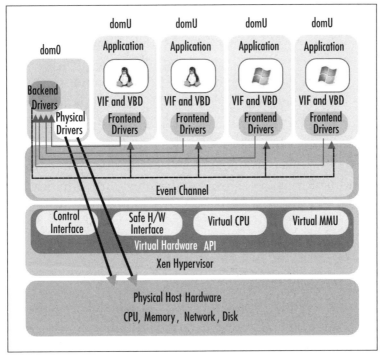

The frontend driver appears to the domU guest operating system as a real device. The guest can interact with it just as it would any other device for which it had the appropriate drivers installed. It can receive I/O requests from its kernel, but since it does not have direct access to the hardware, it must pass those requests to the backend driver running in dom0. The backend driver, in turn, receiving the I/O requests, validates them for safety and isolation, and proxies them to the real device. When the I/O operation completes, the backend driver notifies the frontend driver that the operation was successful and ready to continue, which in turn reports the I/O completion to the operation system kernel.

The concepts we have discussed previously all come into play to make this happen. Device I/O rings and event channels are central to the virtual I/O architecture, as is one additional component—the Xenstore (which we will discuss in a minute). The Xenstore is used to set up a shared memory frame between the domU frontend and the dom0 backend in each domain.

Network I/O

To facilitate network I/O virtualization, Xen provides an abstraction of a virtual firewall-router (VFR). The VFR has one or more virtual interfaces (VIFs) that logically make up the communication interfaces of the VFR. Each VIF looks and acts like a standard network interface card, containing two I/O rings, one for transmission and the other for reception. The VFR contains the rules, as established by the guest OS, to control the movement data through each VIF in a manner similar to firewall rules.

The two I/O rings handle the payload of the network traffic going to and from the guest domain. The guest places transmission requests on the transmit I/O ring. Xen then makes a copy of the request's header and descriptor, validates it using the VFR rules, and, if all is well, pins the appropriate memory frames in the shared memory frame and performs the actual data transfer to the physical interface mapped to the VIF. The backend driver is responsible for all of this packet handling, which can be summarized as:

- **Validation** Ensuring that an attempt to generate invalid traffic has occurred. This is done by analyzing the source MAC and IP address.

- **Scheduling** Using a simple round-robin scheduler, the backend manages the transmission queue from the various running domUs. In addition to the round-robin scheduler, other schemes such as shaping or rate-limiting schemes can be applied.

- **Logging and accounting** The backend driver can be coded and configured to log characteristics of the communication traversing each VIF. The logging can be triggered based on network packet data—for example, when a SYN or FIN is received.

To receive data, empty page frames are used as temporary buffers in the guest operating system, just as they would be in a nonvirtual implementation. Xen demultiplexes incoming network traffic and divides the data up between the corresponding domain VIF. Xen again validates it against the VFR rules and, if all is well, exchanges the page buffer with a page frame in the actual shared memory frame.

Block I/O

Similar to network I/O, block devices are only accessible from privileged domains. dom0 has unrestricted access to physical disks, regardless of their type—IDE, SATA, SCSI, Fibre Channel, and iSCSI. Unprivileged domains utilize block device abstractions called virtual block devices (VBDs). A VBD works similar to a physical disk interface. One of the critical components for a high-performing disk subsystem is the ability of a typical operating system to reorder disk I/O requests intelligently and to efficiently retrieve and write data, reducing disk response times. This is possible through advanced scheduling schemes. In the virtual world, Xen has similar abilities, thus a VBD appears to a guest operating system just like a typical physical block device.

The VBD allows competing domains access to portions of a block storage device by using the backend/frontend driver architecture. As a split device driver, a single shared memory frame is used between the frontend and backend drivers for each VBD forming the device I/O ring used to send requests and receive responses. The backend driver has similar responsibilities as with network I/O, particularly in regards to validation, scheduling, and logging and accounting.

Trusted Platform Module and Other Devices

Practically any device can be abstracted and exported to guest domains using the frontend/backend architecture in paravirtualized guest operating systems. An example is the recent addition of Trusted Platform Module (TPM) devices to the supported Xen model. Virtual TPM (VTPM) devices enable domUs to access their own private TPM in a manner similar to built-in, hardware-based TPM devices. Implemented as a split driver, the guest exports a character device, /dev/tmp0, to User Mode application for communicating with virtual TPM, which is identical to the interface of an actual TPM device. The backend driver provides a single interface in the privileged domain, /dev/vtpm, listening for commands from all of the domains. All communication between guest domains and Xen are accomplished using a single I/O ring for sending requests and for sending responses in the opposite direction.

Driver Domains

Until now, we have talked about an exclusive privileged domain, Domain-0. This domain has access to all hardware devices, and less privileged domains (domUs) perform I/O operations through it. In implementations containing large numbers of virtual machines, or virtual machines that require high levels of I/O utilization, dom0 can become overwhelmed with the burden of supporting the backend drivers for all of the virtual devices, as well as managing the overall Xen system.

Xen provides a way to help offload the burden of extensive consumer load through the creation of driver domains. Driver domains, or isolated driver domains (IDDs), are traditional guest domains that have been granted extended privileges, each with its own devices and consumers, as shown in Figure 2.8. The control interface in the Xen hypervisor allows dom0 to create device-specific guests and assign permissions necessary to directly access the hardware using unmodified device drivers. While this may seem contrary to the purpose and function of guest domains, it offers a boon in improved and balanced I/O performance. It is assumed that each driver runs inside one and only one drive domain (dom0 or other). This maintains the reliability, maintainability, and manageability provided through driver and fault isolation.

Figure 2.8 User of Driver Domains

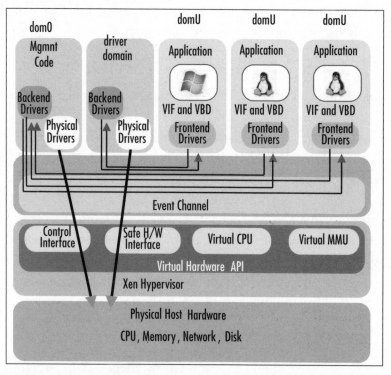

Since IDDs are guest domains themselves, they cannot utilize the conventional mechanisms to interact with other guest domains. They communicate with domUs through device channels, point-to-point communication links that facilitate asynchronous messaging between each side of the channel. dom0 uses the controller interface to introduce the guest operating system and IDD to each other.

One of the key benefits of device-driver domains is fault recovery. Not only are driver faults limited to the domain, and VIFs mapping to that physical interface, but the fault can be detected and the driver restarted. In worse cases, the driver domain itself can be killed and restarted without having to restart the dom0, leaving other virtual environments online and intact.

Software and Hardware IOMMUs

Some new types of devices, however, do not need to utilize the split driver architecture to provide high-performance I/O communication. To understand how this can be accomplished and under what conditions, we will first discuss various I/O Memory Management Units (IOMMUs), hardware constructs that can be emulated in software. IOMMUs provide two main functions, translation and device isolation, as follows:

- The IOMMU translates memory addresses from I/O space to physical space to allow a particular device to access physical memory potentially out of its range. It does this translation by providing an in-range address to the device and either translates the DMA access from the in-range address to the physical memory address on-the-fly or copies the data to the physical memory address.

- Also, IOMMUs can limit the ability of devices to access memory, used for restricting DMA targets.

SWIOTLB

IOMMUs are 32-bit and DMA-capable, and are able to access physical memory addresses higher than 4GB. They can be programmed so that the memory region appears to be contiguous to the device on the bus. However, remapping can add a performance penalty during data transfers. There are several advantages to this, but the one most important for virtualization is isolation. Although IOMMUs are able to translate memory addresses, the translation must be available for the appropriate device only, but masked from other devices. Therein lies the challenge of IOMMUs in current system architectures.

IOMMUs can be found in two forms: software and hardware. The common forms of software IOMMUs are Software I/O Translation Buffer (SWIOTLB) and grant tables. Xen's implementation of SWIOTLB is based on the standard Linux distribution for IA64 since there are no hardware IOMMUs for that architecture. The Xen team has tweaked the implementation as of version 3.0.0, and runs the IOMMU in dom0. Using SWIOTLB is transparent to the drivers, and it uses DMA mapping in its architecture. The one drawback to this feature is that it requires contiguous blocks of physical memory (based on the DMA requirements), although configurable.

Grant Tables

The second form of software IOMMU, grant tables, provides a memory-sharing approach to I/O management. Grant tables allow pages of data to be shared and transferred between domains. These pages can be read, written to, or exchanged for the sake of providing a fast and secure means for unprivileged domains to receive indirect access to hardware. They support higher performance I/O because the guest operating system can make DMA calls directly into pages in its local memory rather than having to copy or flip pages from a privileged domain to a local memory page. However, as with everything else "Xen," it can only access the pages specified in the grant table, so safety is still maintained. Using the *gnttab_grant_foreign_access* hypercall, guest domains can advertise to the hypervisor that a page is available to be shared. Once the sharing is complete and the remote domain has accomplished its work, access is revoked using the *gnttab_end_foreign_access* hypercall.

Grant tables help resolve the problem of IOMMUs needed to provide both translation and isolation. Working together with SWIOTLB, the two provide not only the translation functionality needed in an IOMMU but also protection by permissions managed at the table level. As CPU manufacturers continue to innovate and develop hardware acceleration into their chips, the translation that SWIOTLB may be replaced with hardware IOMMU equivalents, such as AMD's GART or Intel-VT features, but grant tables will probably last a lot longer.

The Xenstore

Referred to earlier in the chapter, the Xenstore is the primary mechanism for controlling activities such as setting up shared memory regions and event channels, managing notifications of guests of control events, and gathering and reporting status information from guests. The structure of the Xenstore is hierarchical in nature, with a directory-like traversal of a collection of key-value pairs. Each domain has a directory hierarchy containing store information, principally configuration info.

All the information is stored in a database, located at */var/lib/xenstored/tdb*. The store addresses certain key aspects of domain functionality. For example, a Xen bus is provided to facilitate device discovery when drivers are present or during the installation of new drivers. This is critical for plug-and-play functionality inside certain guest operating systems. Also, maintaining the configuration of a domain is as simple as updating references in its store hierarchy. Since domains can only modify the contents of their own directories, they are permitted to register for notifications about changes in their store tree and subtrees and to apply changes in a transactional fashion. For example, if you wanted to switch from using the host's physical CD-ROM drive for a guest domain to using an ISO file, you would use a management tool to update the store of that domain, letting the configuration of the */dev/cdrom* device be reconfigured to map to the ISO file—a change which would take place almost immediately. The contents of the ISO become available for use within the guest operating system without having to tear down and re-create the domain.

If you look at the store hierarchy, you'll see that three main paths can be used:

- **/vm** Contains configuration information about the domain.
- **/local/domain** Stores information about the domain on the local node.
- **/tool** Contains information about the various User Mode tools.

You can use the information in the store to develop a custom management interface or to perform simple queries within your Xen environment. Although the development of custom code interacting with the Xenstore is beyond the scope of this chapter, it is still worth discussing the type of information that each of the three paths contains, as well as the shell commands used to interact with the store itself.

The daemon spawned by *xend* at boot time, *xenstored*, exposes several commands you can use to manage the store and its contents, including the following:

- **xenstore-chmod** Permits administrator and developers to manually change the permissions on arbitrary locations in Xenstore.
- **xenstore-list** Outputs the keys, or categories, stored in the store hierarchical directory tree.
- **xenstore-read** Outputs the value associated with a specific key in the store.

- **xenstore-write** Used to change the value of a key within the store.

- **xenstore-exists** Used to check for the existence of a particular key-value pair.

- **xenstore-ls** Outputs the entire store hierarchical database tree, including all nodes and key-value pairs.

- **xenstore-rm** Removes a key from the directory tree.

Using a simple shell script, as follows, we can examine the complete store layout for all three paths for each domain, including dom0:

```
#!/bin/sh

function dumpkey() {
   local param=${1}
   local key
   local result
   result=$(xenstore-list ${param})
   if [ "${result}" != "" ] ; then
      for key in ${result} ; do dumpkey ${param}/${key} ; done
    else
      echo -n ${param}'='
      xenstore-read ${param}
   fi
}


for key in /vm /local/domain /tool ; do dumpkey ${key} ; done
```

Narrowing down the output from this script, we will examine a few significant cross-sections, beginning with the */vm* path. In the following output, configuration information for a guest domain is shown. From this output, we can see its UUID, learn that it uses hardware virtualization (HVM), identify the MAC address and VLAN for its VIFs, and determine what features have been enabled, such as ACPI, USB, and the serial console port.

```
/vm/ba2b02b2-7684-432b-b56f-62bf3e573095/image/ostype=hvm
/vm/ba2b02b2-7684-432b-b56f-62bf3e573095/image/kernel=/usr/lib/xen/boot/hvmloader
/vm/ba2b02b2-7684-432b-b56f-62bf3e573095/image/dmargs=-vcpus 1 -serial pty -acpi -
usb -usbdevice tablet -domain-name ba2b02b2-7684-432b-b56f-62bf3e573095 -net
nic,vlan=1,macaddr=00:16:3E:74:33:97,model=rtl8139 -net tap,vlan=1,bridge=xenbr0 -
net nic,vlan=2,macaddr=00:16:3E:A7:D5:EF,model=rtl8139 -net
tap,vlan=2,bridge=xenbr1
```

```
/vm/ba2b02b2-7684-432b-b56f-62bf3e573095/image/device-model=/usr/lib/xen/bin/qemu-
dm
```

We can also determine uptime using the start_time field and what actions are taken for various events, such as reboot, poweroff, and crash events notifications. We also learn more about the CPU and memory allocations provided to the domain.

```
/vm/ba2b02b2-7684-432b-b56f-62bf3e573095/on_reboot=restart
/vm/ba2b02b2-7684-432b-b56f-62bf3e573095/start_time=1174892778.62
/vm/ba2b02b2-7684-432b-b56f-62bf3e573095/on_poweroff=destroy
/vm/ba2b02b2-7684-432b-b56f-62bf3e573095/on_xend_start=ignore
/vm/ba2b02b2-7684-432b-b56f-62bf3e573095/on_crash=restart
/vm/ba2b02b2-7684-432b-b56f-62bf3e573095/xend/restart_count=0
/vm/ba2b02b2-7684-432b-b56f-62bf3e573095/vcpus=1
/vm/ba2b02b2-7684-432b-b56f-62bf3e573095/vcpu_avail=1
/vm/ba2b02b2-7684-432b-b56f-62bf3e573095/memory=256
/vm/ba2b02b2-7684-432b-b56f-62bf3e573095/maxmem=256
```

In the following output, we trace the /local/domain path. This is a great place to identify information about a domain's virtual I/O devices. You can identify configuration information about the frontend and device setup, including which backend device it maps to, the event-channel port, its current state, and statistics since start-of-day.

```
/local/domain/2/device/vbd/768/backend-id=0
/local/domain/2/device/vbd/768/virtual-device=768
/local/domain/2/device/vbd/768/device-type=disk
/local/domain/2/device/vbd/768/state=4
/local/domain/2/device/vbd/768/backend=/local/domain/0/backend/vbd/2/768
/local/domain/2/device/vbd/768/ring-ref=1664
/local/domain/2/device/vbd/768/event-channel=5
/local/domain/2/data/vbd/0/name=hda
/local/domain/2/data/vbd/0/total=8578932736
/local/domain/2/data/vbd/0/used=1998139392

/local/domain/2/device/vif/1/backend-id=0
/local/domain/2/device/vif/1/mac=00:16:3E:A7:D5:EF
/local/domain/2/device/vif/1/handle=1
/local/domain/2/device/vif/1/state=4
/local/domain/2/device/vif/1/backend=/local/domain/0/backend/vif/2/1
/local/domain/2/device/vif/1/tx-ring-ref=1893
/local/domain/2/device/vif/1/rx-ring-ref=1892
```

```
/local/domain/2/device/vif/1/event-channel=6
/local/domain/2/device/vif/1/request-rx-copy=1
/local/domain/2/device/vif/1/feature-no-csum-offload=0
/local/domain/2/device/vif/1/request-rx-copy-offset=2
```

Finally, we can see information about the operating system that is running inside the guest domain, such as the OS class, version, IP address, and boot environment.

```
/local/domain/2/attr/PVAddons/Installed=1
/local/domain/2/attr/PVAddons/MajorVersion=3
/local/domain/2/attr/PVAddons/MinorVersion=2
/local/domain/2/attr/PVAddons/BuildVersion=1960
/local/domain/2/attr/os/class=windows NT
/local/domain/2/attr/os/major=5
/local/domain/2/attr/os/minor=2
/local/domain/2/attr/os/build=3790
/local/domain/2/attr/os/platform=2
/local/domain/2/attr/os/spmajor=0
/local/domain/2/attr/os/spminor=0
/local/domain/2/attr/os/suite=272
/local/domain/2/attr/os/type=3
/local/domain/2/attr/os/boottype=0
/local/domain/2/attr/os/system32_dir=C:\WINDOWS\system32
/local/domain/2/attr/os/hal=hal.dll
/local/domain/2/attr/os/boot_options=FASTDETECT  PV
/local/domain/2/attr/os/hotfixes/0/installed=1
/local/domain/2/attr/eth1/ip=192.168.100.180
/local/domain/2/data/os_name=Microsoft Windows Server 2003 Standard
Edition|C:\WINDOWS|\Device\Harddisk0\Partition1
```

Summary

The debate continued on which technique is better for companies large and small—full virtualization or paravirtualization. Full virtualization offers an emulation of the physical server's hardware resources (CPU, memory, disk, and network) through extensive binary translation and trapping techniques at the expense of performance degradation. However, because standard operating system distributions can be used without modification, full virtualization reduces the complexity and administrative overhead of deploying virtual machines.

In comparison, paravirtualization optimizes guest operating systems and makes them hypervisor-aware, making for a more symbiotic relationship between guests and the host's hypervisor. With tweaks for CPU and memory virtualization, responsibility of instruction execution is shared between virtual machines and the host, resulting in a lightweight hypervisor. However, because some guest operating systems cannot be modified, there are fewer compatible choices other than full virtualization.

Regardless of the ferocity of this debate, XenSource continues to lead the charge of Xen's paravirtualization team, consisting of its own development resource as well as developers from IBM, Intel, HP, and the open-source community, and has set out to preach the gospel of Xen and evangelize the open-source virtual machine monitor and its commercial derivatives. Combined with the latest server hardware, Xen continues to provide high-performance virtualization and greater compatibility with operating systems, such as the Microsoft Windows family. The key to its strength is the unique architecture, enabling efficient CPU, memory, and I/O virtualization, while providing a very manageable and intelligent platform for developers and administrators alike.

Solutions Fast Track

What Is Xen?

- ☑ Xen is a power-packed virtual machine monitor that allows multiple operating systems to run concurrently on the same physical server hardware.

- ☑ Xen's hypervisor takes its cues from the school of paravirtualization, a technique that presents a software interface that is similar, though not identical, to the underlying hardware.

☑ Xen includes features such as 32- and 64-bit guest support, live migration, and support for the latest processors from Intel and AMD, along with other experimental non-x86 platforms.

☑ The XenServer product family provides a range of virtualization platforms that offer ease of use, robust virtualization, and powerful management.

☑ Xen's hypervisor is available as an open-source release as well as a commercially supported and feature-enhanced suite of offerings, including the XenExpress, XenServer, and XenEnterprise products.

Xen's Virtualization Model Explored

☑ Xen's architecture is currently supported on x86 (with and without PAE) and x64. Limited support is also available for the IA-64 and POWERPC CPU architecture as well.

☑ In Xen's paravirtualization architecture, the hypervisor provides a lightweight support role to the overlying guests, taking the responsibility of access control and resource scheduling while allowing the guest operating systems to maintain accountability and responsibility for higher-level functions. This combination provides high-performance without the expense of the overhead associated with full virtualization.

☑ Xen's approach to paravirtualization is highly focused on maintaining the efficiency of (arguably in order of importance): memory management, CPU, and I/O operations.

☑ Guests are presented in a construct called domains, or the layer of abstraction that lies on top of the physical hardware and the Xen hypervisor and management APIs.

☑ Two types of domains are offered: privileged and unprivileged. Privileged domains, the principle called Domain-0 or dom0, are provided limited access to hardware resources; more important, though, they are granted the ability to create and terminate unprivileged domains, called Domain-Us or domUs, which they have full access to and control over.

☑ The Xen hypervisor executes in Ring-0, thus maintaining full control over all hardware resources. The overlying domains run in Ring-1 of the x86 architecture, providing isolation from one another while avoiding conflict with Ring-3 applications and processes.

☑ Within the user space of dom0 lie all of the management tools used to administer Xen, as well as the ability to interact with the control interface exposed by the hypervisor.

☑ System calls within the operating system are sent to the hypervisor as hypercalls. Communication back to the domains from the hypervisor is sent through an event notification mechanism.

CPU Virtualization

☑ Xen utilizes a trapping mechanism to handle exceptions from faults that occur in guest operating systems.

☑ The Xen hypervisor is responsible for managing the scheduling of guest domain instruction execution with the physical CPUs available in the underlying hardware platform. Several schedulers are available, including a Simple Earliest Deadline First (sEDF) and Credit scheduler optimized for SMP platforms.

☑ Utilizing Borrowed Virtual Time (BVT), Xen favors a work-conserving scheduling scheme while providing a low-latency "fast" dispatch when needed. Xen is able to deliver high levels of CPU performance inside guest domains with minimal overhead in the hypervisor itself.

☑ Xen guests must be aware of both real and virtual time.

☑ Utilizing a calculation of system time, wall-clock time, domain virtual time, and cycle counter time, a guest is able to maintain accurate time, even when idle over an extended period of time.

Memory Virtualization

☑ Memory virtualization is the most difficult and crucial element a virtual machine monitor like Xen must perform.

☑ Safety and isolation are critical to providing a reliable and stable platform for each guest operating system. As a result, Xen must ensure no two unprivileged domains access the same memory area.

☑ Aside from memory reserved to support the guest domains, Xen is allocated a dedicated portion of memory at the top of x86 systems, both with and without PAE. For x86 without PAE, Xen is allocated 64MB; for x86 without PAE, Xen is allocated 168MB.

☑ A similar reservation is provided on x64, although it is considerably larger and more generous. However, it does not benefit from segment limits as in the x86 architecture, which relies on page-level protection for the hypervisor from other memory operations.

☑ Although memory can be spread in a fragmented manner across the actual physical machine memory available on the host, Xen uses a construct called pseudo-machine memory to fool guest domains into believing they have a contiguous range of machine memory to use, making memory allocation very operating system friendly.

☑ Page tables, and the TLB, are used to manage memory frames and maintain the performance of memory operations in the guest operating system. Although each guest domain allocates and initializes its own memory space, Xen is responsible for efficient virtual address translation and ensuring the safety and isolation of memory operations.

I/O Virtualization

☑ Xen makes use of I/O rings in a producer-consumer relationship with the guest domains. The rings are asynchronous and allow flexible control of reordering by the guest and hypervisor. Request scheduling is managed by the hypervisor.

☑ Devices are presented as an abstraction class device, rather than an emulated copy of the physical device.

☑ Using an event notification mechanism to replace typical hardware interrupts, event channels facilitate the reverse communication from Xen to the guests. This is how guests know there's data waiting for them to pick up from I/O devices.

☑ To facilitate communication across the rings, Xen uses a bus to bridge data transfer between a frontend device driver installed in the unprivileged domain and a backend driver in the privileged domain.

☑ Besides dom0, other domains (still domUs in nature) can be created and granted direct access to physical I/O devices using unmodified drivers. These are called driver domains and can be created and used to improve isolation and performance.

☑ Virtual network interfaces (VIFs) and virtual block devices (VBDs) make up the abstraction of the I/O devices and are implemented in Xen along with rules and a shared memory space. They are responsible for validation, scheduling, and logging and accounting via the backend driver.

☑ IOMMU implementations in Xen are accomplished in software using SWIOTLB and grant tables. SWIOTLB provides the address translation for I/O operations, while grant tables manage permission, providing the protection that is needed as well.

The Xenstore

☑ The Xenstore is the configuration database for each domain, which includes dom0 executing in Xen. The file is located at /var/lib/xenstored/tdb.

☑ The store is represented as a hierarchical tree with three paths: /vm, which contains configuration information for the domain; /local/domain, which contains information about the local node; and /tool, which contains information about the tools used.

☑ The store enables real-time configuration management of guest domains. Using seven commands exported by xenstored, the store can be read and updated from a command-line or programmatically.

Frequently Asked Questions

The following Frequently Asked Questions, answered by the authors of this book, are designed to both measure your understanding of the concepts presented in this chapter and to assist you with real-life implementation of these concepts. To have your questions about this chapter answered by the author, browse to **www.syngress.com/solutions** and click on the **"Ask the Author"** form.

Q: Which operating systems can be modified to take full advantage of paravirtualization?

A: At the time of this writing, any Linux distribution based on a 2.6 kernel, NetBSD 3.1 and newer, and Solaris 10 are currently tested and supported for the Xen hypervisor release 3.0 and newer. If you would like to see the most current compatibility list, visit http://wiki.xensource.com/xenwiki/OSCompatibility.

Q: How can I tell if the processor I am using supports HVM?

A: The Xen Wiki maintains a running list of HVM-compatible processors from Intel and AMD at: http://wiki.xensource.com/xenwiki/HVM_Compatible_Processors. If you have a recently released processor that does not appear on the list, check the Intel web site to see if the processor supports Intel-VT, or AMD's Web site for AMD-V support.

Q: I have an HVM-compatible processor, yet Xen won't let me create a full-virtualization domain. Why?

A: Most BIOS implementations give you the ability to disable SVM (AMD) or VMX (Intel) support. In some cases, the default is disabled. Check to make sure you have SVM or VMX enabled. If it is enabled and you still cannot create a full-virtualization domain, be sure Xen recognizes that feature for your processor. You can do this by running "grep vmx /proc/cpuinfo" for Intel or "grep svm /proc/cpuinfo" for AMD and looking for the appropriate flag. If you see the flag, check for the flag in the hypervisor capability set by running "cat /sys/hypervisor/properties/capabilities".

Q: Is it possible to access guest disk images outside of Xen?

A: The answer is both yes and no. Using tools such as iomount and kpartx, you can mount small and large disk images inside dom0 to access data. Be sure the guest is not running, and thus using the disk image, when you mount it, however. Those tools may have issues with some LVM volumes and are meant to work with block devices, not images installed as files.

Q: Do I need a server to run Xen?

A: No. Xen will run on virtually any platform based on the x86 architecture, including desktops and laptops. You must meet the minimum requirements, though. If you have a system with at least a Pentium 4 processor and 1GB of RAM, you should have sufficient resources to support dom0, and at least a domU, without much suffering. See the Xen Wiki for updated information about requirements for the latest build of Xen.

Chapter 3

Deploying Xen: Demystifying the Installation

Solutions in this chapter:

- **Determining Which Xen to Choose**
- **System Requirements**
- **Thinking Before You Start**
- **Installing Xen on a Free Linux Distribution**
- **Installing the XenServer Product Family**
- **Other Xen Installation Methods**
- **Configuring Xen**

☑ Summary

☑ Solutions Fast Track

☑ Frequently Asked Questions

Introduction

With Xen's roots in the open-source community, the original users of the hypervisor were skilled Linux experts that new their way around kernel development. As it has grown in popularity, Xen is now widely available to a diverse array of users of various backgrounds. Getting Xen up and running may appear to be a daunting task to newcomers, and taking advantage of every feature nearly impossible—but if you think yourself among the novices, don't worry. The installation really is not that complicated.

In this chapter, we will demystify the installation of Xen. You will learn what kind of machine you need for different Xen installations, walk through various methods for installing Xen, and, even more important, find out how to configure Xen, get connected, and get your first virtual machine up and running.

Determining Which Xen to Choose

When choosing your Xen platform, you should consider a couple of different options. Since Xen started out as an open-source product and most people are running their host platform, domain0 in Xen terminology, on a Linux machine, you can choose between Community, Commercial, or Enterprise Linux Distributions, or a custom Linux platform created by XenSource.

If you choose a Community Linux Distribution, such as Fedora Core, CentOS, Ubuntu, or OpenSuse, you will get a Xen version that is packaged and tested by the community, with a different set of GUI and command-line tools depending on the packager.

Open-source Linux Distributions give you the freedom to do everything yourself and mix and match tools just the way you like them. The disadvantage of this approach is that you need the experience to install, manage, and deploy them, and when you are in trouble, you either need to be able to rely on a local support partner or on the community.

Enterprise Linux Distributions will give you a fully tested version of the hypervisor, which has been certified to integrate seamlessly with existing tools to install and deploy packages. You will also have a support line to call and vent through when things go wrong, but it's going to cost you some money.

Then there is the XenSource platform, a commercial offering of Xen created by XenSource, the creators of Xen, that has one goal: making Xen easy. If you are not interested in deploying more Linux machines, this is probably the option you should go for. It's a well-supported platform by the original Xen authors and many OEMs, such as IBM and HP.

While getting Xen to run is for some people as easy as installing two packages on their favorite Linux platform, other people will be performing their very first Linux installation altogether. On the other hand, XenSource markets "Ten minutes to Xen" with its XenServer product family. This chapter will guide you through different ways of installing Xen with the goal of having a minimal virtual machine up and running by the end. We will also show you how to install Xen on a mainstream Linux distribution (Fedora Core 6), how to install the XenEnterprise product from XenSource, and install it as an RPM from XenSource on a general distribution.

In a typical Xen environment, you will be running a host operating system called dom0 and multiple guest operating systems called domUs. We will focus on using Linux as dom0, which is the default dom0 for the XenServer product family as well. Although most people use this configuration, some run dom0 under other Unix-style operating systems such as BSD or Solaris.

System Requirements

Depending on your needs, your system requirements will vary. Xen runs on most x86-compatible hardware that is more recent than the P6, or 686, family of processors. Ports to other architectures such as PowerPC are being worked on, but we will not be covering them. Concerning memory, the default 32-bit Xen supports 4GB out-of-the-box. As of Xen 3.0, support for the PAE (Physical Address Extensions) has been added so you can address up to 64GB. Note that on some platforms this feature has been enabled by default, which means you might have problems booting these Xen builds on laptops or older machines.

As general hardware support on driver level, Xen hands all the hardware management over to dom0, this means that all the hardware supported by the average Linux distribution is supported on Xen. Note, however, that Xen was initially developed for server-style hardware, which means that desktop- or even laptop-like features such as suspend and power management were not meant to work, might not have been tested, or might have simply been disabled in the build your distribution ships.

Different types of usage result in different hardware requirements. Let's go over a couple of scenarios.

If you are looking into datacenter virtualization, you will probably need to install as many disks as possible. You should also note the current memory usage of the machines you plan to deploy (or ones similar) and calculate the total sum of these applications, adding a little extra. You don't need to install a graphical interface, and if you are only running Linux, you don't need a VT capable machine. Since your dom0 isn't doing anything besides managing the other machines, it can be really small. If you have small virtual machine instances that can run with a minimal amount of RAM (we often see small servers such as DHCP or DNS server not needing more than 128 or 256MB RAM), you can easily put 10 to 15 virtual machines in a 2GB memory machine.

If you are looking at using Xen to run different test platforms, you will need both a graphical interface on your dom0, which requires more memory than your average datacenter dom0. You'll usually give the different environments more memory so you can install their graphical environments as well.

Windows virtual machines can only be created through full virtualization with support of the Intel-VT or AMD-V CPUs. Most of the new hardware products available today have these features. Intel has a good site, www.intel.com/products/processor_number/index.htm, where you can find the CPUs that have VT capabilities. Most Dual Core processors such as the Xeon MP 7000 series, the Pentium 4 Extreme Edition 955 and 965, Intel Core Duo mobile processors, the Pentium D 9x0, and also Pentium 4 662 and 672 support VT.

Configuring & Implementing…

VT-Support Virtualization on Laptops

The Intel Core duo, which is also used in lots of laptops and the Mac Mini, is VT-capable. The Mac Mini was one of the first machines to support VT. Note, however, that different laptop vendors have disabled VT features, and you either need to enable them in your BIOS or upgrade your BIOS to enable these features. If you want to test your machine to see if it is VT-capable, you can download the Knoppix Xen CD. You can also boot any Linux Live CD and run the following on an Intel machine:

Continued

```
[root@macmini ~]# cat /proc/cpuinfo | grep vmx
flags           : fpu vme de pse tsc msr pae mce cx8 apic mtrr pge mca cmov
pat clflush dts acpi mmx fxsr sse sse2 ss ht tm pbe nx constant_tsc pni
monitor vmx est tm2 xtpr

    or

[root@box ~] cat /proc/cpuinfo | grep svm
    flags           : fpu tsc msr pae mce cx8 apic mtrr mca cmov pat pse36
clflush mmx fxsr sse sse2 ht syscall nx mmxext fxsr_opt rdtscp lm 3dnowext
3dnow pni cx16 lahf_lm cmp_legacy svm cr8_legacy
```

If grep shows you a line like the preceding examples, your CPU is capable of supporting full virtualization. If it comes back empty, you either don't have a VT-capable CPU, or you need to look at your vendor's hardware documentation in order to enable the feature.

Thinking Before You Start

Before you start, you must plan how we will be using your disk. What you want to do with your guest operating system determines how you will be using your disk layout. The easiest way to export a disk is to export an actual physical block device (a hard disk or a partition) from dom0 to your virtual machine. This, of course, limits you to the number of disks you have available or the number of partitions you can make on a disk.

"Old-school" virtualization platforms still tend to use files that are images of hard disks. This doesn't scale at all. It is useful if you want to create an image you want to distribute to other people, something to show around. But if you are building an infrastructure, you will limit yourself while paying a big performance penalty.

When you install your software on a loopback device created on a sparse file, which resides on a huge file system next to different other virtual images, chaos will eventually rule. We already know that copying these kinds of files will be slow and that there is no easy way to replicate, grow, or shrink them. When thinking about these kinds of problems you realize LVM (Logical Volume Manager) is one of the best ways to solve these issues. LVM gives you the opportunity to manage growing volumes over different physical disks. It gives you the opportunity to take snapshots of those disks (easy for backups) and also solves the issue of a maximum 15 partitions on a SCSI disk.

When you are using multiple virtual machines on a machine, the problem is not how to manage five partitions on a disk. Since you are managing such a set of partitions for each virtual machine, you need to be able to add virtual machines and, therefore, partitions on-the-fly. Thus, you want to use LVM. It is a way to look at one, or multiple, disks that goes beyond partitions. You gain much more flexibility such as adding, removing, and resizing "partitions" while not having to reboot to reread the partition table.

LVM deals with Physical Volumes (PVs), Volume Groups (VGs), and Logical Volumes (LVs). PVs are the actual physical disk, or partitions, you want to use LVM on. You can combine multiple different partitions in a group. A group doesn't need to have multiple PVs, but it can have them. Within each group, you then can define Logical Volumes. These logical volumes are what you will create a file system on and use in your virtual machines.

Now imagine that you want to deploy a new server. In your average physical setup, you will want different partitions for the operating system, the log files, the data, and so on. If you want to add different actual partitions for each virtual machine, you will end up forgetting if */dev/hda6* was the root partition of your first virtual machine or if it was */dev/hda9*.

A good practice is to create a Volume Group for your virtual machine instances. The following is an example of Virtual Group creation:

```
-bash-3.00# pvs
  PV          VG          Fmt  Attr PSize  PFree
  /dev/sda8   vm_volumes  lvm2 a-   26.77G 13.90G
-bash-3.00# vgs
  VG          #PV #LV #SN Attr   VSize  VFree
  vm_volumes   1   25   0 wz--n 26.77G 13.90G
```

You then use a consistent naming convention for each of these virtual machines. Thus, a machine called DB2 will have at least a root, a temp, and a swap partition. The following example gives a clear overview of which Logical Volume is being used for which virtual partition.

```
-bash-3.00# lvs

  LV         VG          Attr   LSize    Origin Snap% Move Log Copy%
  root-DB1   vm_volumes  -wi-ao   1.17G
  root-DB2   vm_volumes  -wi-ao   1.17G
  swap-DB1   vm_volumes  -wi-ao 128.00M
  swap-DB2   vm_volumes  -wi-ao 128.00M
  tmp-DB1    vm_volumes  -wi-ao  64.00M
  tmp-DB2    vm_volumes  -wi-ao  64.00M
```

```
varlib-DB1 vm_volumes -wi-ao    4.00G
varlib-DB2 vm_volumes -wi-ao    4.00G
```

Another advantage of using LVM is that you can export an LVM partition as a block device to another machine, such as with iSCSI. That's probably a whole lot easier than copying four 3GB+ files.

So when you are about to install the machine that will serve as a Xen server, don't let the Installer do the partitioning for you. Give it only a limited part of the disk, and then use the rest for LVM. That gives you the freedom to go for both disk images and actual partitions for your virtual machines. Use LVM, do not fully partition, and do not use images.

Of course, you can also choose more advanced methods such as NBD or iSCSI, or even put your root file system on NFS if you prefer to. (Note that putting a loopback file on a remote NFS volume is not advised.)

Installing Xen on a Free Linux Distribution

In this section, we'll discuss how to install Xen on a free Linux distribution.

Fedora Core 6

What is a Fedora? A fedora is a soft felt hat, often in red. When Red Hat decided to build an enterprise distribution, they rebranded the original open-source Red Hat distribution to Fedora Core. The Fedora Project is a Red Hat–sponsored and community-supported open-source project. It is the free as-is, bare Linux version that the new features placed in Red Hat Enterprise Linux will originate from. Fedora can be downloaded from the Internet for free, either via torrents to save bandwidth (from http://torrent.fedoraproject.org/) or via HTTP from http://fedoraproject.org/wiki/Distribution/Download. You can also often find Fedora Core CD's distributed with magazines at the newsstands.

If you are already running Linux, you can burn the downloaded images to a CD by running the following commands:

```
cdrecord -v dev=ATA:1,0,0 -data FC-6-i386-disc1.iso
cdrecord -v dev=ATA:1,0,0 -data FC-6-i386-disc2.iso
cdrecord -v dev=ATA:1,0,0 -data FC-6-i386-disc3.iso
cdrecord -v dev=ATA:1,0,0 -data FC-6-i386-disc4.iso
cdrecord -v dev=ATA:1,0,0 -data FC-6-i386-disc5.iso
```

You actually only need the first two CDs when you want to do a minimal install of Fedora Core 6. If you are on another platform, the manual with your CD writing software will explain how to burn an ISO image.

Now, it's time for a guided tour, where we show you how to get Fedora Core 6 installed and Xen configured. The following steps will guide you through the process

1. Upon putting your freshly burned CD into the server, press **F10** or the appropriate key combination for your platform to boot from the CD-ROM. Fedora will boot to its initial CD menu. Press **Enter**.

2. The first screen will ask us if we want to check the media we just burned. Feel free to skip the media test.

3. The graphical Fedora Core installer should now launch and show you a welcome screen, after which you will be given the choice of either upgrading or installing a new system (see Figure 3.1). If this is a clean installation, you should select to perform a new install.

Figure 3.1 Choose a Fedora Core Installation Type

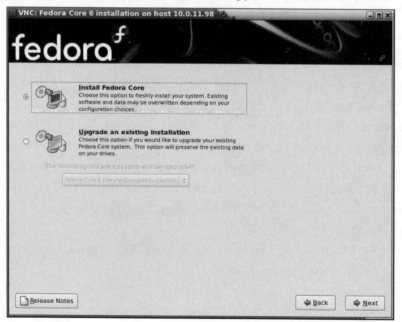

TIP

Switching consoles: Just as with any other regular Linux, you can switch to a different log and console by using **Ctrl + Alt + F2** for a console, **Ctrl + Alt + F3** or **Ctrl + Alt + F4** for different log files, and **Alt + F6** to go back to the installer.

4. The next screen is an important one. A default Fedora Core installation will not give you the Disk Layout you want for a machine that will host different virtual machines. Therefore, I suggest you choose the **Remove All The Partitions From Your Existing Disks** option, and then choose **Review And Modify Partition Layout**.

5. You will be asked to confirm that you want to erase all existing partitions.

6. Fedora will create a boot partition and a Volume Group VolGroup00 where it will create a Logical Volume called LogVol00 (see Figure 3.2) that will take up the whole remaining file system (besides the small boot file systems it creates).

Figure 3.2 Define Your Own LVM Layout

Device	Mount Point/ RAID/Volume	Type	Format	Size (MB)	Start	End	
▽ LVM Volume Groups							
▽ VolGroup00				38016			
LogVol01		swap	✓	1984			
LogVol00	/	ext3	✓	36032			
▽ Hard Drives							

You want a bigger part of that file system for other Logical Volumes that will be used as file systems for virtual machines you will deploy. So you will resize the LogVol00 to about 4 to 6GB, which should be more than enough for a basic dom0 installation (see Figure 3.3).

www.syngress.com

Figure 3.3 Modify the Size of Your Root File System

7. The next screen will provide you with the default values for a normal Grub installation. Grub is the bootloader required by Xen.

8. On the Network Configuration screen, configure your network with a static IP address (see Figure 3.4). Unless your DHCP server hands out static IP addresses based on the MAC address of your network card, you don't want to use DHCP for a server since you won't be able to connect to your server again once your DHCP lease changes.

9. Choose the correct Timezone so that when you have to look at log files someday, you will be able to correlate the timestamps with other events on your network.

10. Choose a strong root password for this machine.

11. The next screen will provide you with the choice to install different software packages (see Figure 3.5). A normal Xen server usually does not need anything else besides the tools to manage the virtual machines, so you can disable the Office Tools and Development Tools option. Our goal is to make dom0 as small and lightweight as possible, so a minimal install is sufficient.

Figure 3.4 Configure Your Network Card

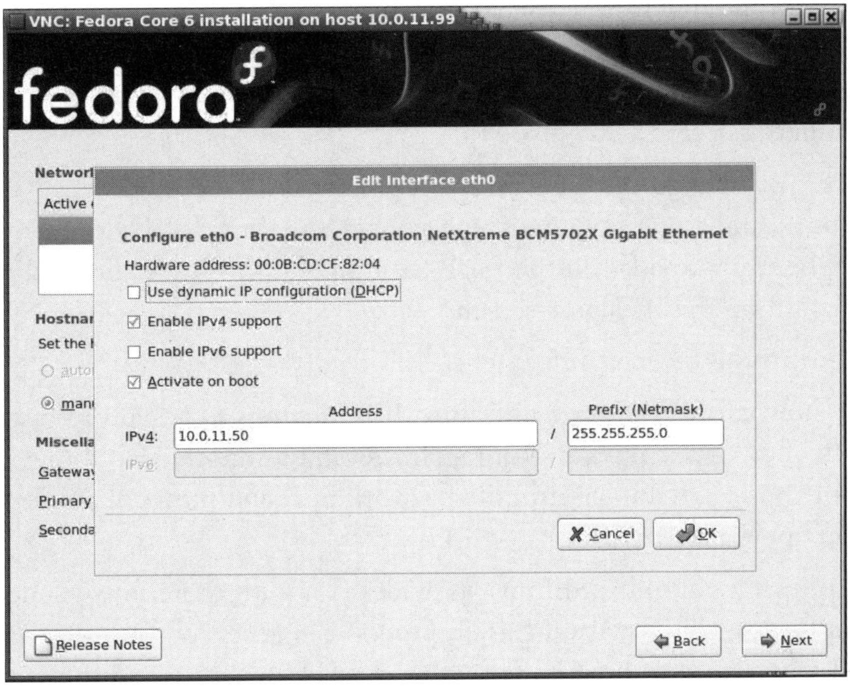

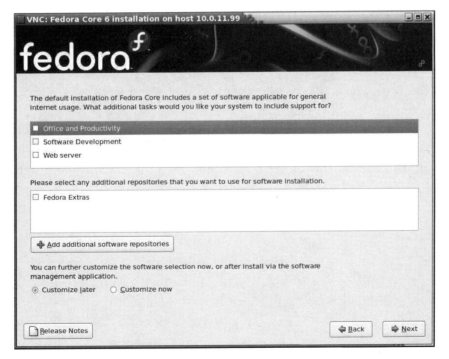

Figure 3.5 Choose a Minimal Installation

12. After this selection, you will be warned about the CDs you will need to perform the installation. Make sure you have these. If you are doing a minimal install, you only need the first two CDs. The machine will start transferring a basic image to its hard disk and continue by installing the packages you have selected.

13. After you change the CDs, your Fedora installation is ready to be rebooted. Your machine will now boot into your freshly installed Fedora Core 6, and will be ready to ask you the final questions for this installation. Click Forward on the Welcome screen.

14. Agree to the License Agreement.

15. For now, disable the firewall feature. It is recommended you re-enable it back after Xen is up and running; however, be sure to keep things simple until you clearly understand the network port and protocol requirements of your applications.

16. Also disable SELinux. SELinux provides you with more fine-grained security constraints such as what a certain process can access or not. Making an SELinux policy to be used with virtual machines is beyond the scope of this chapter and this book.

17. You probably want to enable NTP using either the NTP servers on your internal network or the ones provided by your ISP.

18. Create at least one user so you can log on to the machine while not being root.

19. Since you have disabled both the firewall and SELinux, your machine will now require an additional reboot.

At this point, your Fedora Core 6 is now ready to be used. Our next step will be to install Xen. You can do this either by logging in to the machine remotely on a command line from the login or local desktop, or via the GUI.

Configuring & Implementing...

Building a Local Fedora Core Repository

As of now, we assume your machine has been connected to the Internet and can download packages from a publicly available Fedora Core mirror. If this is not the case, you will need to either reconfigure your network settings so you can access the Internet, or set up a local Fedora Core RPM repository and modify your *yum* configuration accordingly.

An RPM repository is the location where all the RPMs for a distribution and their metadata are stored for later redistribution via the network. Building your own local distribution repository will save you bandwidth and will ensure that if your Internet connection breaks down for some reason you can still continue to deploy new machines while not depending on third-party repositories. You also take the load away from mirrors that are often funding the bandwidth for these repositories out of their own pockets.

Assuming you want to build a local Fedora Core repository, you will need to either copy all the files on the CDs to a directory on your system, such as */data/repository/FC*, and run **yum-arch** in that directory or mount the CD you have on that mount point. In order to have yum use that freshly created repository, you will need to modify the yum configuration. The following is an example of a modified /etc/yum.repos.d/fedora-core.repo:

```
[core]
name=Fedora Core $releasever - $basearch
baseurl=file:///data/repository/FC
#baseurl=http://download.fedora.redhat.com/pub/fedora/linux/core/$releasever
/$basearch/os/
#mirrorl-ist=http://mirrors.fedoraproject.org/mirrorlist?repo=core-
$releasever&ar
ch=$basearch
enabled=1
gpgcheck=1
gpgkey=file:///etc/pki/rpm-gpg/RPM-GPG-KEY-fedora file:///etc/pki/rpm-gpg/RPM-
GP
G-KEY
```

Continued

> You should also modify all the other configuration files in the /etc/yum.repos.d/ directory by changing all the "enabled=1" values to "enabled=0".
>
> The following overview shows you how to install Xen, as well as the accompanying kernel required, via the command line.
>
> ```
> [kris@mine FC6Install]$ ssh kris@10.0.11.50
> kris@10.0.11.50's password:
> Last login: Mon Feb 19 20:38:04 2007 from 10.0.11.43
> [kris@fc6-xen ~]$ su -
> Password:
> [root@fc6-xen ~]# yum install xen kernel-xen
> Loading "installonlyn" plugin
> Setting up Install Process
> Setting up repositories
> Reading repository metadata in from local files
> Parsing package install arguments
> Resolving Dependencies
> --> Populating transaction set with selected packages. Please wait.
> ---> Package kernel-xen.i686 0:2.6.19-1.2911.fc6 set to be installed
> ---> Package xen.i386 0:3.0.3-3.fc6 set to be updated
> --> Running transaction check
> --> Processing Dependency: libxenstore.so.3.0 for package: xen
> --> Processing Dependency: xen-libs = 3.0.3-3.fc6 for package: xen
> --> Processing Dependency: bridge-utils for package: xen
> --> Processing Dependency: mkinitrd >= 5.1.19.0.2-1 for package: kernel-xen
> --> Processing Dependency: libxenctrl.so.3.0 for package: xen
> --> Processing Dependency: python-virtinst for package: xen
> --> Processing Dependency: libxenguest.so.3.0 for package: xen
> --> Processing Dependency: libblktap.so.3.0 for package: xen
> --> Restarting Dependency Resolution with new changes.
> --> Populating transaction set with selected packages. Please wait.
> ---> Package mkinitrd.i386 0:5.1.19.0.2-1 set to be updated
> ---> Package bridge-utils.i386 0:1.1-2 set to be updated
> ---> Package xen-libs.i386 0:3.0.3-3.fc6 set to be updated
> ---> Package python-virtinst.noarch 0:0.98.0-1.fc6 set to be updated
> --> Running transaction check
> --> Processing Dependency: libvirt-python >= 0.1.4-4 for package: python-virtinst
> --> Processing Dependency: nash = 5.1.19.0.2-1 for package: mkinitrd
> --> Restarting Dependency Resolution with new changes.
> ```

Continued

```
--> Populating transaction set with selected packages. Please wait.
---> Package nash.i386 0:5.1.19.0.2-1 set to be updated
---> Package libvirt-python.i386 0:0.1.11-1.fc6 set to be updated
--> Running transaction check
--> Processing Dependency: libvirt = 0.1.11 for package: libvirt-python
--> Processing Dependency: libvirt.so.0 for package: libvirt-python
--> Restarting Dependency Resolution with new changes.
--> Populating transaction set with selected packages. Please wait.
---> Package libvirt.i386 0:0.1.11-1.fc6 set to be updated
--> Running transaction check


Dependencies Resolved


===============================================================================
 Package                Arch         Version          Repository      Size
===============================================================================
Installing:
 kernel-xen             i686         2.6.19-1.2911.fc6  updates        17 M
 xen                    i386         3.0.3-3.fc6      updates          1.7 M
Installing for dependencies:
 bridge-utils           i386         1.1-2            core              28 k
 libvirt                i386         0.1.11-1.fc6     updates          411 k
 libvirt-python         i386         0.1.11-1.fc6     updates           47 k
 python-virtinst        noarch       0.98.0-1.fc6     updates           30 k
 xen-libs               i386         3.0.3-3.fc6      updates           83 k
Updating for dependencies:
 mkinitrd               i386         5.1.19.0.2-1     updates          438 k
 nash                   i386         5.1.19.0.2-1     updates          1.1 M


Transaction Summary
===============================================================================
Install      7 Package(s)
Update       2 Package(s)
Remove       0 Package(s)


Total download size: 20 M
Is this ok [y/N]: y
Downloading Packages:
(1/9): mkinitrd-5.1.19.0. 100% |=========================| 438 kB    00:01
(2/9): libvirt-0.1.11-1.f 100% |=========================| 411 kB    00:01
```

Continued

```
(3/9): bridge-utils-1.1-2 100% |=========================| 28 kB    00:00
(4/9): kernel-xen-2.6.19- 100% |=========================| 17 MB    01:06
(5/9): xen-libs-3.0.3-3.f 100% |=========================| 83 kB    00:00
(6/9): nash-5.1.19.0.2-1. 100% |=========================| 1.1 MB   00:04
(7/9): python-virtinst-0. 100% |=========================| 30 kB    00:00
(8/9): libvirt-python-0.1 100% |=========================| 47 kB    00:00
(9/9): xen-3.0.3-3.fc6.i3 100% |=========================| 1.7 MB   00:06
warning: rpmts_HdrFromFdno: Header V3 DSA signature: NOKEY, key ID 4f2a6fd2
Importing GPG key 0x4F2A6FD2 "Fedora Project fedora@redhat.com"
Is this ok [y/N]: y
Running Transaction Test
Finished Transaction Test
Transaction Test Succeeded
Running Transaction
  Installing: xen-libs              ######################## [ 1/11]
  Updating  : nash                  ######################## [ 2/11]
  Updating  : mkinitrd              ######################## [ 3/11]
  Installing: bridge-utils          ######################## [ 4/11]
  Installing: kernel-xen            ######################## [ 5/11]
  Installing: xen                   ######################## [ 6/11]
  Installing: libvirt               ######################## [ 7/11]
  Installing: python-virtinst       ######################## [ 8/11]
  Installing: libvirt-python        ######################## [ 9/11]
  Cleanup   : mkinitrd              ######################## [10/11]
  Cleanup   : nash                  ######################## [11/11]

Installed: kernel-xen.i686 0:2.6.19-1.2911.fc6 xen.i386 0:3.0.3-3.fc6
Dependency Installed: bridge-utils.i386 0:1.1-2 libvirt.i386 0:0.1.11-1.fc6
libvirt-python.i386 0:0.1.11-1.fc6 python-virtinst.noarch 0:0.98.0-1.fc6 xen-
libs.i386 0:3.0.3-3.fc6
Dependency Updated: mkinitrd.i386 0:5.1.19.0.2-1 nash.i386 0:5.1.19.0.2-1
Complete!
```

If you want to use the GUI, choose the **Add/Remove Software** option from the Applications Menu (see Figure 3.6).

Figure 3.6 Choose Add/Remove Software

This will start the Package Manager, which will first update the list of available packages before giving you a screen where you have a Browse, Search, and List tab. On the **Search** tab, search for "xen." From the result set, select the most recent "kernel-xen" and "xen" package. Upon selecting **Apply**, you will see a listing of your selection. Select **Continue** (see Figure 3.7).

Figure 3.7 Confirm Package Selection

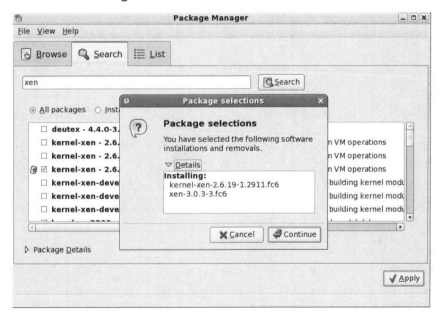

The package manager will now calculate the dependencies for those two packages for you and will ask you to confirm these dependencies before it starts their actual download. Whichever you choose, the next step is to carefully inspect your grub.conf file and find a part similar to the following:

```
[root@fc6-xen grub]# more /boot/grub/grub.conf
# grub.conf generated by anaconda
#
# Note that you do not have to rerun grub after making changes to this file
# NOTICE:  You have a /boot partition.  This means that
#          all kernel and initrd paths are relative to /boot/, eg.
#          root (hd0,0)
#          kernel /vmlinuz-version ro root=/dev/VolGroup00/LogVol00
#          initrd /initrd-version.img
#boot=/dev/hda
default=1
timeout=5
splashimage=(hd0,0)/grub/splash.xpm.gz
hiddenmenu
title Fedora Core (2.6.19-1.2911.fc6xen)
        root (hd0,0)
        kernel /xen.gz-2.6.19-1.2911.fc6
        module /vmlinuz-2.6.19-1.2911.fc6xen ro root=/dev/VolGroup00/LogVol00 no
dmraid rhgb quiet
        module /initrd-2.6.19-1.2911.fc6xen.img
title Fedora Core (2.6.18-1.2798.fc6)
        root (hd0,0)
        kernel /vmlinuz-2.6.18-1.2798.fc6 ro root=/dev/VolGroup00/LogVol00 nodmr
aid rhgb quiet
        initrd /initrd-2.6.18-1.2798.fc6.img
```

In the preceding example, the default boot entry is set to 1, which actually means the second entry, so upon rebooting, the second listed kernel will boot. You will either have to manually change the kernel at boot time by navigating up in the grub menu, or modify this file so the default reads 0. The xen and kernel–xen packages should have installed the following files:

```
[root@fc6-xen ~]# ls /boot/*xen*
/boot/config-2.6.19-1.2911.fc6xen        /boot/vmlinuz-2.6.19-1.2911.fc6xen
/boot/initrd-2.6.19-1.2911.fc6xen.img   /boot/xen.gz-2.6.19-1.2911.fc6
/boot/symvers-2.6.19-1.2911.fc6xen.gz   /boot/xen-syms-2.6.19-1.2911.fc6
/boot/System.map-2.6.19-1.2911.fc6xen
```

Make sure they actually exist and match the versions as listed in your *grub.conf* file. If they are there, it's time to reboot into that new Xen hypervisor, and afterward you will have your first virtual machine up and running.

Yes, the regular Linux version you have just booted into is not running on a regular x86 platform anymore. It is instead running on a Xen Hypervisor. You can check this by running the following command:

```
[kris@fc6-xen ~]$ uname -a
Linux fc6-xen.hs62.be 2.6.19-1.2911.fc6xen #1 SMP Sat Feb 10 16:09:50 EST 2007 i686
i686 i386 GNU/Linux
```

The *fc6xen* tag marks that you are running in a Xen-enabled dom0. If you already started *xend* at boot time, which Fedora does for you, your output of *xm list* should be similar to the following:

```
[root@fc6-xen ~]# chkconfig --list | grep 3:on  | grep xen
xend            0:off   1:off   2:on    3:on    4:on    5:on    6:off
xendomains      0:off   1:off   2:off   3:on    4:on    5:on    6:off
[root@fc6-xen ~]# xm list
Name                                    ID Mem(MiB) VCPUs State    Time(s)
Domain-0                                 0    1059      1 r-----     38.2
```

> **NOTE**
>
> In other distributions, you still might need to start the xend daemon yourself via:
>
>   */etc/rc.d/init.d/xend start*

On some distributions and hardware configurations, the creation of a valid *initrd* can fail. The initial RAMDISK is a temporary file system used to load drivers on the platform before the actual root file system will be mounted. This results in a kernel panic proceeded by an error that the kernel cannot mount its root file system. This is caused by some builds of the Xen dom0 kernel insisting on the *initrd* having the most basic kernel modules inserted manually. You can do this by running:

```
mkinitrd /boot/initrd-2.6.19-1.2911.fc6xen.img 2.6.19-1.2911.fc6xen --with-module
mptbase --with-module scsi_mod --with-module sg --with-module mptscsih --with-
module mptspi --with-module ext3 --with-module sd_mod --with-module ide-disk --
with-module dm-mod --with-module jbd --with-module mptctl
```

The version you mention should match both the kernel version you are trying to build an *intrd* for and the directory of modules with the same version that lives in */lib/modules/$version*. You can find the actual list of modules you need to include by running **lsmod** on your active system and including every module listed there that refers to file systems or storage.

VirtManager

As of Fedora Core 6, the distribution provides you with a nice GUI called *virt-manager* which really eases up the installation of guests… Fedora guests, that is. For now, we will use *virt-manager* to install a Fedora guest from which the data will reside in a loopback device. Fedora Core 6's default build only supports XVDX type disks. You cannot easily use a full disk or an LVM volume for your virtual machine storage. We will review how to use LVM later in this chapter when installing the XenSource-provided RPMs.

Of course, the first step is to install the VirtManager package itself, as in the following:

```
[root@fc6-xen ~]# yum install virt-manager
Loading "installonlyn" plugin
Setting up Install Process
Setting up repositories
Reading repository metadata in from local files
Parsing package install arguments
Resolving Dependencies
--> Populating transaction set with selected packages. Please wait.
---> Downloading header for virt-manager to pack into transaction set.
virt-manager-0.2.6-3.fc6. 100% |=========================| 25 kB    00:00
---> Package virt-manager.i386 0:0.2.6-3.fc6 set to be updated
--> Running transaction check
--> Processing Dependency: gnome-python2-gnomekeyring >= 2.15.4 for package: virt-manager
--> Restarting Dependency Resolution with new changes.
--> Populating transaction set with selected packages. Please wait.
---> Downloading header for gnome-python2-gnomekeyring to pack into transaction set.
gnome-python2-gnomekeyrin 100% |=========================| 3.5 kB    00:00
---> Package gnome-python2-gnomekeyring.i386 0:2.16.0-1.fc6 set to be updated
--> Running transaction check

Dependencies Resolved
```

```
================================================================================
 Package              Arch       Version         Repository        Size
================================================================================
Installing:
 virt-manager         i386       0.2.6-3.fc6     updates           553 k
Installing for dependencies:
 gnome-python2-gnomekeyring  i386      2.16.0-1.fc6     core            15 k

Transaction Summary
================================================================================
Install       2 Package(s)
Update        0 Package(s)
Remove        0 Package(s)

Total download size: 568 k
Is this ok [y/N]: y
Downloading Packages:
(1/2): virt-manager-0.2.6 100% |=========================| 553 kB    00:03
(2/2): gnome-python2-gnom 100% |=========================|  15 kB    00:00
Running Transaction Test
Finished Transaction Test
Transaction Test Succeeded
Running Transaction
   Installing: gnome-python2-gnomekeyring     ######################### [1/2]
   Installing: virt-manager                   ######################### [2/2]

Installed: virt-manager.i386 0:0.2.6-3.fc6
Dependency Installed: gnome-python2-gnomekeyring.i386 0:2.16.0-1.fc6
```

After installing this package, you will once again see a new entry in the Applications | System Tools menu called **Virtual Machine Manager**. Start it. When launched as a non-root user from the menu, you will be prompted for the root password since you will need root privileges to create a virtual machine (see Figure 3.8).

Figure 3.8 Create a New Virtual System

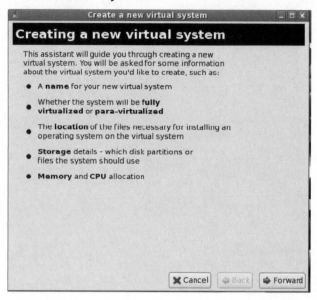

1. Choose to connect to the local Xen Host by clicking **Connect**.

2. Choose **File | New Machine**.

3. Choose a unique and self-explanatory name for your Virtual Machine.

4. Since we are installing a Linux machine, choose to use the Paravirtualized method (see Figure 3.9).

Figure 3.9 Choosing a Virtualization Method

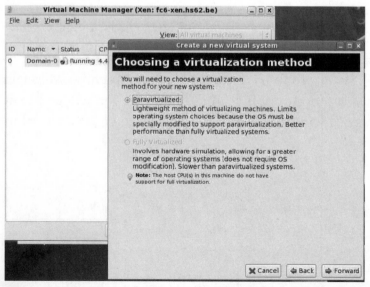

5. Choose a repository where you can install your Guest Virtual Machine, as shown in Figure 3.10.

Figure 3.10 Locating Installation Media

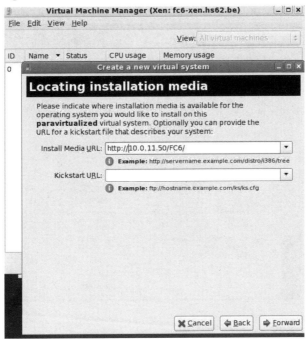

NOTE

To save on bandwidth and speed up the installation process, make sure you have mounted the DVD, or copied the content of your CDs to a local repository. Also, make sure you can access them via a Web browser. Of course, you can choose a remote Fedora Repository, but that will only slow down the installation.

6. You can either choose to use a local file or a full file system or LVM partition. Figure 3.11 shows you a dialog box for assigning storage space for your virtual system.

Figure 3.11 Assigning Storage Space

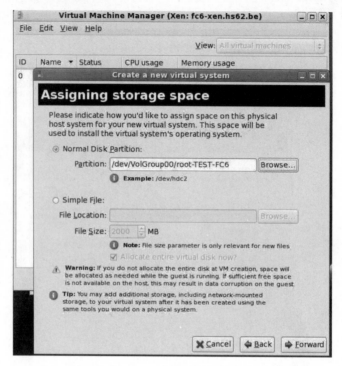

> **NOTE**
>
> You won't be able to mount this LVM partition or disk as a normal file system since Fedora will use this as a full virtual disk. If you don't want this, read on. Later in this chapter we'll discuss how to use actual LVM volumes.

7. After either an empty file has been created or your partition has been chosen, you can also set the default memory parameters. Of course, they depend on how much memory there is in your actual system and how these virtual machines will be used (see Figure 3.12).

8. By Finishing the Installation Wizard, a configuration file matching your choices will be written into /etc/xen/, and your virtual machine will be started for the first time. You'll recognize the Fedora Core installer again, which you have already used to install this physical machine (see Figure 3.13).

Figure 3.12 Allocate Memory and CPU

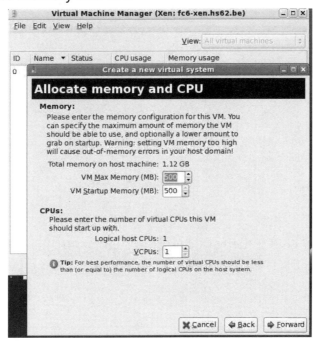

Figure 3.13 Start the Virtual Machine Installation

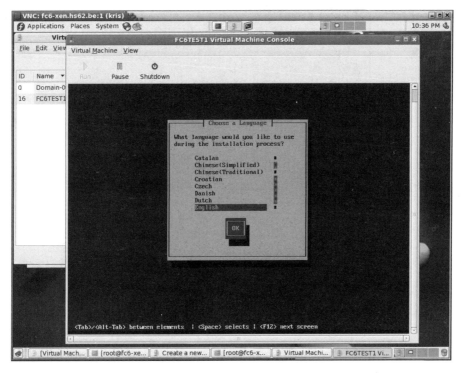

```
[root@fc6-xen xen]# more FC6TEST1
# Automatically generated xen config file
name = "FC6TEST1"
memory = "500"
disk = [ 'phy:/dev/VolGroup00/root-TEST-FC6,xvda,w', ]
vif = [ 'mac=00:16:3e:42:83:34, bridge=xenbr0', ]
vnc=1
vncunused=1
uuid = "f6ebc9f0-8ad4-2868-7297-9822ab6496cd"
bootloader="/usr/bin/pygrub"
vcpus=1
on_reboot    = 'restart'
on_crash     = 'restart'
```

The preceding config file has been generated by virt-manager for the virtual machine FC6TEST1. It doesn't specify a kernel as it is using pygrub.

NOTE

pygrub is a bootloader that can be used instead of the regular domU kernel for booting. It reads the kernel from the domU's file system rather than from the dom0 file system, enabling reboots of a virtual machine even after it has migrated to another physical machine.

However, it does specify that it will be using the logical volume */dev/VolGroup00/root-TEST-FC6* as a full disk (xvda). It will enable VNC access so you can have a graphical console on the machine. It has one virtual CPU and will have a maximum of 500MB of RAM.

After the installation of this virtual machine, it will shut down. From there on, you can use the regular Xen *xm* command-line tool to start your virtual machine as follows:

```
xm create FCTEST1
```

In the *virt-man* GUI, you should now see your freshly installed virtual machine listed (see Figure 3.14).

Figure 3.14 A New Host Running in VirtManager

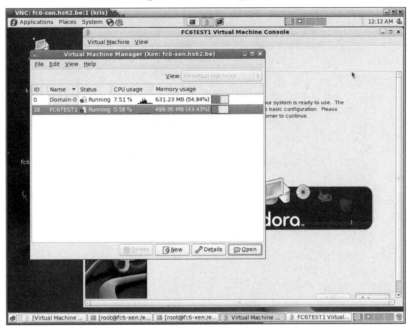

If you select it and then open it, you will be connected to the graphical desktop of that virtual machine, which is waiting for you to finish the installation. From here, you can use either the GUI or the command line to fully manage the virtual machine.

Installing Windows XP

Installing a Windows Virtual machine first of all requires a VT-capable machine. We discussed before in the system requirements how you can test if your machine is VT-capable. Once again, we will be using *virt-manager* to install XP as a virtual machine. The following steps walk you through creating a Windows guest.

1. Rather than choosing Paravirtualization, select **Fully Virtualized** (see Figure 3.15).

Figure 3.15 Choosing a Fully Virtualized Installation Method

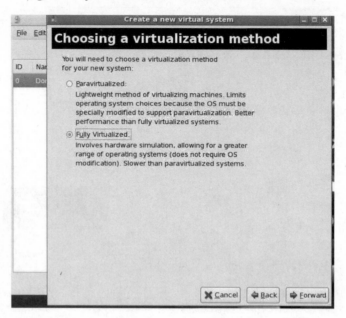

NOTE

If your CPU does not support this feature, you won't be able to select that option and you might need to reboot and modify your BIOS settings or even upgrade to a new BIOS.

2. This time you won't need to select a repository, but you will need to select either a CD mounted in the local CD drive or an ISO image of a CD you have stored somewhere on your file system (see Figure 3.16).

NOTE

You can also use this feature to install Linux distributions not supported by the Fedora installer or other operating systems.

Figure 3.16 Locating Installation Media on CD

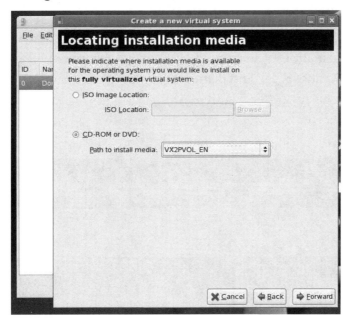

3. Choose a disk or a file image that will host the guest operating system (see Figure 3.17).

Figure 3.17 Adding Storage Space

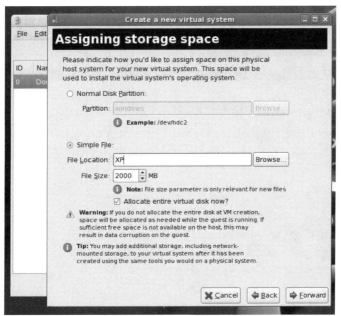

4. Choose the appropriate amount of memory. Be sure to factor in the appropriate amount of memory for the Windows XP operating system and the applications that will run in it.

5. After confirmation of your settings, a virtual machine will be started and will boot the Windows XP installation program from the CD as if it were a regular XP installation (see Figure 3.18).

Figure 3.18 Starting a Fully Virtualized Install

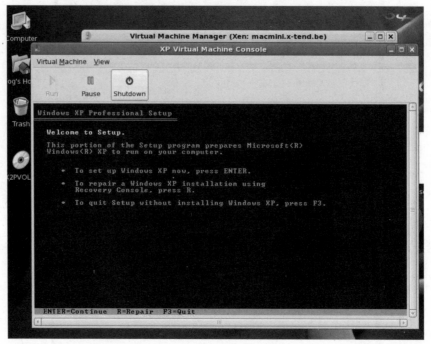

This time, a configuration file has been written by VirtManager, and you can start the virtual machine after installation by using the *xm* command. The following is a sample configuration file.

```
name = "XP"
builder = "hvm"
memory = "1024"
disk = [ 'file:/vhosts/XP.img,hda,w', ]
vif = [ 'type=ioemu, mac=00:16:3e:6d:a4:6b, bridge=xenbr0', ]
uuid = "23a340d1-e82e-da77-6525-4133a9e9e828"
device_model = "/usr/lib/xen/bin/qemu-dm"
kernel = "/usr/lib/xen/boot/hvmloader"
```

```
vnc=1
vncunused=0
apic=1
acpi=1
pae=1
vcpus=1
serial = "pty" # enable serial console
on_reboot    = 'restart'
on_crash     = 'restart'
```

Notice the different options in the configuration file. The kernel is now the hvmloader, as opposed to a real kernel or pygrub. Since Windows, by default, requires a graphical console, you have two choices. Either you connect to the graphical console by VNC, meaning you will need the vnc=1 parameter, or you want to see the Windows machine booting on the desktop where you launch it, using vnc=0 parameter or replacing it with sdl=1. This way you have the choice between direct output on the screen or connecting via VNC remotely.

We have shown you how to install both a Linux and a Windows virtual machine on a standard open-source Linux distribution. As the stable packages in Fedora Core eventually end up being part of the next Red Hat Enterprise release, you will notice that, with a few cosmetic changes left and right, these instructions will also help you install Xen on a RHEL platform and, therefore, also on a CentOS platform.

Installing the XenServer Product Family

Now let's discuss installing the XenServer product family.

What Is XenServer?

XenServer is the commercially supported Xen platform built by XenSource, the authors of Xen. It comes in three different flavors. The first Xen product is XenExpress, which is aimed at the IT Enthusiast or developer. It allows up to four concurrent virtual machines on a dual-socket server with 4GB of memory. It has support for Linux P2V conversions. It can also run Windows Server 2003, Windows XP SP2, and Windows 2000 SP4. It has templates for different RHEL and Debian releases, and also supports SLES 9.2 through 10.1. From the management console, you can manage a single server, but best of all it is free. Should you decide to use one of the other versions, the process is no more difficult than changing the license key.

The next product in the suite is XenServer, which is aimed at the Windows IT Professional. It allows up to eight concurrent VMs on a dual-socket server with up to 8GB of memory. It does not support any Linux guests, but it does support all the aforementioned Windows guests and you can manage multiple servers from the management console. It is not free, but for a price of less than $100 per year, it is an interesting platform to get started on.

Finally, there is XenEnterprise, the more expensive alternative of the three but still a lot cheaper than other commercial products in the same field. It is targeted at larger enterprises, with unlimited VMs and support for as much RAM as your machine is capable of. It has Linux P2V support included and Windows P2V via partner bundles. It supports both Linux and the aforementioned Windows version, and it is the version that supports the more advanced features such as live migration and shared storage first.

Collectively, the XenSource commercial offering is referred to as XenServer, regardless of whether you are talking about XenSource, the Windows-only XenServer, or the flagship XenEnterprise product.

XenServer Requirements

Unlike a Xen installation with Fedora Core, for a XenServer installation you need two machines—one to be installed as the Xen server, and another that will run the XenSource XenServer Administrator Console used to manage the server. The requirements for XenServer are about the same as for a Fedora machine. However, you must take into account the fact that XenServer requires a machine with at least 16GB of free disk space on the same disk, though more is recommended. In addition, XenEnterprise can use up to 32 CPUs.

XenServer is based on a Centos root file system with a SUSE-based kernel. It is meant to be headless and managed from a remote console. It will install its own two 4GB LVM partitions for the XenServer host domain and leave the rest free for the virtual machines themselves. As for the virtual machine templates, a minimal Red Hat Enterprise Linux (RHEL)-based install will take a root file system of 4GB, while the Debian template will take up to 1GB for its root device and 512MB for its swap.

The client machine can be almost anything. We will install the client on the Fedora Core, but you can use a Windows XP or 2000 client or any RPM-based Linux machine with about 100MB of free disk space and a minimum 256MB. For P2V, you, of course, need a network as fast as possible.

If you compare the feature set of a XenServer with the features of the open-source Xen version, you will see there are a lot fewer features in the XenEnterprise GUI. Many of those features are available under the hood, but not as yet from the GUI. Keep in mind that XenEnterprise was meant to be friendly for the non-Linux savvy public that wants to do bare metal virtualization for Windows virtual machines. Linux experts may still lean towards a fully open-source version of Xen, or an Enterprise Linux version, though the commercial version does provide a support channel as well.

XenServer is being marketed as "Ten minutes to Xen," and we will show you that that time is about exactly what you'll need to get up and running.

Getting and Installing XenServer

As mentioned before, XenServer comes in different flavors. You can start with a free XenExpress and then upgrade afterward to other versions. So, after registering or purchasing one of these versions, you will get instructions from XenSource on how to download your install binaries and your license key.

As of XenServer 3.2, Xen now comes as two CDs: One smaller ISO image, which will get you started with a Windows-only virtualization platform, and a second larger ISO image if you want to run Linux-based virtual machines. The latter CD contains the basic templates for different Linux distributions. Assuming you downloaded the ISO image to a Linux machine, you can burn the ISO to a CD as root with the following command:

```
cdrecord -v dev=ATA:1,0,0 -data XenServer-3.2.0-install-cd.iso
cdrecord -v dev=ATA:1,0,0 -data XenServer-3.2.0-linux-cd.iso
```

Installing the Host

The first thing to do is install the server. Assuming you have a machine at your disposal that has the preceding specifications, let's install XenEnterprise. We'll be using XenServer Version 3.2.0 Release Candidate, build 1960, for this walkthrough. After you have burned the ISO to a CD, place it in the server you plan to use and power up the server, either your server boots from the CD-ROM by default or you will have to tell it to do so. As the server boots from the CD, it will boot a Xen hypervisor and Xen kernel, and will boot to a text mode install of a Linux system. The installer is based on Anaconda, which is the same installation program used by Fedora Core, Red Hat Enterprise Linux, and other distributions. It is responsible for the basic configuration of your system and also allows you to automate installations via kick start. Since we are installing a server that is not supposed to have a graphical screen, the installation will be in Text mode.

The following steps will guide you through the installation process:

1. The First screen you get after the installer has finished its hardware auto-detection is the KeyMap configuration screen. Choose the keyboard layout you prefer and then press **Enter**.

2. This CD has three functions. The first is to install a XenServer host (see Figure 3.19), which is the option we need now. The second function is to load a network or block device driver for dom0. The third function is used to do a physical-to-virtual machine conversion. Choose **install XenServer** and press **Enter**.

Figure 3.19 Welcome to XenServer

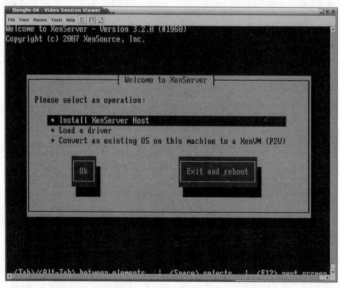

NOTE

Just as with any other regular Linux install in Text mode, you can switch to a different log and a console by using **Alt + F2** for a console, **Alt + F3** or **Alt + F4** for different log files, and **Alt + F1** to go back to the installer.

---

3. Since you are sure this is the correct machine, click **OK** to continue when warned that XenServer will overwrite data on any drives you select during the install process. Note that you don't need to select all the drives in your server.

4. XenServer asks you to read and Accept the End User License Agreement. Please do so.

5. XenServer might warn you about system requirements you have not met. If you don't have a VT-capable machine, or if you do not have enough memory, XenServer will warn you. You, however, are free to continue installing (see Figure 3.20).

Figure 3.20 System Hardware (VT Detection)

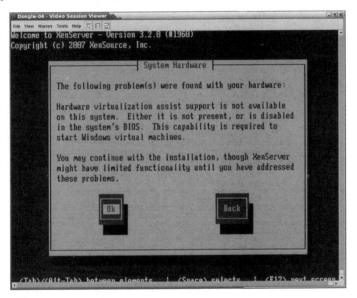

6. The XenServer installer will check if you already have an older version of XenServer installed. If you do, it will ask you if you want to upgrade.

7. Upon detecting multiple hard disks, XenServer will give you the opportunity to choose which disk you want to use and if you want to use and format other disks.

8. Since we are installing from a CD, choose the **Local media (CD-ROM)** option and click **OK** (see Figure 3.21).

Figure 3.21 Select the Installation Source

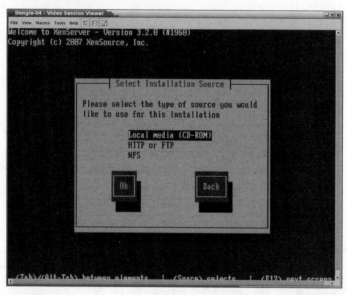

9. When XenServer thinks your machine is not VT-capable, it will encourage you to add the "Linux pack," which is on the second CD you downloaded and which you will need to bootstrap Linux images from (see Figure 3.22).

Figure 3.22 Adding the Linux Pack

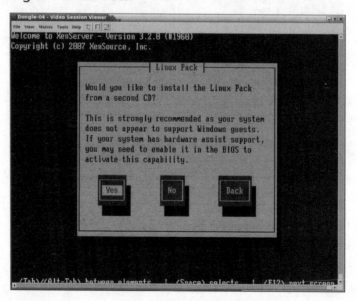

10. If you wish, you can verify whether the CD you created is intact, if you run into problems later during the install, this is worth verifying, but to gain time we can skip the Media Testing for now.

11. XenServer asks you to choose a password, this password can be used to log on to the console of the Xen server and will also be needed to connect to the Xen Server from the Administrator Console. You only need a six–character password, but make sure you choose a strong password you can remember so you don't have to write it down anywhere.

TIP

An easy way to create a strong but easy-to-remember password is to think of a memorable sentence and then use the first letters from each word to compose your password—for example, "Open-Source security is better than security through obscurity!" becomes "OSsibtsto!"

12. Choose the geographical area you are installing the server in. Click OK.

13. Choose the city that is in your Time Zone and click OK.

14. If you have access to an NTP server, you can use NTP; otherwise, you must do a manual time entry. We will choose to use NTP.

15. An NTP server can be announced by your DHCP server or specified manually. Either your internal network administrator knows which NTP servers can be used or you can use a public one (pool.ntp.org). Figure 3.23 shows a dialog box for an NTP configuration.

16. The next step is network configuration. Since you are installing a server, you have two options. Either your DHCP server has the MAC address of this server listed and will hand out a static IP address with all the other network configuration parameters, or you will manually configure a fixed IP address. Do not use a dynamic IP address for a server that you can only manage via a remote GUI since when your DHCP lease changes you might end up obtaining another IP address and you wouldn't be able to connect to your XenServer anymore.

Figure 3.23 NTP Configuration

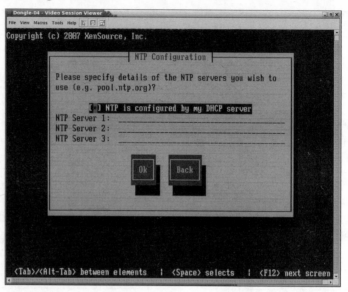

17. For each interface in your server, you will now be given the chance to configure the IP address, subnet mask, gateway, and on the second screen, the hostname and the different DNS servers (see Figure 3.24).

Figure 3.24 Hostname and DNS Configuration

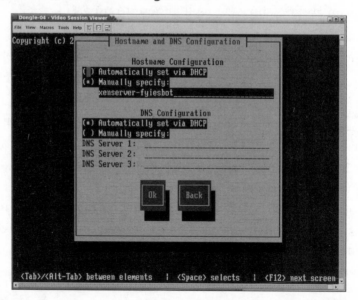

18. You will now get a final warning that all the data on that machine will be destroyed. Click **Install XenServer** if you are sure. After this leave your XenServer's installer do its work. *If you didn't select the extra disk, the next time it will need input from you will be when it is ready to be rebooted. At which time, it will require that you click **OK** again.*

19. If you did select the extra disk, after a while the installer will prompt you to insert the second disk (see Figure 3.25).

Figure 3.25 Inserting the Extra Disk

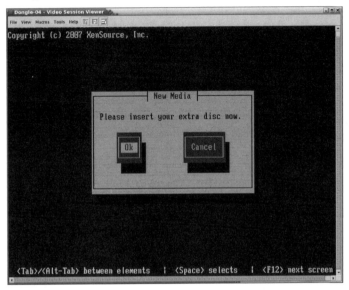

You will also be given the opportunity to verify the new disk, or just go on and skip the verification.

Note that as the second disk is larger, it will take longer to install the second CD compared to the first. After a while, a screen stating "The XenServer installation has completed" will appear. You are now ready to reboot.

Make sure the CD-ROM is not in the drive when the machine restarts again. If everything was installed correctly, you will now see GNU Grub, which will, after a small timeout, boot into Xen. If you need to make changes to the boot parameters (such as giving your dom0 less memory by default), or if want to boot the Xen server in Safe Mode, you can navigate the menu with the **Up-** and **Down-arrow keys** and choose your preferred boot image. If you don't, grub will automatically boot your system and after a few seconds the following message will appear on your screen:

```
XenServer Host 3.2.0-build

System Booted: 2007-03-26 19:40

Your XenServer Host has now finished booting.  To manage this
server please use the XenServer Administrator Console
application.  You can install the XenServer Administrator Console
for Windows and Linux from the XenServer install media.



You  can connect to this system using one of the following network
addresses:


10.0.11.28


xenserver-1t login:
```

You should now be able to log on as user root using the password you chose earlier in the install. Your Xen server is now ready to be managed. As proof that you actually have a Xen machine up and running, you can try an **xm list**.

```
[root@xenserver ~]# xm list
Name                             ID Mem(MiB) VCPUs State    Time(s)
Domain-0                          0      121     1 r-----      47.4
```

To be sure your network connection is working, you can now try to ping any machine on your network using the *PING* command.

```
[root@xenserver ~]# ping -c 5 10.0.11.1
PING 10.0.11.1 (10.0.11.1) 56(84) bytes of data.
64 bytes from 10.0.11.1: icmp_seq=0 ttl=255 time=0.227 ms
64 bytes from 10.0.11.1: icmp_seq=1 ttl=255 time=0.225 ms
64 bytes from 10.0.11.1: icmp_seq=2 ttl=255 time=0.207 ms
64 bytes from 10.0.11.1: icmp_seq=3 ttl=255 time=0.246 ms
64 bytes from 10.0.11.1: icmp_seq=4 ttl=255 time=0.234 ms
```

NOTE

If at a later time you want to modify the hostname or the network configuration of your XenServer host, you won't be able to do so from the command line and you will need to use the regular Linux tools. Since XenServer is based on a Red Hat–style distribution, you must modify the network configuration files located in /etc/sysconfig/network-scripts. The configuration file for your eth0 will be called ifcfg-eth0.

Also, if you first decide you don't need the Linux Pack, but later realize you do need it after all, you can simply mount the Linux install CD and run the install.sh script from the CD.

Client Installation

The XenServer client is a Java-based GUI that can run on either a Linux or Windows platform. It has an installer for both. The Java GUI for Windows resides on the first CD. Just double-clicking the *xenserver-client.exe* will launch the installer, which will guide you through an easy installation. The XenSource XenServer Administrator Console for Linux has been placed on the second Linux CD. In order to install the client on an RPM-based Linux desktop, you need to become root.

```
[user@host ~]$su -
Password:
[root@host ~]#
mount /dev/hdc


[root@host client_install]# df .
Filesystem          1K-blocks       Used Available Use% Mounted on
/dev/hdc              686198      686198         0 100% /media/XenServer-3.1.0-1332
```

Then install the actual RPM packages.

```
[root@client ~]# cd /media/XenServer-3.1.0-1332/client_install/
[root@client client_install]# rpm -vih xenserver-client*.rpm
Preparing...                ########################################### [100%]
   1:xenserver-client-jre   ########################################### [ 33%]
   2:xenserver-client-jars  ########################################### [ 67%]
   3:xenserver-client       ########################################### [100%]
```

The client will be installed in */opt/xensource/xenserver-client*, and you can start the client by running:

```
/opt/xensource/xenserver-client/bin/xenserver-client.sh
```

> **NOTE**
>
> If you are running Beryl, the 3D window manager, your xenserver-client will not work and you will get two gray windows rather than readable text. If you switch back to the default metacity window manager, your application will be usable.

Both the Windows and Linux client will go through the following upon first launch.

1. You will be prompted to accept the license agreement.

2. The administration client will ask you to choose a master password. With this password, you will be able to access the management console again so you can manage different servers from the same GUI (see Figure 3.26).

Figure 3.26 The XenSource XenServer Master Login

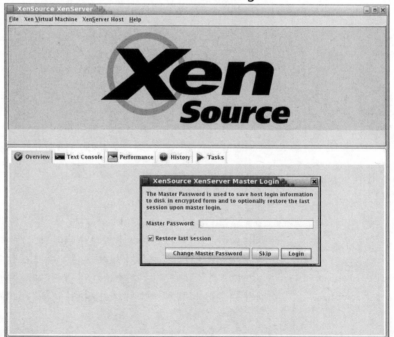

3. The next step is to specify the IP address and the password for the XenServer we just installed.

4. You will now be connected to the management console of a freshly installed and empty XenServer (see Figure 3.27).

Figure 3.27 The XenSource XenServer Dashboard

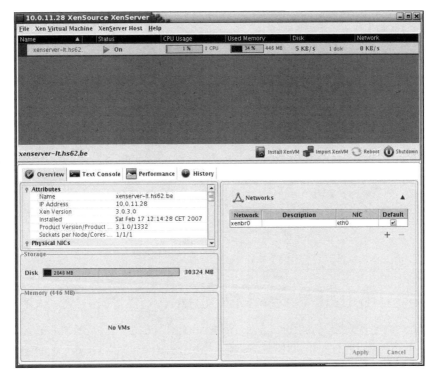

5. The only remaining item is to enable the license key you got from XenSource. From the **XenServer Host** menu, choose **License Key**, then click **...** and select the file in which you saved the license key. Finish by selecting **Apply License** (see Figure 3.28).

Figure 3.28 The XenSource XenServer License Key Installation

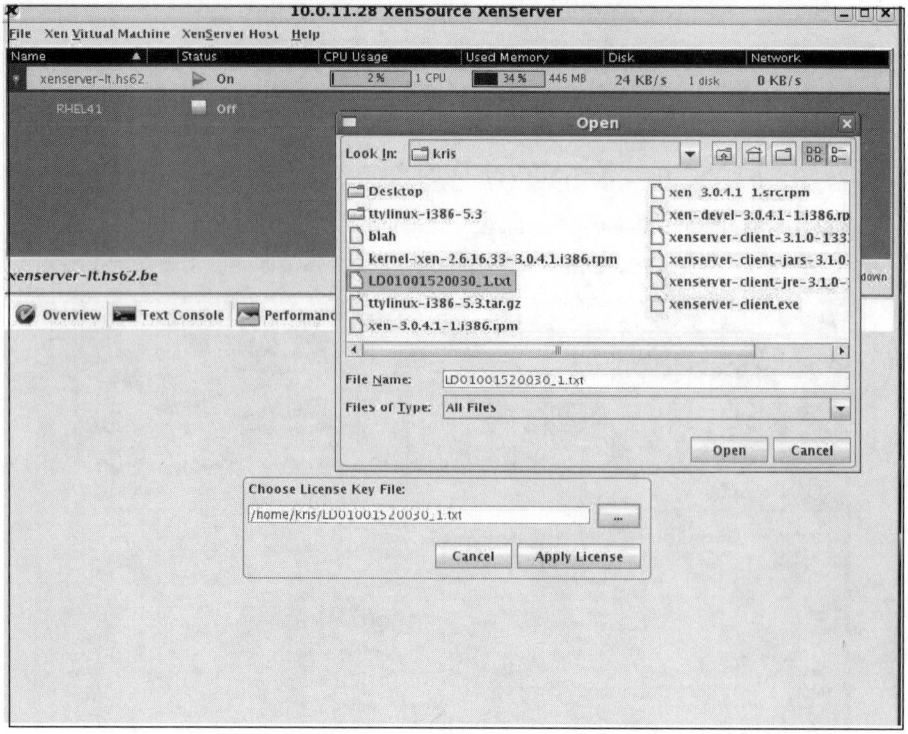

Installing an Initial Virtual Machine on XenServer

Now that you've made it this far, it's time to install your first virtual machine on the XenServer. So if you have already quit the Administrator Console, start it again and log on to your just-installed server.

1. Click the **Install Xen VM** icon in the middle bar.

2. In the lower part, you will now be able to fill in the details about the virtual machine you want to install. Let's start by installing a virtual machine from a Red Hat Enterprise Linux 4.1 repository. First, give it a name and a description. Next, even though you might only have one or two physical CPUs in your machine, you can give your virtual machine more virtual CPUs than you actually have. You, however, cannot give your virtual machine more memory than you actually have. Nevertheless, you can start with a little and grow on-the-fly as you need more memory.

3. On the right-hand side you will see the disk and the network configuration. The RHEL 4.1. template has a one 8GB disk by default. By clicking the +

or − signs right below the overview, you can add more disks or remove them.

4. You will also see your network interfaces. Here you can add more interfaces and connect them to different bridges. The default xenbr0 bridges your physical eth0 to the eth0 in your virtual machine. Note that you will need to have access to a RHEL 4.1 repository. One on your local network, of course, is the fastest alternative.

NOTE

Creating a RHEL repository is as easy as copying the content off all the RHEL CDs you have into one directory. Make sure you have a Web server that will serve these files and you are ready to go.

5. After you click **Install** in the lower-right corner, a virtual machine template will be created and will be started for the very first time. As of this point, you actually already have a virtual machine running—it just needs to be installed now. When you return to the overview, after a while you will see that a virtual machine with the name you chose is "on," and when you click the **Text Console** tab you will see a familiar Anaconda installer. This actually is a slightly modified version of Anaconda that has been adapted to run in a virtual machine. Once it has started, proceed as follows:

1. Choose your language (see Figure 3.29).

2. Choose HTTP as the install media.

3. Configure your network so you can reach your repository. Test network connectivity by pinging the IP you just configured from a host.

4. Select your repository (see Figure 3.30). Test whether you can use the listed repository by connecting to the IP and the URL you provided with your Web browser.

Figure 3.29 The XenSource XenServer RHEL Installation

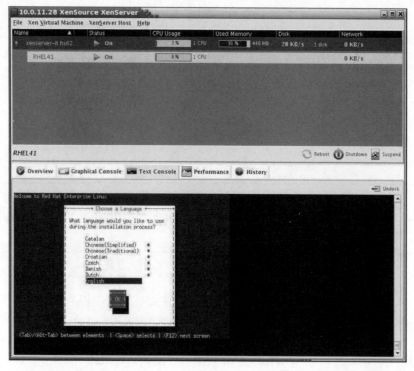

Figure 3.30 The XenSource XenServer RHEL Repository Configuration

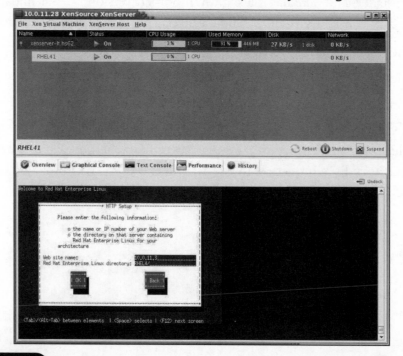

5. The Red Hat installer will download its initial install images from the network. From here it is just a regular RHEL install. The full RHEL 4 manual, which also documents installation in detail, can be found at www.redhat.com/docs/manuals/enterprise/RHEL-4-Manual/x8664-multi-install-guide (see Figure 3.31).

Figure 3.31 The XenSource XenServer RHEL Installation Starting

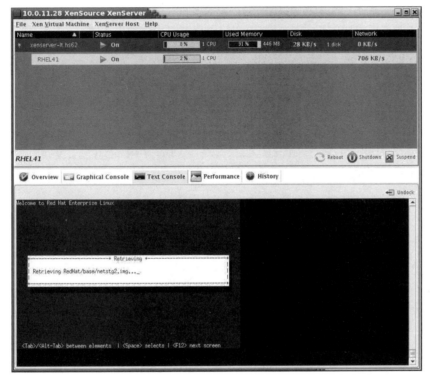

After installation, the Virtual machine will shut down and automatically restart into its freshly installed image. From here, you can use the Xen GUI to stop, start, suspend, and clone as you please.

We just explained how simple it is to install XenServer. You have to agree with us that getting the dom0 up and running is indeed a "Ten minutes to Xen" procedure. The installation of the virtual machines largely is related to the speed of your network. In the following section, we will be documenting how to install the RPMs provided by XenSource on any RPM-based distribution and how to use LVM as a disk backend for your virtual machines.

Other Xen Installation Methods

In this section, we'll discuss other methods for installing Xen.

Using the XenSource Binaries and LVM

You can download the open-source binaries and source code from getxen.org in addition to the XenSource Web site. The getxen.org packages are built by XenSource but are not supported by them; however, they do work on a variety of distributions and often have different features enabled that distributions don't have. One of those features is other disk backends for your virtual machine. Using other backends for your virtual disk means you can download existing images from a distribution and use those on a file system you prepare, rather than having to stick to the tools that a distribution forces you to use.

Jailtime.org provides a variety of distributions you can base your guest virtual machines on. As mentioned earlier, Xen can use both file-backed virtual block devices, which you can create by running:

```
dd if=/dev/zero of=vmdisk bs=1k seek 2048k count=1
```

You can export physical devices (the actual /dev/hda9) or you can use LVM volumes (phy:VolumeGroup/root_volume). We prefer to use Logical Volumes on our machines since they are very flexible to work with. In this section, we will document how to use the XenSource-provided RPM Binaries and how you can build virtual machines with their file systems on an LVM volume.

> **NOTE**
>
> If you are working on the same distribution where you installed virt-manager and the other fedora tools, you will need to uninstall all Xen tools from that distribution first because they will conflict with the XenSource RPMs.

So, the first step is to install the XenSource-provided RPMs on a vanilla machine.

```
[root@fc6-xen kris]# rpm -vih xen-3.0.4.1-1.i386.rpm  ker-nel-xen-2.6.16.33-
3.0.4.1.i386.rpm  --nodeps
Preparing...               ########################################### [100%]
   1:kernel-xen             ########################################### [ 50%]
   2:xen                    ########################################### [100%]
```

The Xen RPMs do not modify your grub configuration, so you will need to add a grub entry for your freshly installed kernel yourself.

```
default=0
fallback=1
timeout=5
splashimage=(hd0,0)/grub/splash.xpm.gz
hiddenmenu
title Fedora Core (XenSource)
        root (hd0,0)
        kernel /xen.gz
        module /vmlinuz-2.6-xen ro root=/dev/VolGroup00/LogVol00 nodmraid
xencons=off
        module /initrd-2.6-xen.img

title Fedora Core (2.6.18-1.2798.fc6)
        root (hd0,0)
        kernel /vmlinuz-2.6.18-1.2798.fc6 ro root=/dev/VolGroup00/LogVol00 nodmraid
rhgb quiet
        initrd /initrd-2.6.18-1.2798.fc6.img
```

Do not remove the regular Linux kernel since you will need it if anything fails. After modifying that grub entry (take a look at the default kernel and verify it is the kernel you want to boot by default), upon rebooting you should arrive in a Xen-enabled kernel.

```
[root@fc6-xen xen]# uname -r
2.6.16.33-xen_3.0.4.1
```

The XenSource rpm will also have started *xend* and xendomains for you. Thus, the output of **xm list** should also look familiar.

```
[root@fc6-xen grub]# xm list
Name                             ID   Mem VCPUs      State   Time(s)
Domain-0                          0   875     1      r-----     89.1
```

Now it's time to install your first virtual machine on an LVM Volume. As we noted earlier, you should still have plenty of space available in the Volume Group you created since you only chose to use 4 to 6GB of disk for the dom0 file system. So let us create a new virtual machine, this time based on LVM.

```
lvcreate -L4096 -nroot-TEST-FC6 VolGroup00
mkdir -p /vhosts/FC6
mount /dev/VolGroup00/root-TEST-FC6  /vhosts/FC6
```

You should usually create a directory */vhosts* where you mount your partitions as they would be mounted in a real machine on your dom0 host. From there, you can install the first FC6 Base packages in a chroot on the actual future root device. First, modify the */etc/yum/repo.d/* files. Uncomment the commented basedir and replace the variables. The beginning of the file should look like:

```
[core]name=Fedora Core $releasever - $basearch
baseurl=http://download.fedora.redhat.com/pub/fedora/linux/core/6/i386/os/
```

You can disable the other repositories for now by modifying the enabled parameter to 0. Start the installation of the Distribution into the chroot with:

```
yum --installroot=/vhosts/FC6/ -y groupinstall Base
```

This installation will take a while depending on the bandwidth you have to the repository as configured in the fedora-core.repo file. After this installation, some small changes are needed to make sure you can open your initial console and log on to your newly created virtual machine.

```
MAKEDEV -d /path/dev -x console
MAKEDEV -d /path/dev -x null
MAKEDEV -d /path/dev -x zero
```

Since you want network connectivity and the ability to log on to the virtual machine, you should also create a */etc/sysconfig/network* file, an */etc/sysconfig/network-scripts/ifcfg-eth0* file, and a working */etc/shadow* and */etc/password* file in to the */vhost/FC6* tree in order to be able to log in to the machine once it is booted. Also copy the /lib/modules directory from the dom0, or install the kernel-xen package again with the same install root so the modules will match the appropriate kernel.

You're almost ready. What you still need is the configuration file for this virtual machine. Most of Xen's configuration files live in */etc/xen*. You'll be creating a separate configuration file for each virtual machine you want to deploy on your Xen host. They look like the following example, and if you create a symlink to the */etc/xen/auto* directory, they will even be started at boot time given that you enable the xendomains script at bootup.

```
[root@fc6-xen xen]# more FC6-LVM
kernel = "/boot/vmlinuz-2.6-xen"
#initrd= "/boot/initrd-2.6-xen.img"

name = "FC6-LVM"
```

```
memory = "256"
disk = [ 'phy:/dev/VolGroup00/root-TEST-FC6,sda1,w', ]
root = "/dev/sda1 rw"
vif = [ 'mac=00:16:3e:06:3b:80, bridge=xenbr0', ]
```

As you can see, the file system you will use this time is
phy:/dev/VolGroup00/root-TEST-FC6—exactly the Logical Volume we just created. The configuration file is rather straightforward, and the Xen packages include
examples. You can add multiple Logical Volumes mapped to multiple partitions. For
example create a mapping like:

```
disk = ['phy:vm_volumes/root-hostname,sda1,w'
        ,'phy:vm_volumes/var-hostname,sda3,w'
        ,'phy:vm_volumes/www-hostname,sda4,w'
        ,'phy:vm_volumes/swap-hostname,sda2,w'
        ]
```

Make sure you unmount the Logical Volume from */vhosts/FC6* before trying to
start the virtual machine. Otherwise, it won't start. You now must start your virtual
machine with the command **xm create config file**. If you add a **-c** to that command, you'll see the machine booting and you should get a login prompt within seconds. From there, you can log in and use your virtual machine just like any other
machine.

The whole process we've just documented is ideal for managing larger deployments since every step you take can be automated. A paper first presented at the
2005 Hamburg Linux Kongress on Automating Xen Virtual Machine Deployments
(which can be found on http://howto.x-
tend.be/AutomatingVirtualMachineDeployment/) documents how you can integrate
SystemImager, which is a Large Scale Deployment framework and a couple of simple
scripts to automate Xen virtual machine deployment.

If you are interested in Physical 2 Virtual Machine migration tools, the previously
mentioned paper, in combination with the golden client framework that SystemImager
comes with is perfectly suited to do such migrations for Linux-based physical
machines.

Configuring Xen

Most people can get Xen up and running without having to touch any of the configuration files we'll be discussing in the next couple of paragraphs. However, both xendomains and Xen have different facets you can tune and tweak.

The main Xen configuration file is xend-config.sxp, which is located in /etc/xen/. If you install the XenSource RPM, it brims with examples and documentation, while other distributions tend to slim down the configuration file and leave you with a preconfigured set of parameters. Note that the commented entries in this file show the default parameters.

Let's look at some more important parameters that can be found in these configuration files. A not unimportant feature is logging. If you want to change the location of your log file or the amount of data it is logging, modify the following:

```
(logfile /var/log/xen/xend.log)
(loglevel DEBUG)
```

Xend can be managed via an httpd server, which you probably want to disable for security reasons.

```
#(xend-http-server no)
#(xend-port 8000)
```

If you plan on configuring live migration of virtual machines, you will need to enable the xend-relocation-server parameters.

```
#(xend-relocation-server yes)
# Port xend should use for the relocation interface, if xend-relocation-server
# is set.
#(xend-relocation-port 8002)
#(xend-relocation-address '')
```

And as with any daemon, you can restrict the sockets to which xend listens via the following parameters.

```
#(xend-address '')
#(xend-address localhost)
```

A more important section for day-to-day usage is the network configuration portion. Whenever a system is booted in a xen-kernel, it will just have an eth0, just like any other system. This will change when the xend service is started. The xend service will activate bridging and the necessary virtual devices that allow network traffic from outside to the virtual hosts. At first, the current eth0, which is the physical network card, will be changed to peth0. For other network interfaces (eth1, ...), the same will happen (peth1, ...). From now on, you have to check the link status on device peth0 instead of eth0.

Next, eth0 will be re-created in the same way as on every other virtual host. The virtual host will only see eth0, which has a corresponding VIF interface on dom0. Eth0 on dom0 (which has ID 0) will be mapped to vif0.0, while eth1 of dom0 will be mapped to vif0.1. On a virtual host with ID 3, the eth0 interface will be mapped against vif3.0. In general, you have a unique vifY.X interface on dom0 for every interface of each virtual host. Y indicates the ID of the virtual host and X the number of the interface (eth0, eth1, ...).

The connection between the physical interface (peth0) and the interface of the virtual host (vifY.X) is made by bridging. The amount of bridges and which interface is bounded to which bridge is handled by the Xen configuration.

```
(network-script network-bridge)


# The script used to control virtual interfaces.  This can be overridden on a
# per-vif basis when creating a domain or configuring a new vif.  The
# vif-bridge script is designed for use with the network-bridge script, or
# similar configurations.
#
# If you have overridden the bridge name using
# (network-script 'network-bridge bridge=$name') then you may wish to do the
# same here.  The bridge name can also be set when creating a domain or
# configuring a new vif, but a value specified here would act as a default.
#
# If you are using only one bridge, the vif-bridge script will discover that,
# so there is no need to specify it explicitly.
#
(vif-script vif-bridge)



## Use the following if network traffic is routed, as an alternative to the
# settings for bridged networking given above.
#(network-script network-route)
#(vif-script     vif-route)



## Use the following if network traffic is routed with NAT, as an alternative
```

```
# to the settings for bridged networking given above.
#(network-script network-nat)
#(vif-script     vif-nat)
```

The xend–config.sxp file is also the file where you configure the minimum memory required for a dom0 196, which is more than enough for a dom0. We're mostly running them with only 128MB of RAM as a minimum. This certainly is enough in a headless environment where the dom0 only serves as a management console for the virtual machines.

```
(dom0-min-mem 196)
(dom0-cpus 0)
```

If you are installing Windows machines as domUs, you can also configure the behavior of a VNC server, or give it a default password.

```
# The interface for VNC servers to listen on. Defaults
#(vnc-listen '127.0.0.1')


# The default password for VNC console on HVM domain.
# Empty string is no authentication.
(vncpasswd '')
```

As mentioned earlier, every configuration file you place or symlink from in /etc/xen/auto will be started by the rc script xendomains at boot time. Xendomains itself also has a couple of configuration parameters that can be modified in the /etc/sysconfig/xendomains parameters.

One of the more important configuration parameters in the xendomains config file is the parameter that defines what to do with a virtual machine that has been started by xendomains when the physical machine is being rebooted. By default, a domain will be saved and restarted, unless you modify the configuration parameters. Also, if you want to save a virtual machine, the xendomains config file has a parameter that defines where to store these images:

```
XENDOMAINS_SAVE=/var/lib/xen/save
```

If you leave the preceding line empty, xendomains will not attempt to save the domains and will shut them down before the physical machine goes down. If you leave this config and you run out of disk space, you might run into trouble rebooting afterwards, so be careful.

Getting Xen on Your Network

As just mentioned, Xen will create a bridge and bind the virtual interfaces of your guest to that bridge. A default bridge configuration will look like

```
[root@fc6-xen xen]# brctl  show
bridge name       bridge id              STP enabled      interfaces
xenbr0            8000.feffffffffff      no               vif1.0
                                                          peth0
                                                          vif0.0
```

Configuring & Implementing…

About brctl

As most of you know, a bridge connects two different Ethernet network segments. All protocols go transparently through a bridge as the connection is being made on Layer 2. Linux Bridging has been around since the 2.2 kernel series and is not specifically related to Xen. It has been rewritten by Lennert Buytenhek for 2.4 and 2.6 kernels. The code itself is in the Linux kernel and you'll need the brctl userspace tool to control it.

Creating a bridge is as easy as running.

```
[root@HOST ~]# brctl addbr xenbr1
```

To see the current state of bridges on your system, you can use

```
[root@HOST ~]# brctl show
bridge name       bridge id              STP enabled      interfaces
xenbr0            8000.feffffffffff      no               peth0
                                                          vif0.0
                                                          vif1.0
xenbr1            8000.000000000000      no               can't get port
```

Continued

```
info: Function not implemented
```

The next thing you need to do is add ports, or interfaces, to that bridge. Such as:

```
[root@HOST ~]# brctl  addif xenbr1 peth1
[root@HOST ~]# brctl  addif xenbr1 vif0.1
[root@HOST ~]# brctl  addif xenbr1 vif1.1
```

Which will then create a bridge for you that looks like:

```
[root@CO-TMS-B ~]# brctl  show
bridge name       bridge id            STP enabled      interfaces
xenbr0            8000.feffffffffff    no               peth0
                                                        vif0.0
                                                        vif1.0

xenbr1            8000.feffffffffff    no               peth1
                                                        vif0.1
                                                        vif1.1
```

Removing bridge ports is as easy as creating them:

```
[root@CO-TMS-B ~]# brctl  delif xenbr1 vif1.1
[root@CO-TMS-B ~]# brctl  delif xenbr1 vif0.1
[root@CO-TMS-B ~]# brctl  delif xenbr1 peth1
[root@CO-TMS-B ~]# brctl show
bridge name       bridge id            STP enabled      interfaces
xenbr0            8000.feffffffffff    no               peth0
                                                        vif0.0
                                                        vif1.0

xenbr1            8000.000000000000    no                can't get port
info: Function not implemented
```

However, before deleting the actual bridge, you must make sure the interface xenbr1 is also down.

```
[root@CO-TMS-B ~]# ifconfig xenbr1 down
[root@CO-TMS-B ~]# brctl delbr xenbr1
[root@CO-TMS-B ~]# brctl show
bridge name       bridge id            STP enabled      interfaces
xenbr0            8000.feffffffffff    no               peth0
                                                        vif0.0
                                                        vif1.0
```

Continued

> If your network requires it, Linux bridging also supports the Spanning Tree Protocol IEEE 802.1d, amongst others, which are responsible for preventing loops in your network. The brctl man page clearly documents its further usage.

If you want to use the eth0 in your machine only for management connections and route all the traffic over other interfaces, nothing can keep you from creating your own xen-network script. You just need to modify the */etc/xen/xend-config.sxp* file to get

```
(network-script my-network-script)
```

Then put your network script in /etc/xen/scripts/. An example might look like:

```
#!/bin/sh
brctl addbr xen-br0
brctl addif xen-br0 eth1
brctl addif xen-br0 vif1.0
brctl addbr xen-br1
brctl addif xen-br1 eth2
brctl addif xen-br1 vif1.1
```

This will actually bind your second and third physical interfaces to your first and second virtual interface. If you want multiple bridges, one bridge per physical interface, you must use a wrapper script. This wrapper script is defined by the xend-config.sxp and will be called when xend is started. The wrapper script will call the original network-bridge script multiple times.

```
[root@XEN-A ~]# grep network-wrapper-bridge /etc/xen/xend-config.sxp
(network-script network-wrapper-bridge)
/etc/xen/scripts/network-wrapper-bridge
#!/bin/sh
/etc/xen/scripts/network-bridge start vifnum=0 netdev=eth0
/etc/xen/scripts/network-bridge start vifnum=1 netdev=eth1
```

Because you will now have multiple bridges, it is not always sure that the correct VIF interface is mapped to the correct bridge. If you want to map each virtual eth0 to the physical eth0, you must write yet another wrapper script, this time for vif-bridge.

```
[root@XEN-A ~]# grep vif-wrapper-bridge /etc/xen/xend-config.sxp
(vif-script vif-wrapper-bridge)
/etc/xen/scripts/vif-wrapper-bridge
```

```
#!/bin/sh

if [ $1 = "online" ]
then
  # load some general functions
  dir=$(dirname "$0")
  . "$dir/vif-common.sh"
  # find the bridge number out of the vif interface name
  brnum=$(echo $vif | sed 's/vif.*\.//')
  bridge=xenbr$brnum
  # store the bridgename in xenstore
  bridge=$(xenstore_write "$XENBUS_PATH/bridge" "$bridge")
fi
# load the real vif-bridge script
/etc/xen/scripts/vif-bridge $1
```

This wrapper script will grab the interface number from the VIF interface and use that number for the xenbr. The generated xenbridge name is stored in the xenstore. The vif-bridge script, which is called at the end, will take the correct bridgename out of the Xenstore.

Summary

Creating an environment to deploy virtual machines takes some thinking up front. We need to make choices about whether we want a Community-supported or Enterprise-supported Linux distribution, or an isolated platform that keeps the Linux system management hidden from us. We need to think about what type of services we want to virtualize and the impact of these choices into CPU selection, disk usage, and memory needs.

Installing Xen, can be done in different ways. In this chapter, you learned how to install Xen and both Linux- or Windows-based virtual machines with either a regular Linux distribution or XenEnterprise on your server, such as Fedora Core, or with the XenSource Enterprise product.

Fedora Core and its successors, including Red Hat Enterprise Linux and CentOS, provide us with an easy-to-install, easy-to-manage platform that eases both the installation and management of Linux and Windows virtual machines. Creating either a Linux or Windows-based virtual machine is just a few clicks away.

XenServer gives you a platform where the Linux management part is hidden from you and you get a well-designed GUI where you can manage different physical and virtual machines. XenServer still is a young product and will gain more features with each release. It is targeted at the Windows IT professional, and though capable, it may not be the product of choice for the seasoned Linux administrator preferring to build and install Xen themselves from a source in their own Linux environment.

Solutions FastTrack

Determining Which Xen to Choose

- ☑ Choosing your Xen distribution is a matter of deciding between freedom and support, and between virtualizing just Windows, or more.

- ☑ If you want freedom, go for a community Linux distribution. If you want support, the Enterprise Linux distributions will help you.

- ☑ XenServer is the obvious product for you if you only plan on virtualizing Windows machines.

System Requirements

☑ Most recent machines you buy already have a VT-capable CPU available. If you plan on virtualizing Windows or other non–modifiable, unsupported operating systems, you will need these capabilities in your CPU.

☑ When buying new hardware, consider the expected disk and memory usage of the virtual machines you plan to deploy. The sum of all of these plus some extra is what your machine should look like.

Thinking Before You Start

☑ A regular Linux distribution will not know upfront that you plan on installing virtualization tools. It will not create a disk layout that is suitable to host different virtual machines. Thus, you should modify the default partition layout at install time.

☑ LVM is the preferred method of managing virtual machine disk volumes. It gives you both freedom and scalability while hiding complexity.

Installing Xen on a Free Linux Distribution

☑ Installing Fedora Core 6 is easy. Use only a minimal install for your domain0 since you will not be running other applications in that domain besides the Xen management tools.

☑ VirtManager provides you with an easy GUI that allows you to install both Windows and Linux virtual machines with a couple of mouse clicks.

Installing the XenServer Product Family

☑ XenSource provides a "Ten minutes to Xen" framework that allows you to quickly install a host operating system that is ready to have new virtual machines installed.

☑ Based on the existing templates, you can install different Linux and Windows distributions from the XenSource client and also manage them from there.

Other Xen Installation Methods

☑ Other distributions might not have pre-shipped Xen RPMS, or not have the VirtManager GUI to ease the installation of virtual instances. You can use yum to create installations in chroot environments on different LVM volumes and thus create reproducible Xen installations.

☑ Other distributions have similar tools like *yast* and *debootstrap*. Also, frameworks such as *systemImager* allow you to create images of other physical or virtual machines and ease physical-to-virtual machine migration.

Configuring Xen

☑ The main configuration files for Xen live in /etc/xen/. This is where all the parameters the *xend* daemon requires and all the different configuration files for the actual virtual machines live. They are usually well documented and example files have been shipped with most distributions.

☑ The easiest way of networking Xen is by using the regular Linux bridging tools. Use them to connect the network interfaces of your virtual machines to the appropriate networks on your physical machine.

Frequently Asked Questions

The following Frequently Asked Questions, answered by the authors of this book, are designed to both measure your understanding of the concepts presented in this chapter and to assist you with real-life implementation of these concepts. To have your questions about this chapter answered by the author, browse to **www.syngress.com/solutions** and click on the **"Ask the Author"** form.

Q: Where do I get Xen?

A: Xen is either included in your distribution already, or you can download either the prebuild RPMS by XenSource from http://getxen.org/ or get the XenExpress Free Starter pack from there.

Q: My machine doesn't boot after installing Xen. What should I do?

A: You most probably are running into a driver problem. The Xen kernel you are trying to boot does not recognize your primary hard disk. If you look carefully at the messages on your screen, you should see an error similar to: Kernel panic: VFS: Unable to mount root fs on sda1. A lot of kernel panics are caused because they can't find the hard disk. This happens because the correct module is not built into the kernel or is not available in the initrd. The xen kernel does not have as many built-in modules as a normal distribution kernel, and the needed modules aren't automatically added in the initrd. The solution is easy: include the needed modules in the initrd. But which module is the correct one? That depends on the hardware in your system. You can start finding the correct modules by reading the dmesg when you boot that system with a working kernel. Creating an Initrd with the matching kernel versions can be done as follows: mkinitrd –v –f —with=ide-generic /boot/initrd-2.6.16.33-xen_3.0.4.1.img 2.6.16.33-xen_3.0.4.1.

Q: Which RPM should I install Xen from? One from my distribution or one from XenSource?

A: Part of that answer depends on what your environment is like. If you are working in an Enterprise Linux environment, you of course will want to use the RPMs that have been shipped with your distribution and will be supported by your vendor. If, however, you are running a Free Distribution, you might want to look at the XenSource RPMs since they have created an RPM with the most features and which has also been created for specific platforms.

Q: Does Xen support my hardware?

A: Xen hardware support is being managed by the dom0 kernel, which means that if your hardware is supported in a general Linux distribution, it will also be supported by Xen. If you are unsure, do not hesitate to contact your local XenSource partner who can help you out.

Q: I got the following error when trying to run xm list: ERROR: Could not obtain handle on privileged command interface (2 = No such file or directory); Error: Unable to connect to xend: No such file or directory. Is xend running?

A: This error usually occurs when you are either running in a non-Xen-enabled environment, or when you haven't started the xend daemon yet. Verify if your kernel is already Xen-enabled by running uname –a, or start your xend daemon by running /etc/init.d/xend start.

Q: I'm running into the following error when trying to start a virtual machine: Error: Device 2049 (vbd) could not be connected. Device /dev/VolGroup00/root-FC6 is mounted in the privileged domain, and so cannot be mounted by a guest. Why?

A: This means one of the virtual disks you have configured for use as a file system in the virtual machine is still being used by another domain. Run df and check the output. It will most probably still be mounted in your dom0. You can solve this by running umount against the volume in question.

## Chapter 4

The Administrator Console and Other Native Tools

Solutions in this chapter:

- **Native Xen Command-Line Tools**
- **XenServer Administrator Console**

☑ **Summary**

☑ **Solutions Fast Track**

☑ **Frequently Asked Questions**

Introduction

The sign of an enterprise-ready technology is an efficient tool to manage that technology. Xen is not any different. Many technologies that promised great potential to companies seeking to contain costs and simplify their operations suffered from poor management tools, leading to little, if any, adoption in the enterprise. This has never been more important than with virtualization products, such as Xen. Fortunately, Xen comes with a robust suite of tools, both command-line as well as GUI.

In this chapter, we will review the native management tools that are available. Tool syntax and options will be explored as well as best practices and use cases for each one. In particular, we will thoroughly review the Administrator Console, used to manage XenExpress, XenServer, and XenEnterprise.

Designing & Planning...

Combining XenServer Tools for Enterprise Administration

Whereas the Administrator Console GUI provides a comprehensive set of functions for managing Xen hosts, virtual machines (VMs), and storage, the command-line interfaces (CLIs) complement and expand that functionality.

The xe CLI, which is on all Xen hosts and is installed on the Administrator Console, provides an efficient way to automate functionality by incorporating or "wrapping" the commands within scripting languages. However, the xe CLI does not provide all the functionality of the sm and xm interfaces, present only on the Xen hosts. Additional scripting can be done directly on the Xen hosts to ease administration tasks.

Because there is a choice of tools for different functions, administrators should select a tool based on their operational conditions. For example:

- Creation or modification to a single VM is easiest on the Administrator Console.

- The Administrator Console does not have a scheduler for administrative tasks, so consider using xe-based cron scripts to schedule periodic tasks.

- Live migrations can be done only through the *xm* command on the Xen hosts.

- Certain storage operations can be done only with the sm CLI.

Native Xen Command-Line Tools

All operations that you can perform on XenHosts and XenVMs you can execute through one of the command-line tool interfaces. In particular, three such interfaces are available with Xen distributions:

- The xe tool provides a management interface for both XenHosts and XenVMs. The xe tool is available both on the XenHosts and on the Administrator Console.

- The sm CLI provides a set of additional storage management options not available to the XenHosts Administrator Console. The sm CLI is available only on XenHosts.

- The xm CLI is the traditional Xen tool for management. It is available on the open source Xen as well as the commercial versions (XenExpress, XenServer, and XenEnterprise). The xm interface maintains the original domain nomenclature of dom0 (XenHost) and domU (XenVMs), and all operations are done against domain names or domain IDs. In addition, certain operations, such as XenVM migration, you can do only through the xm interface. The xm interface is available only on XenHosts.

In this section, we will cover only some of the more common xe commands. Chapter 6 contains more in-depth information.

The xe Command-Line Interface

Here is an example of the syntax for the xe CLI:

```
xe command-name [switches] [param=value ... param=value]
```

command-name refers to the subcommand that is to be run against a XenHost. Commands are classified under three groups:

- Storage commands
- Host commands
- VM commands

Switches refer to authentication and connection string parameters:

- **–u** Username on XenHost.

- **–pw** Password.

- **–pwf** File containing the username and password (prevents command history or process listing from showing username and password in clear text).

- **–h** Host (Internet Protocol [IP] address or hostname of XenHost).

- **–p** Port (if not using the default port).

Installing and Cloning XenVMs

To install a new XenVM, you use *vm-install* with the *xe* command. Here is the syntax:

```
xe vm-install –u USERNAME –pw PASSWORD –h HOSTNAME/IP template-name="TEMPLATE NAME"
–name=VM_NAME auto_poweron=TRUE/FALSE vcpus=1 memory_set=256
```

You can add additional parameters, such as *vif* for network or *vdi* for disk. Upon correct syntax, the output of the command should look something like the following:

```
Adding VIF to install target: host-bridge=xenbr0, MAC=00:16:3E:23:59:32.
Initiating install...
New VM uuid: 5f2852a1-fa96-4e3e-8208-0a05299fc8ed
[DONE]
```

To clone an existing XenVM, use *vm-clone* with the *xe* command. The correct syntax is as follows:

```
xe vm-clone - u USERNAME –pw PASSWORD –h HOSTNAME/IP vm-name="EXISTING_XENVM" new-
name="NEW_VM" new-description="DESCRIPTION FOR NEW XENVM"
```

Starting Up, Shutting Down, Rebooting, Suspending, and Resuming XenVMs

To boot a XenVM, use the following syntax:

```
xe vm-start - u USERNAME –pw PASSWORD –h HOSTNAME/IP vm-name=XENVM_NAME_HERE
```

To shut down a XenVM, use this:

```
xe vm-shutdown - u USERNAME –pw PASSWORD –h HOSTNAME/IP vm-name=XENVM_NAME_HERE
```

To reboot a XenVM, use this syntax:

```
xe vm-reboot - u USERNAME –pw PASSWORD –h HOSTNAME/IP vm-name=XENVM_NAME_HERE
```

Here is the syntax for suspending a XenVM:

```
xe vm-suspend - u USERNAME -pw PASSWORD -h HOSTNAME/IP vm-name=XENVM_NAME_HERE
```

And here is the syntax for resuming a XenVM:

```
xe vm-resume - u USERNAME -pw PASSWORD -h HOSTNAME/IP vm-name=XENVM_NAME_HERE
```

To ensure that the correct information is passed as input for each parameter, be sure to verify the syntax with *xe help*, which will show basic help about syntax and usage for all of the *xe* commands.

Shutting Down and Rebooting XenHosts

To shut down a XenHost, use this syntax:

```
xe host-shutdown - u USERNAME -pw PASSWORD -h HOSTNAME/IP
```

To reboot a XenHost, use this syntax:

```
xe host-reboot - u USERNAME -pw PASSWORD -h HOSTNAME/IP
```

Query Options for XenHosts

Here is the syntax to query a host for existing XenVMs:

```
xe host-vm-list - u USERNAME -pw PASSWORD -h HOSTNAME/IP
```

To query a host for physical network interfaces, use this:

```
xe host-pif-list - u USERNAME -pw PASSWORD -h HOSTNAME/IP
```

To query a host for existing templates, use this:

```
xe host-template-list - u USERNAME -pw PASSWORD -h HOSTNAME/IP
```

And to list vbridges, use this:

```
xe host-vbridge-list - u USERNAME -pw PASSWORD -h HOSTNAME/IP
```

XenServer Administrator Console

The Administrator Console is a remote Java-based application that manages the configuration and operations of XenServer hosts and VMs. The Administrator Console provides a subset of the functionality that is available through the command-line tools. However, this subset encompasses most day-to-day operations, such as creation of XenVMs, power on/off, XenHost reboots, and so on. In addition, the

Administrator Console provides basic performance monitoring graphs of CPU, memory, network, and disk utilization for both XenHosts and XenVMs.

System Requirements for the Administrator Console

Table 4.1 outlines the requirements for the Administrator Console.

Table 4.1 Administrator Console System Requirements

Component	Minimum	Recommended
Operating system	N/A	Red Hat Enterprise Linux 4.x Novell (SUSE) Linux Enterprise Server 9.x Windows XP
		Windows 2000
		Windows Server 2003
CPU speed	750MHz	1GHz or faster
RAM	384MB	1GB or better
Disk space	100MB	N/A
Networking	1 network interface card (NIC)	N/A

Installing the Administrator Console

You can deploy the Administrator Console on Red Hat and SUSE, as well as a variety of Windows operating systems. Installation on either Windows or Linux is fairly simple.

Installing the Administrator Console on Windows (XP/2000/2003)

You can find the installation binaries for the Administrator Console on the XenEnterprise installation CD-ROM. The following steps will walk you through the installation process:

1. Insert the XenEnterprise Installation CD into the CD-ROM of the system that will host the Administrator Console.

2. Run the xenserver-client.exe install program from the client_install directory.

3. Click the **Yes button** to continue the installation (see Figure 4.1).

Figure 4.1 XenServer Administrator Console 3.2.0 Setup

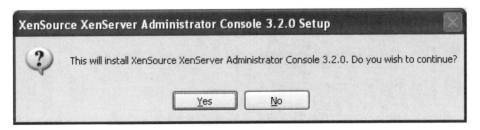

4. Click the **Next button** to continue the installation (see Figure 4.2).

Figure 4.2 XenServer Administrator Console 3.2.0 Recommendations

5. Click **Next** (see Figure 4.3).

6. If the destination folder is acceptable, leave the default location; otherwise, enter or browse to your preferred install directory and click **Next** to continue (see Figure 4.4).

Figure 4.3 License Agreement Screen

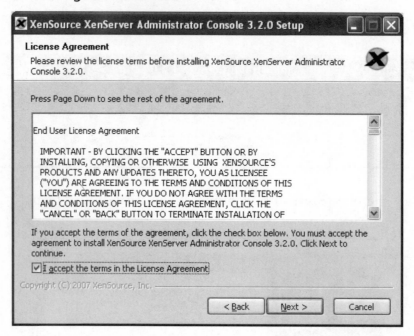

Figure 4.4 Installation Location

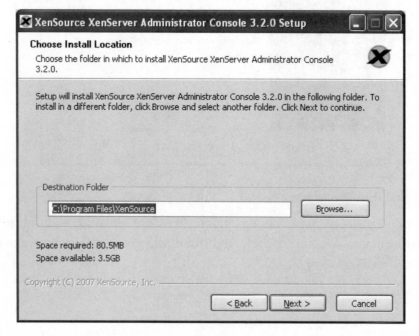

7. To accept the default Start menu folder click the **Install button** (see Figure 4.5). The Show Details button will display the actions of the installer (see Figure 4.6).

Figure 4.5 Start Menu Folder Selection

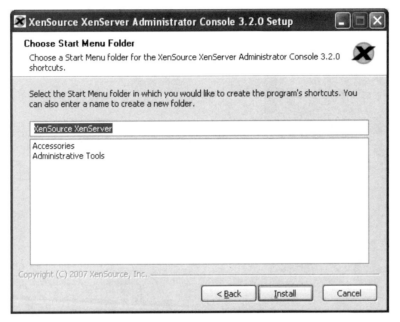

Figure 4.6 Installation Progress

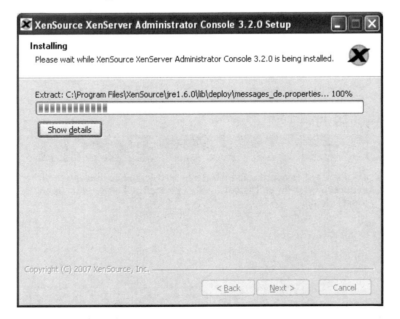

8. To start the Administrator Console, click the **Run XenServer Administrator Console check box** and then click the **Finish button** (see Figure 4.7).

Figure 4.7 Administrator 3.2 Installation Completed

9. The Master Login screen prompts you for your password. This password is used to encrypt host login information locally, such as the XenServer host IP address. Every time you log on to the Administrator Console, you are prompted for the master password. Once you have entered the password, click the **Login button** (see Figure 4.8).

Figure 4.8 Master Login Screen

NOTE

The master password is local to the computer hosting the Administrator Console, and is used only to log into the Administrator Console and encrypt configuration information. The XenServer host password is the password that was given during the installation of the XenServer host, and is used to log the Administrator Console onto the XenServer host.

Installing the Administrator Console on Linux

You can find the installation binaries for Linux on the XenServer Linux Pack CD. To install the Linux Pack, follow these steps:

1. Insert the XenServer Linux Pack CD into the CD-ROM of the workstation to be used to host the Administrator Console

2. *cd* to the client_install directory. The following packages are in the directory:

    - xe-cli–3.2.0–1960.i386.rpm

    - xe-cli–debuginfo–3.2.0–1960.i386.rpm

    - xenserver-client–3.2.0–1960.noarch.rpm

    - xenserver-client-jars–3.2.0–1960.noarch.rpm

    - xenserver-client-jre–3.2.0–1960.i386.rpm

3. Install all the packages in the directory, using this command:

```
rpm -ihv *.rpm
```

NOTE

The xe-cli-3.2.0-1960.i386.rpm and xe-cli-debuginfo-3.2.0-1960.i386.rpm packages are not part of the Administrator Console GUI. They provide a CLI to access and control the XenServer host.

Using the Administrator Console

To log on to the Administrator Console on Windows, select **Start Menu | XenSource XenServer | Administrator Console**. On Linux, use the following command:

```
xenserver-client
```

> **NOTE**
>
> Because the Administrator Console is a Java-based GUI application, make sure the Linux distribution has a functional window manager installed.

After launching the application, you will be prompted for the XenServer host IP/hostname and the root password (see Figure 4.9).

Figure 4.9 XenServer Host Login Screen

Once you have been authenticated, the Administrator Console screen will appear (see Figure 4.10).

Figure 4.10 The Administrator Console Screen

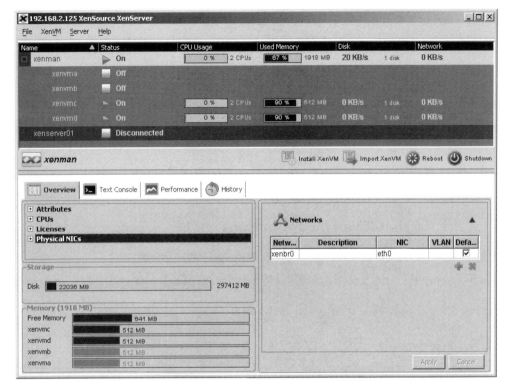

The Administrator Console is functionally divided into three parts:

- The menu bar
- A top pane, which contains a listing of XenHosts and XenVMs and several contextual action buttons
- A bottom pane consisting of multiple tabs for Overview, Consoles, Performance Graphs, and History

You typically can perform actions from the menu bar, from the contextual buttons in the top pane, or within the tabs of the bottom pane.

Working with Hosts

In this section, we'll discuss the steps for connecting to a host and powering off or rebooting a XenHost.

Connecting to a XenHost

To connect to a host click the XenHost and do one of the following:

- Click the **Connect button** on the top pane.
- Select **Connect** from the **Server menu**.
- Right-click the **XenHost** and select **Connect**.

Powering Off/Rebooting a XenHost

You can power off/reboot hosts from the Administrator Console by selecting the host and doing one of the following:

- Click the **shutdown/reboot buttons** on the top pane.
- Select **Shutdown/Reboot** from the **Server menu**.
- Right-click the host and select **Shutdown/Reboot**.

Figure 4.11 shows the additional host operations from the menu bar.

Figure 4.11 Server Menu

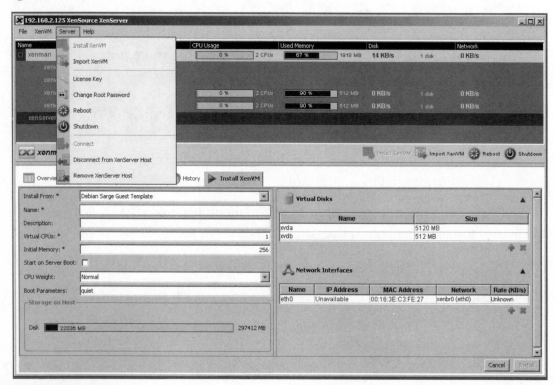

Deploying and Configuring XenVMs

You can use various operations to deploy XenVMs. We explore installing, cloning, exporting, and physical-to-virtual conversions in depth in Chapter 6.

Creating Xen Virtual Machines

Creating VMs in the Administrator Console is a straightforward process:

1. Select the Xen host on which the XenVM will be created.

2. Select **Install XenVM** by clicking the **Install XenVM button**, or by selecting it from the **Server menu**. The lower pane will display the Install XenVM tab (see Figure 4.12).

Figure 4.12 Installing XenVM

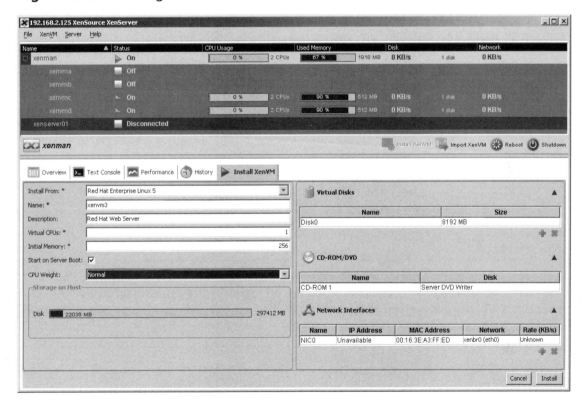

To install XenVM you need to provide information in the following sections of the screen, as shown in Figure 4.12:

- **Install From:** Refers to the template to be used for this XenVM. Currently, Xen supports only the Debian Sarge template.

- **Name:** The name of the XenVM (not the OS hostname of the XenVM).

- **Virtual CPUs:** The number of VCPUs that will be presented to the XenVM. This will depend on the type of license being used (only the Enterprise license allows multiple VCPUs).

- **Initial Memory:** The amount of memory allocated to the XenVM.

- **Start on Server Boot:** Whether to start the XenVM automatically after the XenHost is booted.

- **Virtual Disks:** The disk name and size fields are directly editable. You can specify additional virtual disks by clicking on the plus sign.

- **CD-ROM/DVD:** Automatically detects the XenHosts CD/DVD drive. The Disk field is a drop-down menu with additional entries for P2V tools, and Windows XenSource tools.

- **Network Interfaces:** Lists the xenbr0 network. You can select additional networks by clicking the plus sign.

Cloning XenVMs

Another way to create a XenVM is through cloning. Cloning copies the virtual disks and the configuration files of the original XenVM.

! **W**ARNING

You need to be careful when cloning XenVMs: Windows clones need to have their SSIDs reset and both Windows and Linux clones need to have their network identity changed to avoid IP or hostname conflicts. Refer to Chapter 6 for additional information.

To create a XenVM clone, follow these steps:

1. Select the XenVM to be cloned.

2. Shut down the XenVM to be cloned.

3. With the powered-off XenVM selected, click on the **Clone button**. The lower pane will ask whether to continue with the cloning process. Click the **OK button**.

The cloning process will begin. Notice in Figure 4.13 that the state of the original XenVM (xenvma) is set to cloning, and no information is displayed for the CPU or memory usage (the XenVM is shut down and is not consuming any resources). The new XenVM has the name Clone of xenvma and shows a status of Installing.

Figure 4.13 Cloning Screen

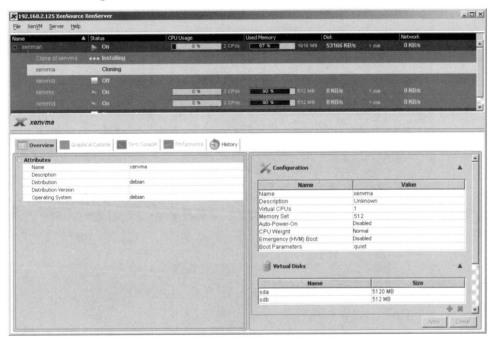

Once you've created the clone, you can modify the fields in the Configuration section of the Overview tab. In addition, you can add virtual disks, but you cannot remove the existing ones.

Additional XenVM Operations

Here is a list of additional XenVM operations:

- Power on/off
- Suspend/resume
- Reboot

- Export
- Force shutdown/reboot
- Uninstall

Performance Monitoring

Although not a comprehensive monitoring platform, the Administrator Console provides basic performance information for both XenHosts and XenVMs (see Figure 4.14). The information displayed is for the most recent 12 minutes and includes data on CPU (percentage), memory (MB), network (bandwidth), and disk utilization (KB/sec).

Figure 4.14 Performance Tab

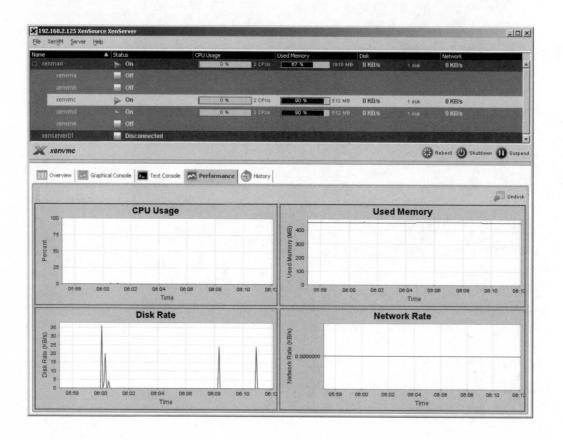

Summary

Different tools are included with XenExpress, XenServer, and XenEnterprise for managing all components in a Xen implementation. The GUI provides a quick and smart interface for routine operations such as XenVM creation, cloning, and modification, and for XenHost and XenVM power/shutdown and performance monitoring.

The command-line tools provide additional functionality and the ability to automate functionality by creating scripts and using native OS utilities (on the administration workstation and on the XenHosts) to schedule maintenance operations.

The tools are simple to install and use, but be aware of the requirements of the XenVM operating system during creation and cloning activities to avoid potential pitfalls of identity duplication.

Solutions Fast Track

Native Xen Command-Line Tools

☑ The Administrator Console, a remote Java-based GUI interface, can manage all XenHosts in an IT environment.

☑ xe is a comprehensive command-line tool for managing XenHosts and XenVMs.

☑ sm is a command-line tool available on XenHosts for storage management.

☑ xm is a XenHost CLI, for the local management of XenHosts, XenVMs, and storage.

XenServer Administrator Console

☑ The Administrator Console provides a subset of the functionality that is available through the command-line tools. However, this subset encompasses most day-to-day operations.

☑ Through operating system scripting languages and utilities, you can use the different CLIs to extend the functionality of Xen implementations.

☑ You can deploy the Administrator Console on Red Hat and SUSE, as well as a variety of Windows operating systems. Installation on either Windows or Linux is fairly simple.

Frequently Asked Questions

The following Frequently Asked Questions, answered by the authors of this book, are designed to both measure your understanding of the concepts presented in this chapter and to assist you with real-life implementation of these concepts. To have your questions about this chapter answered by the author, browse to **www.syngress.com/solutions** and click on the **"Ask the Author"** form.

Q: When would the Administrator Console be a better choice for administration?

A: The Administrator Console definitely has a role as a first-step tool for XenVM maintenance, such as creation and cloning, as well as power on/off activities. Its performance screen gives a snapshot that can help you to determine hot spots quickly.

Q: Does every tool share the same functionality?

A: No, each tool has a specialized function. The Administrator Console (as of version 3.2 of XenSource's XenServer family), for example, does not have all the functionality of any of the command-line tools. And although the xe and xm interfaces share many capabilities, you can use the xe interface remotely, whereas you can use the xm interface only on the local XenHost.

Q: What do I need to create scripts with the command-line tools?

A: Each operating system supported on the Administrator Console, and with the xe tool, has available scripting languages/shells. Even with only a little experience in scripting, system administrators can extend functionality by creating scripts that automate functionality.

Q: Are other tools available for managing Xen implementations?

A: Yes, a sampling of third-party tools is provided in Chapter 5.

Managing Xen with Third-Party Management Tools

Solutions in this chapter:

- **Qlusters openQRM**
- **Enomalism**
- **Project ConVirt and XenMan**

☑ **Summary**

☑ **Solutions Fast Track**

☑ **Frequently Asked Questions**

Introduction

As the popularity of Xen increases, the need to manage all of those Xen installations also goes up. Fortunately, many software companies have come to the rescue and have developed their own management solutions for the Xen Virtual Machine Monitor and its guests. Many of these third-party management tools are available as free, open source alternatives to the existing product line, and others are part of a value-added suite with commercial support and maintenance.

If you have decided to implement a Xen-based virtual infrastructure, or if you already have one but are looking for additional management capabilities in your tool set, this chapter will introduce a few of those that are currently available. Although not an all-inclusive list of available management applications, these products represent some of the more popular choices that Xen administrators have chosen to help keep their implementations under control.

Qlusters openQRM

Qlusters, Inc. is a provider of open source data center provisioning and management software for physical and virtual environments. Its most popular product is openQRM, an open source systems management platform that helps to automate enterprise data centers and keep them running. openQRM is a mature, established product that integrates with existing components in complex data centers to create scalable and highly available infrastructures.

Founded in 2001, Qlusters has grown to be a contender as a data center technology and services provider. openQRM has had a lot to do with the company's success and is currently used by multiple data centers worldwide to improve uptime and reduce operations costs. Qlusters is the founding member of the Open Management Consortium, which creates open source alternatives to proprietary management systems. The company is headquartered in Palo Alto, California, with offices in New York City and Tel Aviv, Israel.

NOTE

For more information about Qlusters and the work going on at the Open Management Consortium, visit www.qlusters.com and www.open-management.org, respectively.

Xen Management with openQRM

Qlusters has recently made available an extension to openQRM that brings advanced virtualization and Xen management capabilities designed to permit simplified deployment, creation, and management of Xen hosts and virtual machines (VMs). This offering bolsters openQRM's capability to provision, manage, and monitor both virtual and bare-metal environments while improving system administrator and hardware efficiencies.

Overview

Once installed, openQRM helps IT professionals rapidly adapt and repurpose their systems to best meet their needs, which includes redeploying or migrating their OS/application environments among various physical and virtual configurations as needed. In addition, the latest version of openQRM helps administrators increase or decrease the memory consumption of a Xen partition on-the-fly while making it possible to add, remove, and assign VMs to specific physical units on any host without having to restart the system.

openQRM is not a tool itself, but is actually a collection of data center management tools that covers many of the areas of systems management. openQRM provides provisioning of the entire software stack, both operating system and installed applications, on physical servers and VMs running on VM monitors such as Xen. openQRM also has a policy engine that allows you to configure resources to be automatically provisioned based on external business needs as well as the requirements of internal organizations.

Out of the box, openQRM includes, but is not limited to, the following functionality:

- Provisioning of physical machines and VMs, or guests
- Monitoring of all major subsystems, including CPU, memory, disk, and network
- Providing high availability through rules and actionable events

You will find that openQRM's provisioning capabilities will be the biggest asset this tool has to offer. openQRM allows for the separation of applications and resources. The application and the operating system are captured in an image and stored on central network storage. You can then deploy the image to a suitable resource, such as a Xen guest. Determining what images to use on which machines is defined by an entity called a virtual environment (VE). The VE definition holds everything necessary to deploy a given image on any range of hardware, including hardware requirements, which images to use, high-availability requirements, and provisioning policies.

When provisioning, the openQRM server selects the appropriate resources from a pool of idle, or unused, resources and assigns them to the VE. The selection is done based on the VE's configuration. The image is then deployed. This deployment triggers the resource to commence running the service that the VE represents. When the VE stops because the service it's running is no longer needed, the resource is de-assigned from the VE/image and is considered idle, waiting to be reallocated elsewhere to host another business-valued service.

openQRM supports several types of deployments, including network-based and local deployments. Network-based deployments include the following:

- PXE with NFS storage

- PXE with software-based Internet Protocol (IP) SAN storage (iSCSI)

- Hardware iSCSI host bus adapters (HBAs)

Local deployments include the following:

- Physical machines or VMs

- Special support for virtual Xen machines

General Concepts for the Xen/openQRM Mix

Conceptually, the formula for an openQRM environment consists of lots of bare-metal physical systems with lots of available resources (CPU, memory, I/O) and boot-from-network support, and the following four additional components:

- A storage server, which can export volumes to your clients such as iSCSI or NFS volumes

- A file system image, captured by openQRM or one that you created from scratch

- A boot image, which the nodes use to network-boot

- A VE, which we discussed earlier in this chapter

openQRM allows you to take any given boot image suitable for your specific hardware (or, as we will discuss shortly, your domU) and combine it with a file system image. Now, the fact that you can mix and combine boot images and file systems makes it extremely interesting. Although this is a novel concept, there are certain idiosyncrasies that you may run into. For example, when adding newer or different hardware types to the VE's pool of resources, you may have to make some minor modifications to your bootstrap environment to account for the differences between the old and new equipment. Though not difficult, it does add another layer of complexity (somewhat unnecessary, at that) to the provisioning process that openQRM facilitates.

This is where provisioning to VMs rather than physical hosts demonstrates the value that virtualization provides. Because Xen presents an identical set of hardware to each of the hosted guests, regardless of the underlying hardware, you can introduce next-generation hardware into your VEs without having to modify your boot images or file system images. This creates a huge potential for fast provisioning of VMs without having to clone or kick-start a new operating system instance.

With openQRM, you can build a booting environment for Xen guests and physical nodes that works independently of the image that will actually be booted. Unless you are using the Local NFS plug-in, deploying does not mean that you are installing a new operating system on a server, but rather that you are simply booting a guest or physical node and putting it in production. Various kinds of deployments are made possible with openQRM:

- **Single deployment** One image is run on a single guest.

- **Shared deployment** The same file system is run on multiple machines. In this deployment scenario, you can define pools of resources for each file system with the intent of load-balancing between those instances.

- **Partitioned deployment** Instead of using dedicated hardware for a booted node, you can partition the physical host into multiple VMs, even using the same file system images.

Once you boot your nodes from the network, they arrive in an idle state. When you tell openQRM you need a new virtual platform, one of the idle nodes then gets promoted to a production node based on existing resources and the matching requirements from the metadata in a VE.

Plug-ins and Licensing

openQRM itself is a freely distributed open source application licensed under the Mozilla Public License (MPL). This license includes the following plug-ins:

- **DHCP** This plug-in is a Dynamic Host Configuration Protocol (DHCP) server used to manage the nodes and give them the capability to network-boot and receive their IP addresses. DHCP is optional because you can use your own DHCP server; however, you need to take certain steps to configure your existing DHCP server.

- **iSCSI** This plug-in installs iSCSI-enabled kernels for use with openQRM, allowing you to store your file system images on an external storage array that supports the iSCSI storage protocol.

- **LDAP** This plug-in allows user authentication through a centralized Lightweight Directory Access Protocol (LDAP) server instead of using internal user credentials stored on each server.

- **TFTP** If you do not have an existing Trivial File Transfer Protocol (TFTP) server, this plug-in provides one that allows managed openQRM nodes to boot from the network.

- **Windows** This plug-in gives openQRM the capability to manage Microsoft Windows systems, including the capability to monitor the nodes and perform start/stop operations.

In addition to these, the open source community has made several other plug-ins available, including the following:

- **SSHLogin** This plug-in allows administrators to establish an SSH connection to managed openQRM nodes directly from the Web-based GUI.

- **VNCLogin** Similar to SSHLogin, this plug-in allows administrators to connect to nodes using VNC.

- **WedminDHCP** This plug-in provides a graphical interface to manage and configure openQRM's DHCP server plug-in or any external DHCP server that openQRM is configured to use.

- **Nagios** This plug-in allows tight integration with Nagios, including management of the services Nagios will use to monitor each VE. It also allows administrators to view both openQRM and Nagios management GUIs from the same console.

- **Xen** This plug-in gives openQRM the capability to be Xen-aware and allow openQRM's partitioning process to integrate smoothly with the Xen VM monitor.

Although there is a Xen community plug-in, it is important to note that Qlusters announced in March 2007 that it is supporting Xen officially through its commercially licensed suite of plug-ins. The openQRM extension for Xen management adds substantial functionality needed to support Xen in small, medium, and large deployments. In addition to the core functionality discussed earlier, some of the added functionality in the latest extension release (3.1.4) includes:

- Live migrations of guest domains from one Xen host to another

- An intuitive and dynamic network interface and virtual interface (VIF) for guests and hosts, including adding or removing additional network cards and configuring through which physical network card on the Xen host traffic should be routed

- Extending a handed-over Logical Volume Manager (LVM) device from the Xen host to the partition without restart, useful for on-the-fly increases to Xen guests on virtual hard disks

In addition to Qluster's Xen plug-in, the following plug-ins are also available to enhance your Xen-based virtual infrastructure to make it more robust, flexible, and available:

- **QRM-HA** This plug-in adds a high-availability option to the openQRM server. In essence, you can cluster multiple openQRM servers in an active-passive configuration, allowing passive openQRM to take over should the active openQRM fail or become unavailable. The running nodes and environments will be unaffected by such a failover.

- **Power Management** Using technologies available through the IPMI standard (mostly used in Dell and IBM x86 hardware) and HP's Integrated Lights-on (iLO) management which ships with each ProLiant server, openQRM can power-off physical nodes when they are not needed, reducing the overall power consumption in your data center. When the demand necessitates the powered–off nodes, openQRM will power them back on automatically.

- **Provisioning Portal** The Provisioning Portal is a set of plug-ins which provides an integrated Web portal for the "end users" of the data center to commit their requests for systems and services. The portal makes provisions for new requests, approvals (or denials), and automated provisioning based on the parameters outlined in the original request.

Although you can install all of the components (the openQRM server, MySQL database, and all the plug-ins) on the same management server, it is recommended that you separate some of the roles to their own dedicated server, as illustrated in Figure 5.1. Note that the figure also illustrates the QRM-HA plug-in for high avail-ability.

Figure 5.1 An Advanced openQRM Deployment Scenario

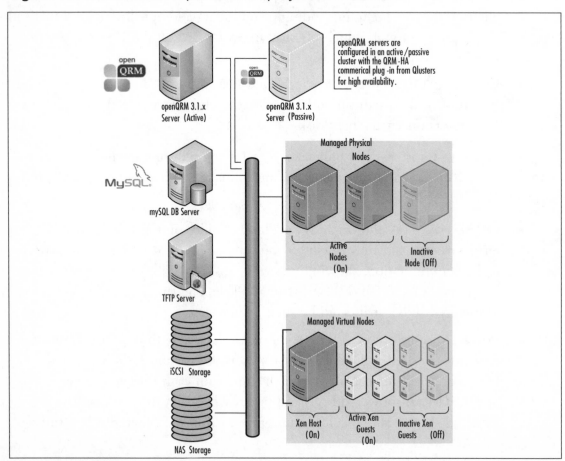

As more and more organizations utilize virtualization technologies as the foundation of their network infrastructure, Qlusters is striving to become your choice for Xen management by continuing to develop and extend openQRM's capabilities to meet the growing needs of the data center.

Installing openQRM

This section will review the steps you can take to install and configure openQRM and the Xen extension. We will base our installation of both the openQRM server and the extensions we will discuss on the latest releases available at the time of this writing. There are three ways you can get openQRM 3.1:

- Use the openQRM-Pro trial package. This package includes a complete set of components and a super-simple installation script that makes sure you have everything preconfigured and ready to work. If you want to quickly evaluate openQRM-Pro, this is the route for you.

- Download the RPMs from SourceForge. These packages allow you to install and use the base openQRM and configure it yourself. If you are a more advanced user and would like to configure openQRM for your needs, this is the route for you.

- Download the sources and build it yourself. If you want to use openQRM on your favorite distribution of Linux and you are an advanced user, this may be the route for you.

Configuring & Implementing...

Evaluating openQRM

There are two ways to evaluate openQRM for your environment. First, the Avastu team working in cooperation with the openQRM team has released a virtual appliance to get you up and running quickly. This appliance is based on CentOS and the 3.1.2 release of openQRM Server. It is fully functional and will not time-expire.

Qlusters also offers a trial package of its openQRM Provision (openQRM-Pro) version. openQRM-Pro is the open source openQRM management application combined with the commercial Provisioning Portal plug-in. By downloading this package, you can easily set up and test openQRM's

Continued

functionality in minimal time. The package contains a simple and preconfigured install script that will set up all components for you.

You can find the virtual appliance at:

www.openqrm.org/openqrm-virtual-appliance.html

You can find more information about the openQRM-Pro trial package at:

www.openqrm.org/provisioning-use-case/openqrm-provision-use-case-
details.html

System Requirements

Before beginning with our installation walkthrough, you need to ensure that you
have met all of the prerequisites and requirements for a successful installation.
openQRM has many dependencies that you can install either separately or via spe-
cially configured packages included with openQRM. We will install all of the
requirements on the same server for simplicity's sake. In a production environment,
you should spread the roles around to maximize the robustness and reliability of your
openQRM deployment.

To install all components on the same machine, you should meet the system
requirements outlined in Table 5.1.

Table 5.1 openQRM System Requirements

Requirement Category	Details
Hardware	x86 or x64 system with: At least a 1GHz processor 512MB of RAM 500MB of hard disk space available
Storage	Access to NFS or NAS-based shared storage for network boot file system images. If you plan to install the iSCSI plug-in, you will need access to a properly configured IP SAN. All managed nodes must have access to the shared storage.
Software (OS)	openQRM has been officially tested on the following operating systems: Red Hat Enterprise Linux 3 (RHEL 3) Red Hat Enterprise Linux 4 (RHEL 4) SUSE Linux Enterprise Server 10 (SLES 10) *Note: Other distributions may work, but are not officially supported.*

Continued

Table 5.1 continued openQRM System Requirements

Requirement Category	Details
Software (openQRM)	Download the following RPM packages: openqrm-core-base openqrm-plugin-tftpd openqrm-plugin-dhcpd openqrm-extras-local_nfs openqrm-extras-mysql openqrm-plugin-xen You can download the packages or source binaries at: http://sourceforge.net/project/showfiles.php?group_id=153504 *Note: Although the Xen plug-in may not be part of a typical install, it is needed for our purposes in terms of managing Xen with openQRM.*
Networking	One or two separate Ethernet adapters. For testing purposes, you will need a minimum of one 100BaseT (Fast-Ethernet) adapter. However, for production, it is recommended that you have two gigabit adapters in the openQRM server: one for the openQRM interface (to handle management traffic to the nodes) and the other for the public local area network (LAN) interface to the rest of the world.
Managed nodes	All managed nodes must have PXE-enabled network adapters that support PXE 2.1. The adapter's BIOS must be enabled, and the managed node's BIOS must be configured appropriately to enable PXE-boot in the system's boot order before the hard drive. Although the managed node can work with a single network adapter, it is recommended that it have two: one for network boot and one for LAN access.

NOTE

Although version 3.1.4 is the most recent at the time of this writing (released March 30, 2007), version 3.1.3 was the last release to be posted with prepackaged Red Hat RPMs. Debian packages and openQRM source are available, though.

Installing openQRM 3.1.x Server

With all of your preparation ready, you are now ready to install openQRM. Begin by getting the RPMs listed in Table 5.1 installed. If you choose to install and use NFS as a local image repository on your openQRM server, you may want to also install the NFS utilities. You can accomplish this by running:

```
yum install nfs-utils
```

MySQL is also a requirement for openQRM. You may decide to install MySQL separately or let the openQRM installer assist you in downloading the package and installing it. Either way, MySQL installation and configuration are outside the scope of this book. If you want more information on MySQL installation, or the binaries to download, visit www.mysql.org.

Configuring & Implementing...

New and Existing MySQL Installations

You do not need to have MySQL installed for openQRM. Both the MySQL Server and the MySQL Client are installed as part of the openqrm-core-base installation package. However, if you plan to use an existing MySQL Server installation from the package distributed with Red Hat or CentOS (MySQL 4.1 or higher), be sure to complete the following steps after running it.

You may receive the following error when attempting to start openQRM after installation and configuration (see the next section) when using a default MySQL install (non-openQRM):

```
668 FATAL [ContainerServices] (main:Initial TX) openQRM server does not
support REPEATABLE-READ transaction isolation level. Please check your
database configuration.
```

If you receive this error message, modify your TRANSACTION ISOLATION LEVEL to READ COMMITTED by running the following command:

```
mysql> SET GLOBAL TRANSACTION ISOLATION LEVEL READ COMMITTED;
```

If this resolves your problem, commit the change permanently by editing /etc/my.cnf and adding the following under the *[mysqld]* directive:

```
[mysqld]
transaction-isolation = READ-COMMITTED
```

Continued

> Be sure to save the file and restart both MySQL and openQRM (in that order) by running:
>
> ```
> service qrm-server start
> service mysqld start
> ```

Once you have all of the packages we identified for our walkthrough installed, your next step is to install and configure openQRM with the installation procedure. The core RPM has placed all the files that you need in /opt/qrm. Proceed with the following steps:

1. Launch the installation and configuration script by running */opt/qrm/qrm-installer -i -c.* This will bring you to the openQRM Installer, as shown in Figure 5.2.

Figure 5.2 The openQRM Installer

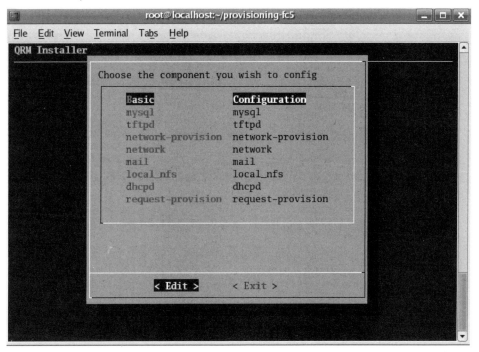

2. Configure each item, following the on-screen instructions and editing the default values, where applicable, to match your test or production environment. The most critical item is "Basic Configuration," as this has the parame-

ters for network communication, directory paths, and database connection items. Note that some plug-ins cannot be configured at this point; they are configured using the openQRM Web console once they are installed and running. When all items have been configured, select **Exit**.

3. The installer then goes through a series of "sanity checks," checking for MySQL, the qrm-core binaries, and the binaries for all of the plug-ins that you selected as part of the installation process and configured in step 2.

4. MySQL will prompt you to restart. Select **y**.

5. You are then brought to a license prompt. If you are installing the MPL-licensed open source version (no commercial components), just press **Enter**. If you have a license for any commercial components, follow the on-screen prompts.

6. You will then be prompted to initialize the system entities. Select **y**. This will configure the PXE server and create the default boot image, based on the kernel and using a default initrd. Note that if you need to customize the initrd, you can find it at /opt/qrm/etc/templates/initrd-qrm.tgz.

7. The qrm-init script will then run, finishing the installation of the qrm-core plug-in.

8. Follow the instructions for the remaining plug-ins.

When the installation has successfully completed, you should see the following:

```
################################################################
          Installation finished
  Plugins with status SUCCESS : mysql qrm-core tftpd dhdcp iscsi local_nfs
  Plugins with status ERROR :


################################################################
```

You should confirm at this point that no plug-ins failed (are listed with status ERROR). For more information about the *qrm-installer* optional switches and for another sample walkthrough, visit www.openqrm.org/installation-guide/openqrm-3.0-installation-guide—-installer-options.html.

At this point, you should have a functioning openQRM system, if everything installed correctly. Navigate to the openQRM Web console by browsing to http://youropenqrm:8080. The default username and password are both *qrm*. You should see the openQRM Dashboard, as shown in Figure 5.3.

Figure 5.3 The openQRM Dashboard

Installing the openQRM Xen Plug-in

With openQRM Server and the core plug-in installed (at a minimum), we will now focus on getting the Xen community plug-in installed and configured for use. This section explains in detail how to gain further efficiencies in Xen system management with openQRM with Xen integration.

To begin, you should download the version of the Xen plug-in that matches your openQRM Server version. For most Red Hat distributions, the latest version as of the time of this writing is 3.1.3. You can download and install it by running the following command:

```
rpm -iHv qrm-xen-plugin.rpm
```

Optionally, you can visit Sourceforge.net to download the source binaries and compile and install them manually. This is often the only option, depending on which Linux distribution you are working with, as Debian, Red Hat, and Solaris packages are usually the ones available prepackaged for download.

Configuring & Implementing…

Building the Xen Plug-in

To build the Xen plug-in, download the Xen plug-in source package from Sourceforge.net and unzip it in your openQRM source directory. Change to the ../src/plugins/xen directory and run:

```
make clean && make && make install
```

This will compile the components for the Xen plug-in, including the Xen hypervisor, the Xen tools, and the special Xen Linux kernel for your domain-0. If compilation fails, be sure that you have the latest compiler and kernel headers installed on your build system, and that they are properly referenced. A common issue with compiling software on some distributions with a kernel of 2.6.20 or higher is that one of the kernel headers, config.h, has been renamed to autoconf.h. If the compiler complains about missing files, be sure they actually exist.

For the "config.h renamed to autoconf.h" issue, the easiest solution is to create a symlink in your kernel source directory. You can do this with the following:

```
cd /usr/src/kernels/$(uname -r)*/include/linux
ln -c autoconf.h config.h
```

The next step is to register the Xen plug-in within the openQRM Server by running the following:

```
/opt/qrm/bin/qrm-plugin -u qrm -p qrm xen register
```

Once it's registered, you can configure the plug-in by performing the following steps:

1. Launch the openQRM configurator by running */opt/qrm/qrm-configurator*.

2. Select the plug-in menu item and be sure that the Xen plug-in is selected (enabled).

3. Return to the main configuration menu and select the menu item to configure the plug-in.

4. Select **Xen** and follow the wizard's instructions.

As you work through the wizard, you will need to provide the IP address for the source system being used to create a Xen host file system image, a logical name for the storage server, the full path to the file system image directory, and its regular and management IP addresses. For the storage type, the default is NFS, although you can specify iSCSI if you have that plug-in installed. You will also need to provide the IP address of the default gateway in your network. Table 5.2 provides a sample configuration for the Xen plug-in.

Table 5.2 Sample Configuration of Xen Plug-in

Configuration Item	Value
Source Xen host's IP address	192.168.1.10
Storage server name	nfs-server
Storage server path	/diskimages/Xen-Hypervisor
Storage server IP address	192.168.1.100
Storage server management IP address	192.168.1.101
Storage server type	NFS
Default gateway	192.168.1.1

5. Run the following commands to install and enable the Xen plug-in on the openQRM Server. The installation procedure creates the boot image, *Xen-Hypervisor*; the storage server, NFS server; and the file system image, *Xen-Hypervisor*.

```
/opt/qrm/bin/qrm-plugin -u qrm -p qrm xen install
/opt/qrm/bin/qrm-plugin -u qrm -p qrm xen run_once
```

6. Restart the openQRM Server by running:

```
/etc/init.d/qrm-server restart
```

TIP

File system image creation can be time-consuming and very I/O-intensive on the live Xen server. If possible, migrate all running VMs with the *xm migrate* command to another Xen host or hosts with sufficient resources. If this is not possible, create the file system image during hours of low utilization to not impact business processes that rely on applications hosted in its guest domains.

7. In the Virtual Environment (VE) view of the openQRM Server, you can create a new VE from the previously listed components. Choose a name and configure the VE to use Xen partitioning. Also, select it to be a **Multi-server**. Figure 5.4 shows a Xen VE in an unstarted, or inactive, state. The VE is called XenDom0.

Figure 5.4 A Xen VE in the openQRM Console

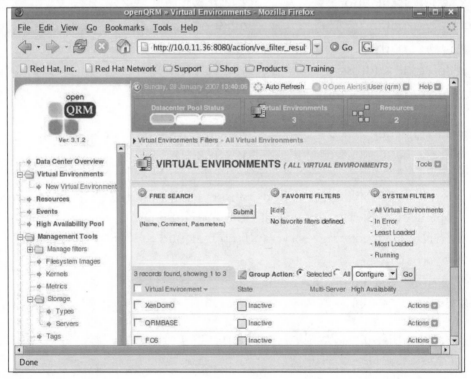

Managing Xen with openQRM

In this section, we will discuss how to manage Xen with openQRM.

How the Xen Plug-in Works

To remote-boot a Xen server, a special assignment/de-assignment procedure is needed. For this purpose, the Xen plug-in registers an **event listener** that listens to both assignment and de-assignment in the openQRM Server while creating and using the special Xen PXE-Linux configuration files generated by the assignment utility attached to the event listener. The Xen event listener also takes care of the de-assignment of the Xen VE, which restores the original PXE-Linux configuration for network boot.

The tricky thing about booting a Xen host on openQRM is that it generally does not have any IP or network boot information in its /proc/cmdline, even if it is configured in its PXE-Linux configuration file. This is because the kernel that initially boots on a Xen host is the Xen hypervisor, not a traditional Linux kernel. The Linux kernel is started, or bootstrapped, as dom0 after the hypervisor loads. To have this special boot mechanism conform with openQRM, the Xen assignment process triggered via the event listener creates the correct /proc/cmdline by appending parameters for the Xen host in the PXE module configuration for the dom0 kernel.

Once a Xen host has been provisioned and booted by openQRM's network boot functionality, it still needs to be managed. You can do this by sending administrative commands to the Xen host via *qrm-execd* from the openQRM server. These commands control start guest, stop guest, create guest, and delete/destroy guest (or in openQRM lingo, *partition*) actions on the Xen host. Each partition has a separate configuration file created by the qrm-xen-manage utility on the Xen host. The configuration files are stores as /var/lib/xen/VirtualMachines/[mac-address]/[mac-address].xen.

The regular Xen control tool, xm, is used to manage each openQRM-provisioned domU. IP addresses for each domU are gathered by DHCP on the Xen host on behalf of the guest's Media Access Control (MAC) address which then assigns them to the guests via the Xen configuration file. The *create* procedure for the Xen guests also configures a /proc/cmdline conformant to openQRM so that they are able to boot the regular *initrd*.

Using openQRM with Xen Integration

Now that we have everything installed, we are ready to start managing our infrastructure with openQRM. To begin, though, we need to make sure that we have resources available to boot into our Xen image. Figure 5.5 illustrates the resources view of the console. You will notice that there are two nodes, called Node 1 and

Node 2. The console will list the resources available in each node, in particular the CPU count and speed, amount of memory, and amount of disk storage in gigabytes.

Configuring & Implementing...

Networking Tips for Xen Host Virtual Environments

It is a best practice to have a minimum of two network adapters in a Xen host managed by openQRM. One adapter is used for network boot and network volume or iSCSI traffic. The other adapters would be used as bridges for guest network traffic as well as dom0 traffic for native Xen management purposes. Although the first adapter (often eth0) will grab an IP from the DHCP server to PXE boot and TFTP sessions, it is recommended that the Xen host image contain a valid network configuration for the other adapters (eth1, eth2, etc.) to avoid having to manually intervene and configure the VE after it has been provisioned.

The simplest approach to this would be to configure each adapter to use DHCP to obtain its IP configuration. If you want to ensure that each VE has a particular IP address, you can take advantage of lease reservations in your DHCP configuration, because you will know network adapter MAC addresses ahead of time.

Figure 5.5 Available Resources Shown in the openQRM Console

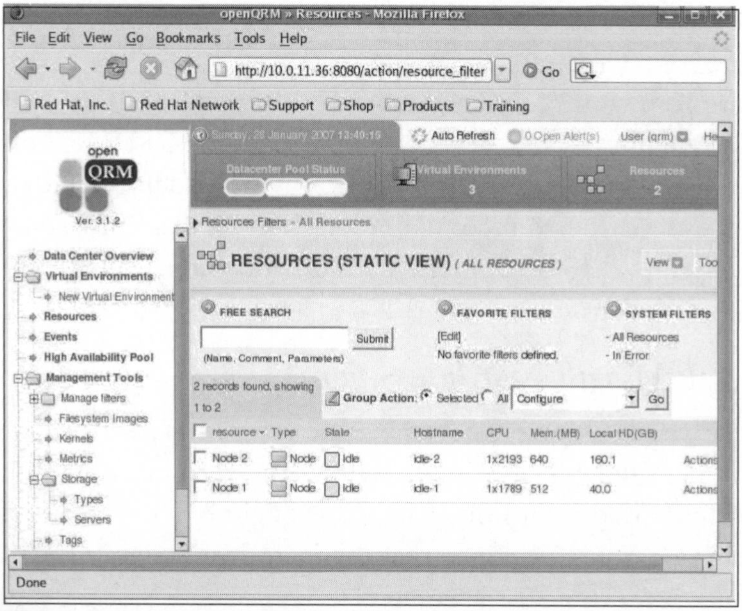

Once you have identified the physical systems on which you want to start the Xen host VE, you can assign those systems as new VEs. When the Xen host VE starts, it will initiate the Xen hypervisor and the special Xen Linux kernel, Xen-Hypervisor in our example. Just as with any Xen host installation, the kernel will boot and become domain-0 (dom0) with all of the standard control tools available to you. You can determine whether everything is working correctly by logging onto the Xen host and running the following Xen command:

```
xm list
```

This should return a list of the current active Xen guest domains, and chances are you will see only dom0 because we have not created any guests yet.

TIP

If you are having problems starting dom0, you may need to rebuild the Xen plug-in using the kernel binaries from your Linux distribution rather than using a downloaded precompiled package. Refer to the sidebar "Building the Xen Plug-in," earlier in this chapter, for additional information.

With your Xen host VEs image-provisioned and booted on a physical resource, we will now review how to use openQRM to manage guest domains, or domUs. In openQRM terminology, guests are referred to as *partitions*, and the act of creating a guest is called *partitioning the resource*. To create a new partition, follow these steps:

1. Click on the resource used for the Xen host VE and find the partition tab added by the Xen plug-in. A configuration page for creating partitions opens when you click on it. Here you can assign things such as the number of virtual CPUs and the amount of RAM, and even set up physical CPU affinity to control which CPUs the guest can be scheduled against (see Figure 5.6).

2. Configure the parameters to start one partition by using one CPU with, for example, a 700MHz CPU speed and 256MB of RAM. Ensure that the amount of RAM configured for the partition does not exceed the available memory on the Xen host, which needs about 120MB of RAM itself.

Figure 5.6 Creating a Partition's Profile

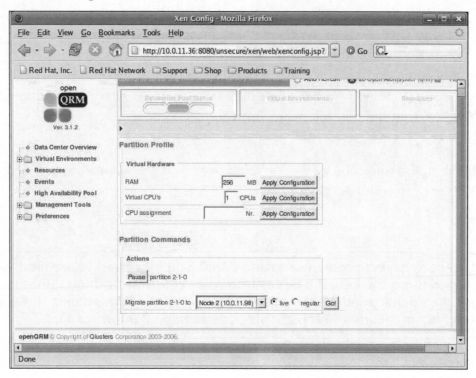

3. Pressing **create** creates and starts the partition on the Xen host VE. It will become available, though idle, in the resource view as a new Xen resource. The available Xen partitions created and started can now be used as a resource for any VE in the openQRM managed network.

4. To start a VE on a Xen partition, go to the partition's configuration page and select **Xen partition**.
   This causes the openQRM server to choose a free Xen partition to start the VE. No further changes are required. Figure 5.7 shows an active partition running an FC6 image and another partition inactive but ready for provisioning.

5. Manage your VE running on Xen partitions in the usual way using the **Actions** menu.

Figure 5.7 Xen Partitions in the openQRM Console

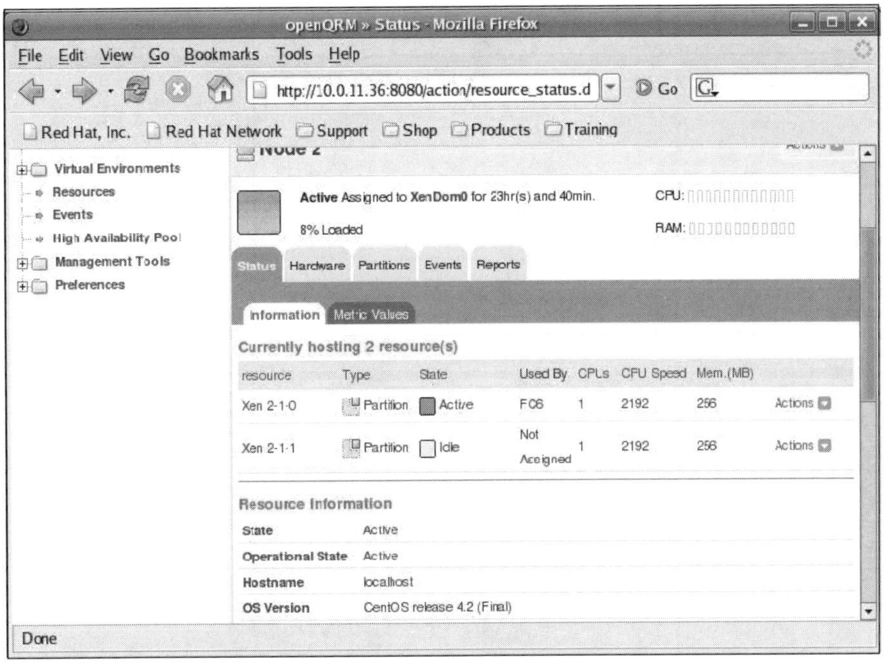

Provisioning with openQRM-Pro

If you are interested in having some business processes wrapped around your openQRM management, you may want to consider the commercial Provisioning Portal plug-in. This component adds a provisioning request and approval mechanism to openQRM. The tool is deployed as a separate servlet, allowing you to grant access to users without having to expose the openQRM Administrator Console.

As mentioned before, a simple way to test openQRM-Pro functionality is to download the trial package available on the openQRM Web site. Once you've installed it, you can navigate to the Provisioning Portal login screen (see Figure 5.8) and manage request activities. Although a thorough review of these activities and what happens in the background is beyond the scope of this book, we have included some screen shots to further introduce you to the possibilities of the Provisioning Portal. The process workflow and automation present the real value-add to the commercial products, providing functionality such as submitting new requests (see Figure 5.9), approving or denying requests (see Figure 5.10), and managing provisioning schedules for approved requests (see Figure 5.11). The documentation that is included with the trial package download provides additional information.

Figure 5.8 Login Page for the Provisioning Portal

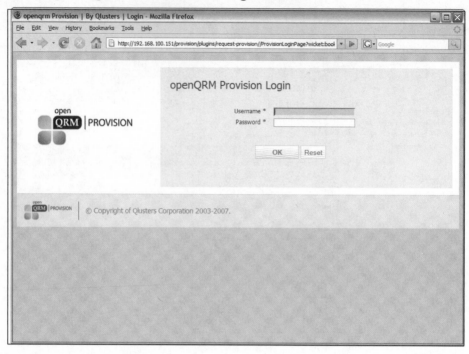

Figure 5.9 Submitting a New Request

Figure 5.10 Pending Requests Waiting for Approval or Denial

Figure 5.11 Managing Approved Requests

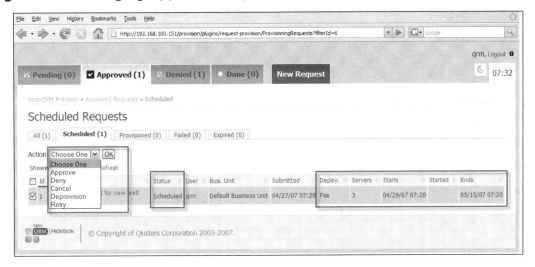

Enomalism

Enomalism was founded in November 2005 by Enomaly Inc., an open source consulting firm located in Toronto. Enomaly has been focusing on solving the challenges of cost and complexity for enterprises that run large technical server infrastructures. As a result, it has combined industry-proven open source components with its experience in designing and operating large-scale, mission-critical software systems, resulting in the Enomalism management application.

Enomalism is an open source, Web-based, virtual server management application built specifically for the needs of a flexible hosted application environment. It was designed to answer the challenges of fragmented hosting environments by providing an interface to provision concurrent isolated servers using the Enomalism Virtualized Grid (EVG) environment and the Elastic Computing Platform (ECP).

Overview of Enomalism

With Enomalism, you can manage multiple physical servers as a single server using a specialized tool set which includes the following:

- Centralized user provisioning system

- Virtualized server creation wizard and templates which facilitate virtual server configuration

- Application deployment mechanism

- Integration into third-party applications via a Web services API

- Centralized LDAP user management

The latest release of Enomalism, version 0.7, builds upon several open source applications, including, but not limited to, the following:

- **Turbogears** A Python Web application framework.

- **Kid** An XHTML frontend templating engine.

- **CherryPy** Middleware that allows you to program Web applications by writing event handlers that return data to templates.

- **MochiKit** A JavaScript library to make programming in JavaScript more Python-like.

- **OpenLDAP** Originally requiring the Fedora Directory Server, Enomaly has replaced the dependency with this more common and widely used directory service.

Enomalism is available in two versions: a free open source edition, and a commercial enterprise edition. The open source edition includes features such as a control center dashboard, resource management, infrastructure-as-a-service components for ISVs, real-time disk management tools, an SSH client, a Web service-based API, and a virtual appliance management system for running VMs as virtual appliance packages. The enterprise edition adds to the open source edition by including multi-server migration for enhanced workload management, enhanced disk management, an enhanced serial console called Twisted, and the ability to create and package VMs as virtual appliances. Enomalism is distributed under the GNU Lesser Public License (LGPL), because it relies on GPL libraries but does not modify any of that code.

Installing Enomalism

This section will review the requirements and general steps that you can follow to install your own Enomalism management system. The installation is actually modularized into several smaller installations for the various core components upon which Enomalism functions.

System Requirements

To begin, Enomalism requires the Fedora Core 6 distribution. Any hardware that meets the requirements for FC6 installation will suffice for installing Enomalism. Enomaly has stated that Ubuntu Edgy 6.10 or the recently released 7.04 version may work, but they are not officially supported.

From a software perspective, you must have the following installed prior to installing Enomalism:

- GCC.

- Python 2.4 or newer.

- Openssl.

- Apache with mod_ssl. This is optional, but strongly recommended for production deployments.

Other modules discussed earlier in this section will be detected (if installed) or deployed by the Enomalism installation process itself.

WARNING

Since version 0.63, Enomalism can manage only those systems that are running the XenSource 3.0.4 hypervisor or newer. Enomalism cannot manage versions 3.0.3 and older. We mention this because as of the time of this writing, many common distributions, including Fedora Core 6, Red Hat Linux 5, and SUSE Linux Enterprise Server 10.2, include Xen as an integrated package, but the hypervisor is at the 3.0.3 release. In order to manage those

Xen deployments, you may need to uninstall the package that came with the distribution and install the latest release from source.

Also, if you plan to manage XenSource's commercial XenServer product family, keep in mind that version 3.1 is based on the 3.0.3 hypervisor. You will need to upgrade to the latest release, version 3.2, to manage XenServer with Enomalism, as it is based on the 3.0.4 hypervisor.

If you need to download the open source Xen 3.0.4 binaries, visit www.xensource.com/download/index_3.0.4.html.

Installation Walkthrough

To install Enomalism, follow these basic steps:

1. Download the latest release at http://sourceforge.net/project/showfiles.php?group_id=164855.

2. Untar the downloaded file into /opt.

3. If you are upgrading from a previous version of Enomalism, be sure to back up the entire /opt/enomalism directory, and then simply untar the new release on top of the original.

4. For new installs and upgrades, go to /opt/enomalism and run the install script, preinstall.py. It's that simple!

NOTE

You must install to /opt/enomalism. Do not try to place the Enomalism binaries in another directory or path.

Because Enomalism requires Xen, if you have not already done so, be sure to install Xen 3.0.4 or newer along with the Xen kernel before starting any Enomalism processes. For assistance with installing Xen, see Chapter 3.

Using Enomalism to Manage Xen

With everything installed and configured, you can now administer your Xen environment. Because Enomalism is installed in the dom0 of the Xen host, there is no need to register or point the management tool to a Xen environment to manage. You simply need to browse to the Enomalism Web GUI at http://yourxenhost:24514, as shown in Figure 5.12.

Figure 5.12 The Enomalism Login Screen

After logging in, you will see the Virtualized Management Dashboard, as illustrated in Figure 5.13. It is through this dashboard that you can monitor and perform a variety of actions against your Xen guests. The dashboard itself is divided into two tabs. The first tab, System Summary, provides you with information regarding the status, name, parent (or Xen hostname), and CPU and memory utilization for each domU. As shown in Figure 5.14, you also have point-and-click control over the domUs for the following activities:

Figure 5.13 The Virtualized Management Dashboard

Figure 5.14 Controls for domU Management

1. **Shutdown** This will power-off the domU, invoking any shutdown processes for the operating system running inside the guest. Note that shutdowns may not be graceful.

2. **Pause** This will suspend the running domU. If the domU is already paused, this icon is replaced with a green arrow icon to "unpause" the guest.

3. **Destroy** This is a hard shutdown, the equivalent of pulling out the power cable of a physical server.

4. **Delete** This performs the "Destroy" activity followed by removing the guest's configuration, files, and references in Enomalism.

5. **Permissions** This will open a new window to allow you to administer permission to the guest for enrolled users and groups.

6. **Resources** This will open a new window with two tabs. The first is used to control the hard drive(s) for the guest, including changing its sizes. The second tab allows you to configure various components of the guest, including the amount of memory, the number of virtual CPUs, setting the VNC password, enabling or disabling VNC and USB, and configuring the virtual serial console.

7. **SSH, VNC, or AJAX Terminal** Depending on the configuration, this will allow you to interact with the guest's operating system using the integrated SSH client, an AJAX-based terminal, or the VNC client.

8. **Firewall** An interesting and useful component, the firewall allows you to set up basic firewall rules, including the protocol (TCP/UDP/both) and ports allowed for network communication to and from the guest.

The control icons visible to you depend on the state of the Xen guest. For example, if a guest is already shut down, you will not see the Shutdown icon, but rather the Start icon. You will not see the SSH or Pause icons, either, on a shutdown guest.

The other dashboard tab, Administrative Tools, will present you with four icons and tools to administer your Enomalism environment. As shown in Figure 5.15, you have tools to administer users, provision new domUs, export or migrate domUs, and gain access to the VMCast appliance feed.

Figure 5.15 The Enomalism Administrative Tools

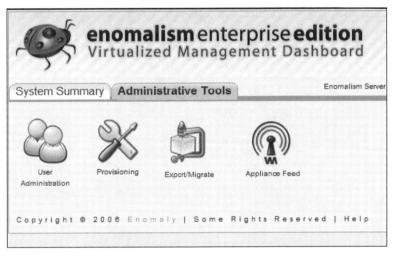

User administration will be straightforward for those used to LDAP, though it may prove to be challenging for those not experienced with directory services when setting up diverse organizations, containers, and users. Provisioning is also straightforward, and should provide you with the ability to rapidly deploy new guests and virtual appliances. Export and migration tools are very useful for moving guests around and, in the enterprise edition, creating your own virtual appliance that can be applied to a farm of Enomalism-managed hosts.

That leads us to the appliance feed tool. This is a unique concept from the Enomaly team, and it really shows the power that virtualization will bring to IT organizations for internal and external use. Tied to Enomaly's VMCasting initiative, the appliance feed provides you with Web access to a catalog of available virtual appliances, making it easy to find one that meets your needs, download it, and deploy it. Unlike other mechanisms currently available to deploy virtual appliances, this Web tool eliminates the need to manually download, register, and run appliances on your virtual host. Figure 5.16 illustrates a feed with two available images, a Debian 3.1 image and a Fedora Core 6 image. Enomaly and the open source community promise more images, which promises to change the whole paradigm on systems management and deployment.

Figure 5.16 Enomalism Appliance Feed for VMCasting

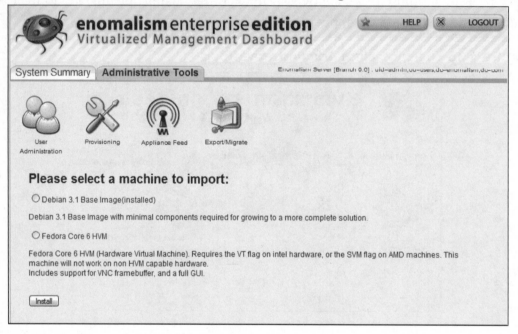

For more information about Enomalism, VMCasting, and the GeoElastic alliance, visit Enomaly's Web site, www.enomaly.net.

Project ConVirt and XenMan

Project ConVirt is an active, open source project with the goal of tackling the administrative and infrastructure management challenges that adoption of virtualization platforms presents to the traditional data center. The XenMan Administrator Console is Project ConVirt's first release.

XenMan is a graphical management tool aimed at operational life cycle management for the Xen virtualization platform. XenMan should be helpful to you regardless of whether you are a seasoned Xen administrator or are just seeking an introduction to Xen virtualization. With XenMan's secure, multinode administration, performance management, and provisioning capabilities, you can manage your entire environment from a single, centralized console. Most common administrative tasks, such as starting, stopping, monitoring, and provisioning VMs (or domUs), typically involve just a few mouse clicks with XenMan. You can also use this point-and-click style to perform system management operations such as scanning operating system configurations or preparing individual servers for maintenance.

XenMan is distributed under the GNU General Public License (GPL).

Overview of ConVirt

ConVirt is a very active project and, as such, XenMan is under constant development release and change. The features, however, are still focused on the following:

- **Multiserver management** Use XenMan to manage all of your Xen hosts and their guest domains.

- **Centralized view** Use a single console to monitor and view what is happening across your virtual infrastructure, including resource utilization, guest deployments, task status, and configuration of both hosts and guests.

- **Security** Based on the SSH tunneling approach, XenMan enhances, if not surpasses, the security provided with the core Xen control tools.

- **Repository of images** Use XenMan to maintain a store of images for rapid domU deployment. You can also automate deployments using the Image Store SDK.

- **Remote server operations** Manage your virtual infrastructure from "virtually" anywhere that you have access to the XenMan console.

Currently, XenMan allows both single and multiple host administration and image provisioning. It does not provide a mechanism for live migrations, centralized user administration (via LDAP, for example), or extensibility and automation through common Web protocols, such as SOAP and XML-RPC (similar to what XenSource, openQRM, and Enomalism provide). The console is not Web-enabled yet, but all of these features are included in the development road map for the product.

Installing ConVirt

XenMan is distributed as both a source/binary tarball as well as an RPM package for various Red Hat distributions. Community packages for Debian, SUSE, and others are also available.

System Requirements

Regardless of which deployment option you choose, you must meet some basic system requirements. For the management server running XenMan's server components, you must have Xen 3.0.2 installed and running, and the SSH daemon must be running. For the client system, Xen must be installed, although you do not need to be booted into the Xen kernel with xend running. You also need to have X server functioning (because XenMan is a GUI-based application), be able to connect to the management server via SSH2, and have the Paramiko library installed.

The Paramiko library is a Python module that implements the SSH2 protocol for secure connections to remote machines. Note that this library is also distributed under LGPL.

> **NOTE**
>
> The Paramiko library also has its own prerequisites—in particular, Python, version 2.3 or higher, and Pycrpyto, version 1.9 or higher. The library has been tested as stable with Red Hat FC 1 and higher, RHEL 3 and 4, Debian Sarge 3.1, and Ubuntu Edgy 6.10. So although you can compile XenMan successfully on other distributions, you will be limited to those that support this library.
>
> If you need to install this library, you can download it and learn more about the project at www.lag.net/paramiko.

Installation

To deploy from the tarball, follow these steps:

1. Download and extract the source tarball from https://sourceforge.net/project/showfiles.php?group_id=168929. The latest release is xenman-0.6.tar.gz.

2. Make sure your environment fulfills XenMan's prerequisites, as listed earlier.

3. If you haven't already, deploy python-paramiko in your environment.

4. Execute the default configuration script if you see one for your distribution. For example, if you are running SUSE, you would run configure_defaults-suse.sh located in ./distros/suse/.

5. If you see a default configuration file for your distribution in the same directory, rename it to xenman.conf and copy it to the top of the installation directory. For example, if you were running Fedora Core, you would run the following command:

```
cp ./distros/fedora/xenman.conf ./xenman.conf
```

NOTE

If you do not see a default configuration file specific to your distribution, XenMan will create one for you upon startup.

6. Create a local copy of the image store by running the following command. This will create the image store at /var/cache/xenman/image_store.

```
sh ./mk_image_store
```

7. Make sure XenMan has execute permissions by running:

```
chmod 0755 ./XenMan
```

8. Once you have finished the installation, you can run XenMan by simply running *XenMan*.

To deploy from RPM, download the appropriate package for your distribution, if available. For example, if you are running SUSE, you would download the RPM for SUSE and run the following command. Once it's installed, follow step 8 as outlined in the steps for tarball installation.

```
rpm -Uvh xenman-0.6-1.suse.noarch.rpm
```

WARNING

If you have an earlier version of XenMan installed, you must uninstall it first. If it was installed via RPM, simply run the command *rpm -e xenman*.

Using ConVirt to Manage Xen

Once your environment is set up and configured, you can use XenMan immediately to start managing your Xen-based virtual infrastructure. The following sections are a summary of common operations you can perform as outlined in the XenMan documentation for the following:

- The XenMan dashboard
- Server pool operations
- Server operations
- VM operations
- The image store

The Dashboard

The XenMan Dashboard is a consolidated listing of all known managed servers along with critical performance, availability, and configuration metrics for each host. It provides the user the ability to view the state of the entire Xen environment at a glance. The following are common administrative tasks:

- **Launch** The Dashboard is the default screen when the XenMan GUI is launched, but you can return to it by selecting **Server Pool** in the navigator on the left and then clicking on the **Summary tab** on the right-hand side.

- **Operations** Left-clicking a row in the Dashboard selects the associated managed server. You can then perform the following actions:

  - **Double-click** Connect to the managed server and drill down into a more detailed view. This selects the server's node in the navigator on the left-hand side and brings up the Summary tab for the server on the right.

  - **Right-click** Context-sensitive menu. Most server operations can be executed directly from here.

  - **Sort** Clicking the column header will re-sort the listing based on the clicked column (not available for all columns).

- **Data** Each row in the Dashboard corresponds to a managed server, as shown in Figure 5.17. The fields are:

  - **Server** The name of the managed server.

- **Connection** Connectivity status to the managed server (i.e., whether XenMan has an active connection to the server).

- **VM Summary** A compact listing of VM status on the server.

- **VM CPU(%)** Aggregate processor usage by VMs running on the server. This does not include the dom0's processor usage.

- **VM Mem(%)** Aggregate memory usage by VMs running on the server. This does not include the dom0's memory usage.

- **Server CPU(s)** Number and clock speed of the physical processors on the managed server, if available.

- **Server Mem** Total, usable physical memory installed on the managed server, if available.

- **Version** The version string being reported by Xen at the managed server.

Figure 5.17 XenMan Dashboard and Metrics

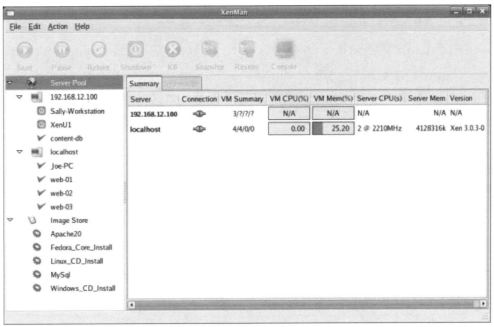

Server Pool Operations

XenMan shows a Server Pool node to refer to a collection of managed Xen hosts. XenMan supports only a single server pool in the current release. The local Xen installation is automatically added to the pool, and you can add additional Xen hosts to the pool for centralized management. The following are some common server pool tasks that you can confirm in the XenMan console:

- **Add Server** You can add additional remote managed servers by using the Add Server operation. You will need to provide the information regarding the hostname, Xen port (usually 8005), and credentials for the connection.
- **Remove Server** You can remove a server from the list by selecting it and choosing Remove Server.

Server Operations

The following is a list of all operations that you can perform against a specific Xen host:

- **Start All VMs** Start all VMs on a selected server.
- **Shutdown All VMs** Shut down all VMs on a selected server.
- **Kill All VMs** Kill all VMs on a selected server.
- **Provision VM** Allows you to create a new VM with very few parameters.
- **Open VM Config File** Allows you to add a new VM file to the list, which you can then edit using the Settings context menu or start using the Start button.

VM Operations

The following is a list of all operations that you can perform against a specific Xen guest (domU), as shown in Figure 5.18:

- **Edit VM Settings** Change the configuration settings for the selected VM.
- **Edit VM Config File** Edit the VM's configuration file directly.
- **Show Console** Launch a text or graphical console of the guest operating system.
- **Start** Start the selected VM.
- **Pause** Toggle button to pause/resume running of the VM.
- **Reboot** Reboot a selected VM.
- **Shutdown** Shut down a running VM.

- **Kill** Hard-kill a VM.

- **Snapshot** Save the state of a running VM to a file.

- **Restore** Restore a VM from a stored snapshot.

- **Remove VM Config File** Remove the VM filename from the list of VMs registered to XenMan.

- **Delete** Delete the VM file and associated Virtual Block Devices (VBDs) or LVMs.

Figure 5.18 VM Operations Available in the XenMan GUI

The Image Store

XenMan allows administrators to define their images and create VM configurations from them. For example, you may have a scenario where you need to frequently deploy four different types of machines: RHEL 4, CentOS, SUSE, and Ubuntu. You can configure XenMan to point to kernel and RAMDisk images of each distribution and deploy many VMs using predefined images. This collection of images is referred to as the *image store*. XenMan ships with a default image store containing a few useful provisionable images. You may also construct your own image descriptions and provisioning schemes and add them to the image store.

The following is a review of some of the operations you can perform to manage the image store:

- **Location** The image store is listed in the navigator. Clicking or expanding the Image Store node results in a listing of the available, provisionable images.

- **Image Operations** Use these operations to manage a specific image:

  - **Click** Selects the image and displays useful information about it in on the right-hand side. When creating an image, you can place important information which can be viewed at this point that gives a brief description of the image, prerequisites, and deployment instructions, as shown in Figure 5.19.

Figure 5.19 Summary Information Displayed for a Provisionable Image

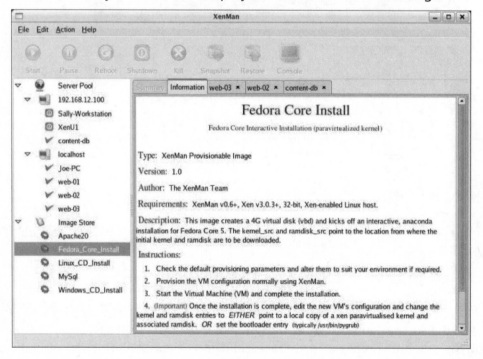

- **Right-click** Brings up a context menu with various image-specific tasks. These include Provision to start the provisioning process (see Figure 5.20), Edit Settings to alter the definition of the image, Edit Script to alter the

mechanism used to provision VMs using this image, and Edit Description to modify the description associated with this image.

Figure 5.20 Setting Parameters for VM Provisioning

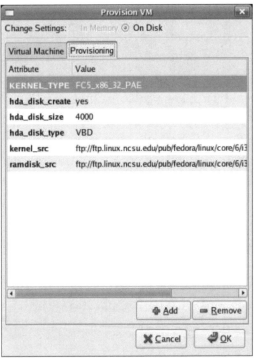

Summary

Xen's adoption in data centers of all sizes has led a diverse range of use cases in development, test, and production environments. As administrators have begun to reap the benefits of virtualization with Xen, they have also begun to feel some pain in the management of Xen hosts and their guest domains. Although the native management tools do provide some efficient ways to manage aspects of a Xen-based virtual infrastructure, only the XenServer Administrator Console available with the commercial XenSource offering has the convenience of graphical administration. However, even this tool is limited in functionality and compatibility, as you cannot use it to manage open source Xen deployments.

Fortunately, many companies have recognized the challenges that administrators faced and have presented tools to address the issues of monitoring, provisioning, and overall systems management. Most are open source, and many are freely distributed, making little (if any) impact on an organization's budget. Others offer an even more robust set of features for a nominal cost that even the tight budget can still support.

Although there are many offerings, we have taken the time to review three of the most popular in use today: Qlusters openQRM, Enomalism from Enomaly, and XenMan, part of Project ConVirt. These applications show that you can achieve great value through virtualization if you manage it with the right tool.

Solutions Fast Track

Qlusters openQRM

☑ openQRM offers a wide range of systems management features for both physical and virtual environments, making it a one-stop shop for your systems and resource management needs.

☑ Administrators can manage their entire workload across both physical and virtual resources through policies that dynamically interact with partitions and nodes to ensure that service levels and business processes continue without impact.

☑ openQRM offers a unique way to provision guests, or partitions, without having to install or deploy a new operating system instance. It is also the only tool in the group that manages Windows and Linux servers, both physical and running inside a Xen domU.

☑ Most of the functionality is available in the free, open source edition, although advanced plug-ins such as QRM-HA and the Provisioning Portal are available only through commercial offerings from Qlusters.

☑ Although offering lots of functionality, openQRM does expose an API for programmatic interaction with the QRM server.

Enomalism

☑ Bringing the concept of geographic computing to the common data center, Enomalism provides a unique, if not elastic, approach to Xen management.

☑ Using a centralized dashboard, administrators can view their Xen environment and control activities manually or in an automatic and dynamic way to meet business and workload needs in real time.

☑ You can manage system users as well as the systems themselves through a central LDAP directory service. Administrators can assign and control system resource parameters and reassign resources as needed.

☑ Enomalism features the Enomalism Virtual Appliance package management interface that automates the processes of installing, upgrading, configuring, and removing software packages using the VMCasting system, based on RSS feed technology.

☑ An open and accessible API enables easy third-party integration with other management products, while supporting industry standards such as SOAP.

Project ConVirt and XenMan

☑ XenMan provides an intuitive interface for managing and administering multiple Xen systems. Through XenMan, administrators can manage host and guest performance and utilize its robust provisioning capabilities.

☑ XenMan gives you complete control of hosts and guests. Through a series of clicks, you can start, stop, deploy, and configure your VMs and their hosts.

☑   Utilizing a unique approach to image repository management, XenMan employs an image store to store, define, and provision images to managed systems.

Frequently Asked Questions

The following Frequently Asked Questions, answered by the authors of this book, are designed to both measure your understanding of the concepts presented in this chapter and to assist you with real-life implementation of these concepts. To have your questions about this chapter answered by the author, browse to **www.syngress.com/solutions** and click on the **"Ask the Author"** form.

Q: We want to create a policy that prohibits anyone, including administrators, from interactively logging into a Xen host. If I use these tools, will we ever have to use the native management tools?

A: Although all three products discussed in this chapter offer an extensive feature set and functionality, they are not a direct replacement for the native tools. There may be occasions when you will need to use the control tools available in dom0—for example, when the host is not available on the network. Also, future releases of the tools may not keep pace with the functionality introduced by Xen in upcoming versions, in which case you will either need to delay your upgrades or make sure that your administrative processes still let you manage hosts locally.

Q: My data center has a mixture of virtualization technologies. I would like to minimize the number of tools that I have to use and maintain. Which tool best fits my need?

A: Although all three offer great management capabilities, only openQRM allows you to manage VMware and Xen hosts in a single console. On top of that, you can also manage your physical hosts, running either Windows or Linux.

Q: Can I receive support for any of these tools?

A: Yes and no. Only openQRM and Enomalism offer a commercial package that adds functionality and support to the equation. However, all three tools are widely used around the world to manage Xen environments, and as such, they have a strong user base that is willing to help you in user forums accessible online. In most cases, you can have your questions answered by posting to these forums.

Q: My company is using XenSource's XenEnterprise. Should I use these third-party tools to manage my VMs?

A: In most cases, the answer is yes. These tools supplement the functionality available in the XenServer Administrator Console. Many features have been included that are not even available in the Administrator Console, making them valuable to your organization. With that said, you should exercise caution when implementing changes to your hosts. Installing additional packages onto a XenServer host may void any support agreement with XenSource, and its CentOS-based dom0 has been minimized and meets certain criteria of functionality and resource consumption.

Q: I need help deploying my Xen hosts as well as Xen guests. Which tool fits my need?

A: openQRM allows you to create a "golden image" of a Xen host and provision that to available physical resources as needed or desired. Although the other two are more focused on VM provisioning, other tools are available which we did not cover in this chapter that will help you with Xen host deployments.

## Chapter 6

Deploying a Virtual Machine in Xen

Solutions in this chapter:

- **Workload Planning and Virtual Machine Placement**

- **Installing Modified Guests**

- **Installing Unmodified Guests**

- **Installing Windows Guests**

- **Physical-to-Virtual Migrations of Existing Physical Servers**

- **Importing and Exporting Existing Virtual Machines**

☑ **Summary**

☑ **Solutions Fast Track**

☑ **Frequently Asked Questions**

Introduction

Understanding the interaction between XenVMs and Xen Hosts requires that administrators understand their workloads. Once they understand their workloads for every application, they can decide which XenVMs work well together and which ones will contend for resources.

Once the Xen Hosts are installed, administrators will have to create the XenVMs. Xen provides different techniques for provisioning XenVMs. Users can create a new XenVM by installing from media or network shares, they can clone a XenVM, they can export a XenVM and use it as a template, or they can convert the OS on a physical host to a "virtualized" XenVM.

Workload Planning and Virtual Machine Placement

As discussed in previous chapters, the appeal of virtualization includes the ability to maximize the utilization of IT assets, reduce administrative overhead, and accelerate provisioning times, among others. At first glance, virtualization is mostly about CPU and memory utilization, but as most of us that have been implementing virtualization technologies for years can attest, both network and disk I/O can also have a major impact in workload combination decisions.

To accomplish an optimal workload mix, thorough research has been done on current physical server utilization and an understanding of the additional horsepower impact of newer servers and I/O subsystems. To help with this task, both commercial and open source products are available that can assist in mapping physical-to-virtual workloads.

Memory

Memory is one of the most expensive system components, and one that should not be underestimated. Xen allows administrators to reserve a minimum amount of memory specific to each virtual machine (VM) upon startup.

Understanding physical server memory utilization is a paramount factor in VM placement. If a Xen host is oversubscribed, the XenVMs can run into physical memory contention, creating a potential performance impact and, in some cases, causing processes and VMs to crash.

CPU

One of the areas where server consolidation has the most impact is CPU utilization. With CPU processing power doubling every couple of years, it is possible that when analyzing the physical server CPU speed, coupled with the power of those processors in comparison with current ones, a huge opportunity for workload consolidation exists.

Make sure that systems with similar high demands on processor resources will not cause contention hot spots as XenVMs running on the same Xen Host.

WARNING

Make sure you understand multicore processor technology. On Intel and AMD multicore processors, increasing the number of cores does not provide a linear increment in processing power, even with dedicated cache and multiple buses.

Designing & Planning...

Modeling CPU Consolidation

A simple rule of thumb when modeling load on an existing physical server to a newer processor platform is to multiply the utilization of the processors by the speed (clock cycles) and number of processors:

Number_of_Processors x Old_Processor_Speed x %_Utilization = Total_consumed_processor_speed

For example:

4 processors x 1GHz x 40% = 1.6GHz

This last example only illustrates a straightforward number of cycles of processing used. And although other factors in workload processing consolidation, such as concurrency and context switching, result in a more complex equation, from experience this rule of thumb has served well as the foundation for VM placement and consolidation.

Network

The network is probably the most overlooked resource when migrating physical servers to VMs. With today's increasing bandwidth at the network infrastructure, it is easy to overlook the cumulative demands of physical servers on the network.

Understanding that total network usage for all the VMs will now be exceeding the physical interface(s) of the Xen Host is paramount to successful migration.

Designing & Planning…

High Availability, Replication, and Backups

Every IT organization has requirements in terms of system availability and data protection. Most solutions that meet these requirements have to move data between systems in the form of a network-based backup, via clustering, or by logically replicating the data from one system to another.

These solutions can have different demands on networks: steady streams of low-impact or periodic bursts, or, in the case of network-based backups, steady, high-impact streams.

High availability High-availability solutions, such as clustering technologies, often require different networks for different functions. In most cases, a minimum of two networks are required: a public network through which clients can communicate with the servers, and a private network that is used for heartbeats, or messaging, between cluster nodes. In addition, most clustering solutions best practices include redundant networks or alternative networks, which would limit the available networks to other XenVMs.

Replication Replication refers to the transport of data from one application to another. Different application types, such as RDMBS and e-mail systems, use proprietary methods to accomplish replication, but the result is that either a subset or all of the data in the original has to be transported to the replica. All of this traffic occurs over the network (whether virtual or physical), and may be synchronous or asynchronous. In either case, either a steady stream of data or a periodic burst will occur on the network, and may impact the performance of all VMs on a specific Xen Host.

Backups Although administrators can back up XenVMs using cloning or exporting techniques (we won't discuss the merits and

Continued

constraints of those techniques here), it is still highly recommended that you back up using traditional network-based methods in which a network server is attached to the media (tapes, disks, virtual tapes, etc.) and to which clients send copies of files and data.

Backup applications will take advantage of any available bandwidth to accomplish the backups in as little time as possible. So, cohabiting XenVMs that have high data volumes and frequent data changes will impact the performance of those VMs during backup periods.

Also, be sure to take into consideration how much data needs to be backed up and how frequently it changes.

In addition to the issue of bandwidth, network isolation due to security might also be required, and taking into account that the XenVM's virtual network interface cards (NICs) and the Xen Host's physical NICs are on the same subnet, and that any Xen Host can have, at most, three NICs, users might find themselves in situations that limit where they can place the XenVMs.

Installing Modified Guests

Modified guests are guest operating systems that are optimized by replacing the kernel with a Xen-aware version and providing Xen-optimized disk and network drivers that "understand" the underlying virtualization layers.

The process of installing modified Linux guests requires an "exploded" network share of the installation binaries (not the ISOs of the CD-ROMs/DVDs). Although it is not necessary to have a boot server (the XenVM will boot and then prompt for the network share), having one allows for fully automated deployments of Linux XenVMs.

In the following subsection, we will discuss how to install Red Hat ES 4 from a network share.

Installing Red Hat Enterprise Linux 4

Red Hat ES 4 installation requires the use of a network share. The network share can be run on the NFS, FTP, or HTTP protocol, depending on the user's preference and/or existing solutions. In addition, each protocol has a list of requirements and dependencies that need to be met, including connectivity, binaries, and security considerations.

To install a Red Hat ES 4 XenVM, follow these steps:

1. Log on to the **Administrator Console**.

2. Select the **Xen Host** on which to deploy the Red Hat ES 4 XenVM.

3. Click the **Install XenVM button**. The Install XenVM tab will appear in the bottom pane, as shown in Figure 6.1.

Figure 6.1 The Install XenVM Tab in Red Hat ES 4

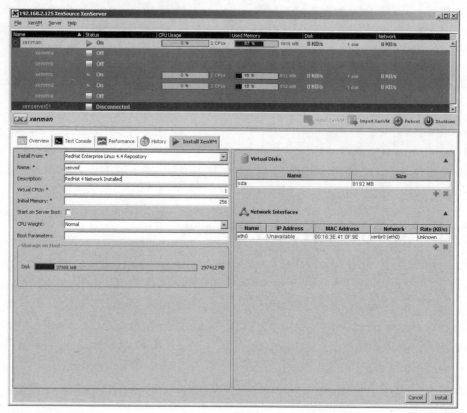

The Install XenVM pane consists of the following fields and sections:

- **Install From** A pull-down menu that allows you to select the operating system template that will be used for the XenVM. This template does not contain OS images, but rather produces a default configuration for the components in this type of XenVM (the number of virtual CPUs, disks and disk sizes, NIC definitions, etc.).

- **Name** The unique alphanumeric identifier for the XenVM (this is not the hostname of the resulting operating system).

- **Description** A nonmandatory field that allows you to identify the function or other characteristics of the XenVM.

- **Virtual CPUs** The number of virtual CPUs that will be presented to the XenVM.

- **Initial Memory** The amount of dedicated memory for the XenVM.

- **Start on Server Boot** A check box that indicates whether to start this XenVM when the Xen Host boots.

- **CPU Weight** A drop-down menu that allows you to select the relative CPU resource allocation for this XenVM. The values in the menu are Low, Normal, and High. You also can define more granular CPU weight distributions from the command-line interface (CLI).

- **Storage On Host** A display of the storage allocation to the Xen Host.

- **Virtual Disks** Displays the virtual disks to be used for this XenVM. To add or remove virtual disks click on the plus (+) or delete (X) symbol. A new virtual disk will appear, or the selected virtual disk will be removed.

- **CD-ROM/DVD** Allows you to select the media device to present to the XenVM.

- **Network Interfaces** Presents you with the default NIC for the XenVM. Clicking the plus or remove symbol will add NICs or remove the select NIC from the screen. If more than one network is defined on the Xen Host, the network column becomes a drop-down menu allowing you to select the correct network for that interface.

4. Once you have filled in all of the mandatory fields, click on the **Install button** in the bottom pane. The Red Hat pseudographical install screen will appear (see Figure 6.2). At this point, you have not indicated where the install files are located, or a boot server from which to boot. This boot image is actually provided by the Xen Host, and is selected based on the Installation Type field shown in Figure 6.2.

Figure 6.2 The Red Hat Install Screen

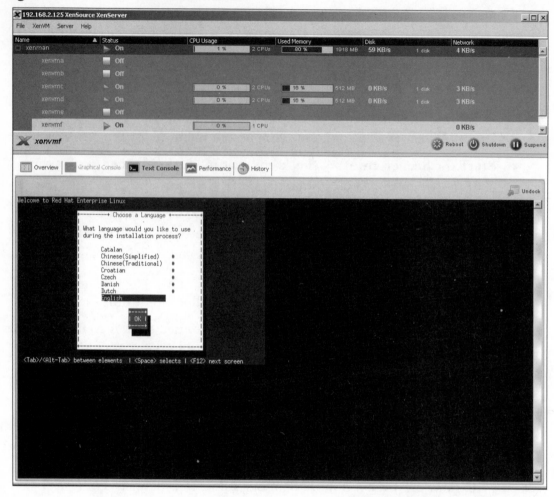

5. Select the appropriate language and tab to the **OK button**. Once the OK button is highlighted, press the **Enter key**. The screen will change, and the installer will prompt for the location of the media, as shown in Figure 6.3.

6. Select the type of media to be used by using the up/down arrows. Then tab until the OK button is highlighted and press **Return**. The new Red Hat ES 4 XenVM will request a network identity from the network (tftpboot/dhcp servers), as shown in Figure 6.4.

Figure 6.3 Network Install Media Location

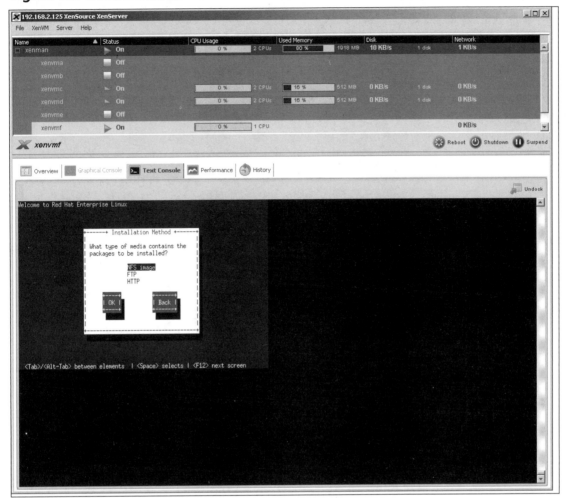

Figure 6.4 Searching for Hostname and Domain Information

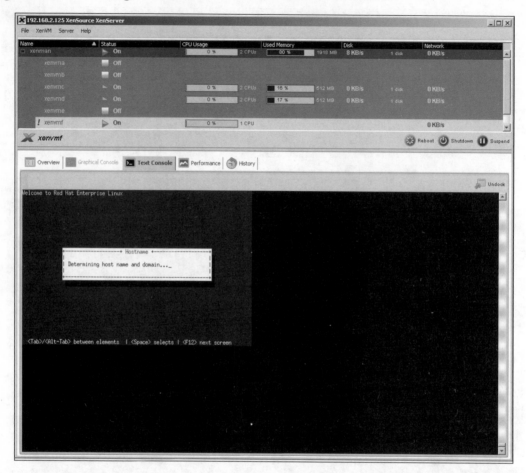

7. If no DHCP/TFTPBOOT server can be found, the installer will ask for network information to be entered manually.

8. After you supply the network information and click the **OK button**, the installer will prompt you for information on the network share to use:

    ■   If you selected **NFS** as the media type, the installer will prompt for the hostname/IP address of the NFS server, and the installation directory, as shown in Figure 6.5.

    ■   If you chose **HTTP**, the installer will prompt for the URL of the server, including the path to the installation files.

    ■   If you selected **FTP**, the installer will prompt for the hostname/IP address of the server along with the authentication credentials to be used.

Figure 6.5 Entering Media Share Network Information

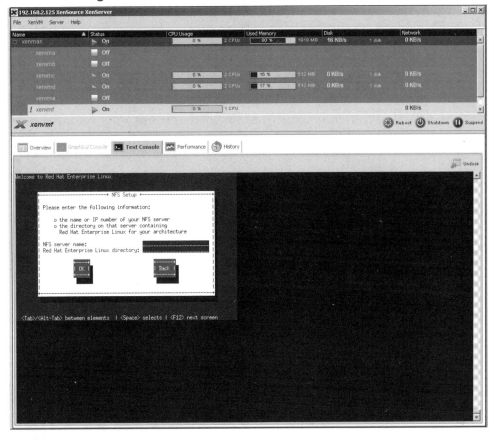

9. Once you've entered the share information, tab to the **OK button** and press **Enter**. At this stage, the installation will commence, and the installer will prompt you for all the configuration information. Refer to the Red Hat Enterprise Linux documentation for complete installation instructions.

Installing Unmodified Guests

Support for installing unmodified guests is available only for Red Hat Enterprise Linux 5, SUSE Linux Enterprise Server 10 SP1, and Windows XP/2003 (Windows XP and Windows 2003 installations are covered in the section "Installing Windows Guests," later in this chapter).

One of the characteristics of unmodified hosts is that you can install them directly from vendor media, as opposed to modified guests, which you can install only through network methods.

As discussed earlier in this book, *unmodified guests* refers to operating systems that can actually run in emulated mode. And although unmodified guests can run permanently, they use more resources because they use emulation drivers instead of the Xen-provided drivers.

Installing Red Hat Linux Enterprise 5

You can install Red Hat 5 either from vendor media or via a network share. We will discuss the process of installing from the original CD-ROMs and then paravirtualizing the resulting XenVM.

1. Log on to the **Administrator Console**.

2. Select the **Xen Host** on which to deploy the Red Hat 5 XenVM.

3. Click on the **Install XenVM button**. The Install XenVM tab will appear in the bottom pane, as shown in Figure 6.6.

Figure 6.6 The Install XenVM Pane

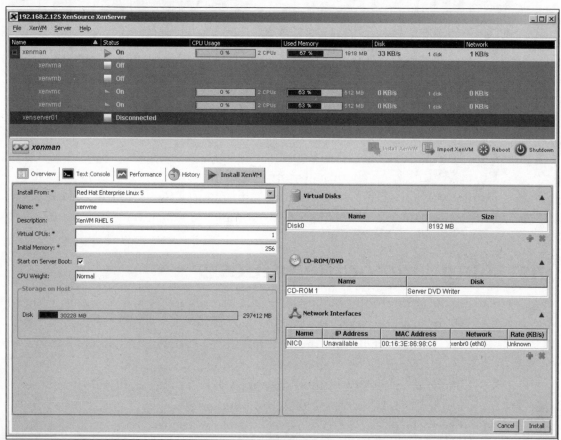

4. Once you have filled in all of the mandatory fields (*), click on the **Install button** at the bottom of the Administrator Console window. The History tab in the lower pane will indicate the progress of the install.

5. The Overview tab in the bottom pane will display the characteristics of the newly created XenVM; however, the XenVM will not be powered on, as indicated in the upper pane in Figure 6.7.

Figure 6.7 Installed XenVM

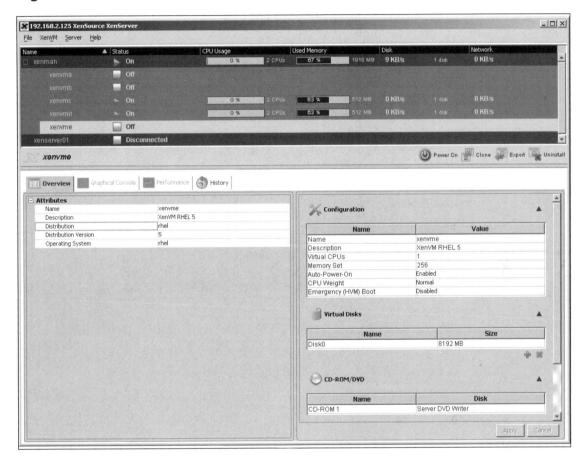

6. Insert **Disc1** of the Red Hat Enterprise Linux 5 distribution into the CD-ROM/DVD of the Xen Host.

7. Boot the **XenVM** by selecting it from the upper pane and clicking the **Power On button**. The new XenVM will go through its boot sequence from CD-ROM/DVD. Figure 6.8 shows the Red Hat install splash page in the XenVM's Graphical Console tab.

Figure 6.8 Booting the New XenVM from Vendor Media

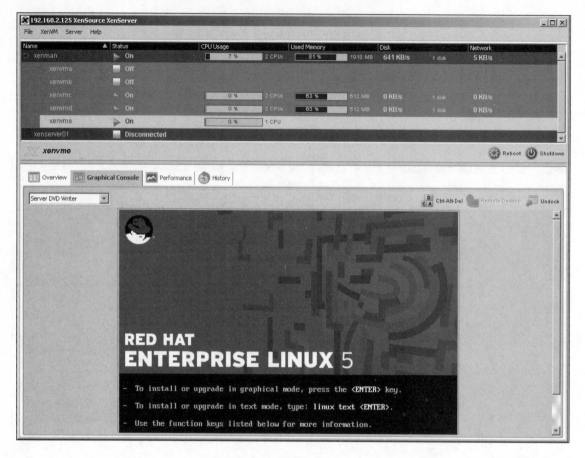

8. Click inside the lower pane to get TTY control. To continue the install in graphical mode, press **Enter**. The boot sequence is displayed on the Graphical Console tab, as shown in Figure 6.9.

9. The installation will prompt for user-defined parameters. Make sure to refer to the Red Hat documentation for installation details.

10. Once the installation is complete, the installer will prompt you to eject the CD-ROM/DVD from the Xen Host's bay and click on the **Reboot button**. The Graphical Console will display the reboot process.

Figure 6.9 The Boot Sequence for XenVM

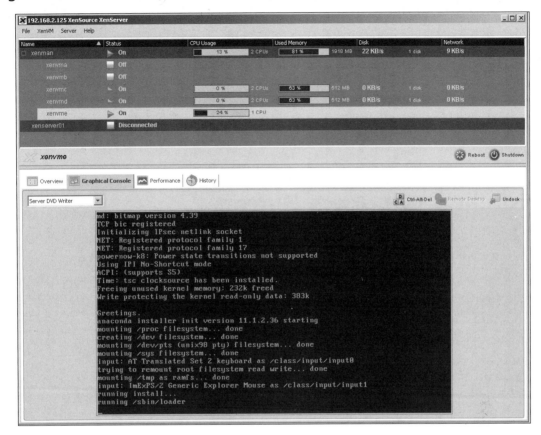

11. When the XenVM has rebooted completely, it is ready for use. At this point, however, the XenVM has not been paravirtualized, and as such, it is not performing to capacity. Select the **XenSource Linux P2V tools CD** from the CD-ROM/DVD pull-down. This will make the ISO image available for the XenVM to use, but will not mount it.

12. Mount the ISO image with the following command:

```
# mount -t iso9660 /dev/hdd /cdrom
```

13. Copy the contents of the mounted ISO image to a separate location. This is required because the Vendor Install media must be in the physical bay when the paravirtualization script is called. When the copy command is complete, enter *unmount /cdrom*:

```
# cp -ra /cdrom /"$TEMP_AREA"
```

14. Insert the **Red Hat Enterprise Linux 5 Disc1** into the Xen Host's CD-ROM/DVD.

15. Run the xen–setup tool:

```
# $TEMP_AREA/xen-setup/xen-setup
```

16. After the xen–setup script completes successfully, reboot the XenVM. After the reboot, verify that the kernel for the XenVM has been paravirtualized:

```
# uname -a
```

Installing Windows Guests

Finally, Windows guests are supported in Xen. This is a much-anticipated event, as Windows operating systems have the lion's share of installations worldwide.

Much like Linux unmodified guests, you can install Windows guests from vendor media and they are unmodified upon first installing the XenVM. However, a quick run around the resulting operating system will show that paravirtualization is absolutely necessary for any semblance of performance.

It's important to understand what happens under the covers:

- First, the Xen Host provides the Windows installer with an emulated IDE and NIC drivers, just to allow the installation to complete.

- After the installation has completed, you will need to install the XenPV tools for Windows, which replace those drivers with optimized versions.

Windows Guest Installation

In this section we will discuss the steps for installing a Windows guest.

1. Insert the **Windows CD-ROM** in the Xen Host on which you want to deploy.

2. Log on to the **Administrator Console**.

3. Select the **Install XenVM button**, after selecting the desired **Xen Host**. The Install XenVM tab appears, as in Figure 6.10.

Figure 6.10 The Install XenVM Windows Tab

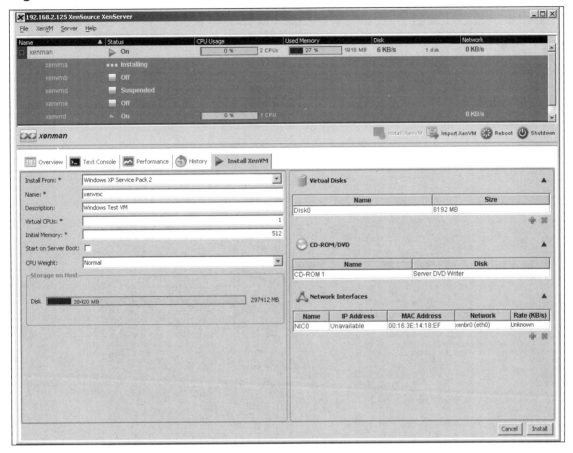

4. After entering the appropriate information to identify the XenVM (and selecting the **Server DVD Writer**), click the **Install button** in the lower pane. The lower pane will be switched to the Graphical Console for the new XenVM, as shown in Figure 6.11, and the Windows Installer screen will appear.

Figure 6.11 The Windows Installer Screen

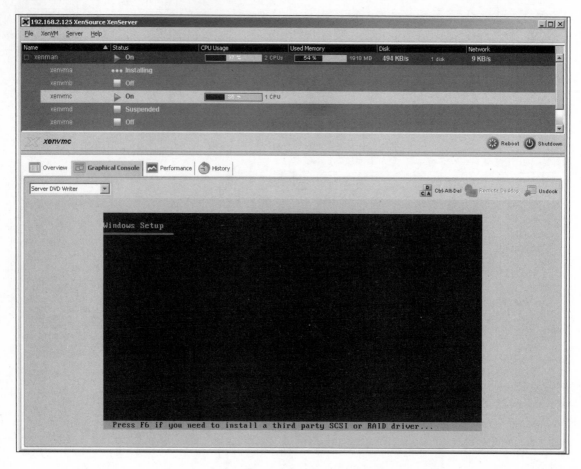

5. After you work your way through the Windows installation, the OS will be booted completely. In the lower pane, the Media drop-down menu will appear. Select the PV Tools for Windows option from the menu (see Figure 6.12).

Figure 6.12 The Xen PV Tools from Media Drop-Down

6. The End User License Agreement (EULA) will appear on the screen (see Figure 6.13).

Figure 6.13 The Xen PV Tools EULA

7. Click on the **Accept the terms of the License Agreement check box** and then click on the **Next button**.

8. Follow the installation instructions. To finalize, the installer will reboot the Windows XenVM. At this point, the resulting XenVM is fully paravirtualized and ready to use.

Physical-to-Virtual Migrations of Existing Systems

Physical-to-virtual (P2V) migrations consist of copying and modifying the operating system files of a physical server to either a logical volume on a Xen Host or a network share. Once the files have been copied, the result is a bootable XenVM.

P2V migrations are now industry-standard, as one of the main advantages of virtualization is the ability to reduce the physical data center footprint. Xen provides a P2V tool in the installation media, but third-party vendors have developed extended-functionality products to assist companies with their migrations.

The P2V tool provided by Xen works only on Linux physical hosts, and then only on those with PAE support. You cannot migrate Windows physical servers with Xen's provided P2V tool; however, several third-party vendors support Windows migrations.

P2V Migration

To migrate a physical server to a XenVM, follow these steps:

1. Boot the **physical server** from the Xen installation media.

2. At the **Welcome to Xen screen**, tab to the **OK button** and press **Return**.

3. After the installer has reviewed the server components, two choices will appear. Select the **P2V option**, then tab to the **OK button** and press **Return**.

4. Click the **OK button** on the **Welcome screen**.

5. The next screen requires the networking information for the resulting XenVM. You can choose to either allow the Dynamic Host Configuration Protocol (DHCP) for all interfaces, or manually configure them. Once completed, tab to the **OK button** and press **Return**.

6. After the installer has verified that the physical host is running a supported version of Linux, tab to the **OK button** and press **Return**.

7. Enter a **name** and **description** for the XenVM. This is not the hostname as registered in the operating system, but rather the name displayed on the Administrator Console or through the CLI.

8. Enter the **desired size of the root disk**, or accept the defaults, and then select **OK** and press **Return**.

9. Select the **target location** for the resulting file system. The options are Xen Host or an NFS server. Once you've made your selection, tab to the **OK button** and press **Return**.

10. Enter the **IP address** of the Xen Host, tab to the **OK button**, and press **Return**.

11. Enter the **root password** for the Xen Host, and select **OK**.

12. After the progress bar has completed, select **OK**. The physical server will eject the Xen Installation CD-ROM and reboot the server. Make sure to take out the media before the reboot.

13. You can verify that the installation completed by launching the **Administrator Console** and selecting the **XenVM name** given in step 7.

Importing and Exporting Existing Virtual Machines

Exporting is a mechanism for copying a XenVM. You can then use the copied XenVM as a template (like a clone) to create similar XenVMs with the characteristics of the original. In addition, you can import the exported XenVM to a different Xen Host (a mechanism that you can use to increase XenVM availability, or in disaster recovery solutions).

The process involves copying the virtual disks (VDIs) of the exported XenVM along with an XML document describing the configuration, as shown in Figure 6.14. The files are copied from the Xen Host to the Administrator Console. The Administrator Console will need enough disk space to store the VDI images.

NOTE

The VDI images will be compressed and are usually smaller than the actual size of the disk.

Figure 6.14 Sample XML of Exported XenVM

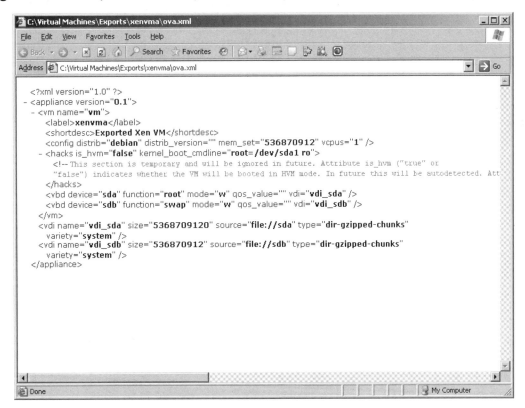

Exporting XenVMs

Before starting the export process, administrators need to ensure that the Administrator Console server has enough disk space to store the exported XenVM files:

1. Log on to the **Administrator Console**.

2. Select the **XenVM** that will be exported. You must shut down the XenVM in order to export it. If the XenVM is still running, click on the **Power Off button**.

3. Once you've shut down the XenVM, click on the **Export button**. Figure 6.15 shows the Export tab that appears.

Figure 6.15 The Export XenVM Tab

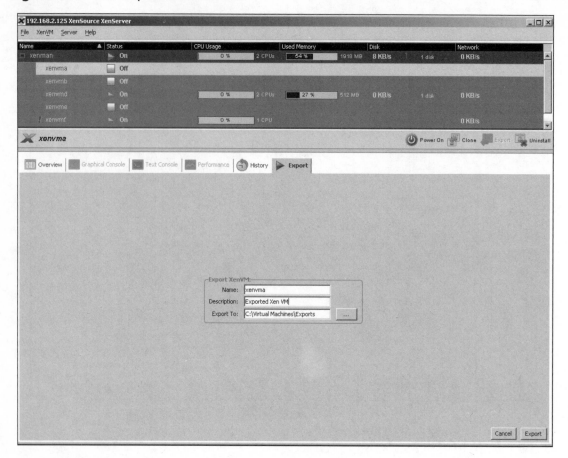

Three fields appear:

- **Name**

- **Description**

- **Export To** The directory on the Administrator Console in which to save the exported XenVM.

4. Click on the **Export button** to begin the process. The lower pane will switch to the History tab for the XenVM and a progress bar will appear showing the status of the export. Export can take a long time, depending on the number and size of the virtual disks and the network bandwidth available between the Xen Host and the Administrator Console.

Importing XenVMs

Importing a XenVM consists of moving the exported XenVM's files to a Xen Host. The process is the reverse of the export operation; copying the VDI files and XML file from the Administrator Console to the Xen Host.

To import a previously exported XenVM, follow these steps:

1. Log on to the **Administrator Console**.

2. Click on the **Xen Host** to which the XenVM will be imported.

3. Click on the **Import XenVM button**, and the Import XenVM tab appears in the lower pane. Figure 6.16 illustrates the Import XenVM tab.

Figure 6.16 The Import XenVM Tab

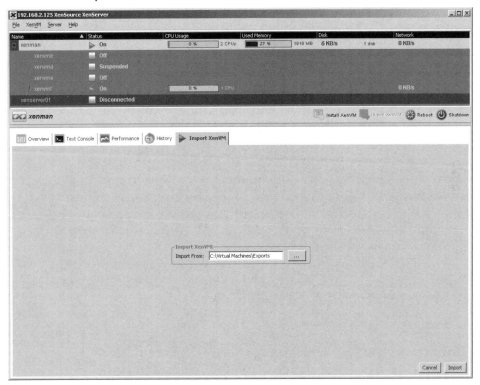

4. In the **Import From: field**, enter the location of the export XenVM directory, and then click the **Import button**. The lower pane will immediately change to the History tab for the imported XenVM. The import process may take awhile, as the VDI files are being copied over the network and then reassembled on the Xen Host.

Designing & Planning…

Export/Import XenVM As an Enterprise Tool

The ability to "transport" a XenVM via export/import is one of Xen's most powerful yet underrated features. In today's IT landscape, where business demands are progressively greater and budgets are lower, having a flexible tool that can decrease provisioning times, increase overall availability, and reduce disaster recovery costs is indeed a necessity.

Exporting a XenVM allows administrators the flexibility of moving XenVMs from one physical Xen Host to another. Downtime for XenVM migrations due to hardware maintenance and hardware migrations can be reduced. In addition, administrators can export XenVMs and use them as templates for creating additional XenVMs on other Xen Hosts, cutting down on provisioning times.

However, exporting and importing XenVMs can be time-consuming, and this is something to consider if you are planning to use this mechanism as a way to migrate XenVMs among Xen Hosts.

In addition to exporting and importing XenVMs, Xen provides an interface to "migrate" XenVMs from one Xen Host to another. From a high level, live migrations consist of moving the active memory pages and the NIC definitions (along with Internet Protocol [IP] address and ARP tables) for a XenVM between Xen Hosts. In addition, both Xen Hosts involved in the operation require simultaneous access to the VDI definitions of the XenVM and the same local area network (LAN).

Currently, the XenSource Administrator Console does not have an interface for performing live migrations of XenVMs. However, the XM CLI provides a mechanism to accomplish live migrations:

```
xm migrate --live XenVM_NAME XEN_HOST_NAME
```

This command will move the XenVM named *XenVM_NAME* to the *Xen_HOST_NAME* physical server from its current Xen Host.

Although you can move a XenVM with either mechanism, both have benefits and constraints:

As discussed earlier, exporting requires that the XenVM be powered off. In contrast, live migrations move the XenVM between Xen Hosts in "real time" (depending on the application, the XenVM might need to be quiesced).

Continued

However, live migrations require shared storage, which adds a cost to the infrastructure. Exporting XenVMs doesn't require such costs, but takes significantly longer to accomplish.

You can use exported XenVMs as templates to create additional XenVMs, whereas live migrations don't actually copy the XenVMs files; they just move control of the VDIs to another physical host.

Summary

XenVM deployment is at the heart of Xen's functionality. In most cases, administrators will start by creating some test XenVMs from either the Administrator Console or the CLI. As users get more comfortable, additional deployment techniques such as cloning or exporting/importing are employed. And after the value of Xen has been tested and proven, users will start using physical-to-logical migrations as an indispensable tool.

Soon, administrators will discover that not all XenVMs can be placed together, as they contend for any or all of the resources on the Xen Host. At that stage, exporting the XenVMs to a different Xen Host allows administrators to balance the workload more evenly.

At a more developed stage, administrators understand that moving XenVMs from one Xen Host to another needs to be more streamlined and dynamic. Enter live migrations, which allow administrators to reduce and even eliminate the downtime associated with moving the XenVMs to another physical host, but for which the IT group has to make additional investments in infrastructure.

Solutions Fast Track

Workload Planning and Virtual Machine Placement

- ☑ Understanding physical application requirements is paramount to planning the workload for a virtual environment.

- ☑ You determine workloads by measuring the use of CPU, memory, network, and disk I/O on either the physical host or the XenVM.

- ☑ With today's enterprise infrastructure components, disk I/O and the network are usually simpler to consolidate.

- ☑ CPU and memory are often the most critical components in workload balancing, and usually they are the most expensive resources on the physical servers.

Installing Modified Guests

- ☑ Modified guests refer to operating systems that are "paravirtualized" during the installation process, such as Red Hat Enterprise Linux 4.*x* and SUSE 9.*x*.

- ☑ You can install modified guests only from a network share. Supported protocols for installation network shares are NFS, HTTP, and FTP.

Installing Unmodified Guests

- ☑ Unmodified guests are based on operating systems that do not need to be paravirtualized in order to run as a XenVM.

- ☑ Operating systems that support unmodified guests include Red Hat Enterprise Linux 5, SUSE 10.1, and Windows XP/2003, and they require the use of processors with virtualization extensions built in, such as the Intel-VT and AMD-V.

- ☑ In contrast to modified guests, you can install unmodified guests from vendor media, such as CD-ROM or DVD.

- ☑ Although you can deploy unmodified guests without being paravirtualized, it is highly recommended that you modify them once installed, as performance will improve dramatically.

Installing Windows Guests

- ☑ Windows guests are installed as unmodified guests. Administrators then have to paravirtualize them.

- ☑ Windows XP, 2000, and 2003 are supported.

- ☑ In order to run Windows XenVMs, the Xen Host has to have a processor with virtualization extensions. Currently, only physical hosts with the Intel-VT or the AMD-V processors are supported.

Physical-to-Virtual Migrations of Existing Physical Servers

☑ P2V migrations are accomplished by booting the physical servers from the Xen install CD and copying and modifying the contents of the boot disk to the Xen Host.

☑ Although you can convert all operating systems supported in XenVMs from physical to logical, only Linux operating systems are supported with the Xen installation media. Windows operating systems require third-party tools to be converted.

☑ P2V migrations allow administrators to minimize the impact of converting physical servers. In addition, P2V migrations also minimize risk by keeping the original server intact.

Importing and Exporting Existing Virtual Machines

☑ Exporting an existing VM involves copying the virtual disk definitions from the Xen Host to the Administrator Console. In addition, an XML definition file is copied and is used to "reproduce" the identity of the XenVM.

☑ You can use XenVM exports to move the VM from one physical host to another. You also can use exports as a way to create templates and simplify deployments.

☑ You import a XenVM when the resulting files from an export are moved from the Administrator Console to a Xen Host.

☑ Export and imports of XenVMs can take a relatively long time, depending on the size of the VDIs and the network bandwidth available between the Xen Host and the Administrator Console.

Frequently Asked Questions

The following Frequently Asked Questions, answered by the authors of this book, are designed to both measure your understanding of the concepts presented in this chapter and to assist you with real-life implementation of these concepts. To have your questions about this chapter answered by the author, browse to **www.syngress.com/solutions** and click on the **"Ask the Author"** form.

Q: What are the pitfalls of migrating a physical server to VMs indiscriminately?

A: Not all workloads perform well together. Take into consideration the resource requirements of each physical server before deciding which Xen Host to migrate it to, and even whether migration is a viable option at all.

Q: Why can some Linux operating systems be installed directly from media, whereas others require a network-based install?

A: Hardware virtualization is a relatively new development in the x86 arena. Older operating systems are not "virtualization-aware," so they will not run as an unmodified XenVM. In contrast, the latest batch of Linux from Red Hat and SUSE "understands" virtualization.

Q: Is export/import a viable technique for implementing workload balancing?

A: It really depends on the availability requirements of the underlying application. Exports and imports can require long periods of time to complete, as the data from the XenVM is transported to and from the Administrator Console over the network. If the application can be down for those periods, export/import may be a viable technique.

Q: Are live migrations quicker than export/import?

A: Yes, they are; however, live migrations require higher technical and financial commitments. Live migrations reduce downtime greatly when you're trying to achieve workload balancing; however, they require higher-bandwidth network and shared storage (SAN). These requirements increase the environment's complexity and create additional administrative overhead.

## Chapter 7

Advanced
Xen Concepts

Solutions in this chapter:

- **The Virtual Split Devices Model**

- **Advanced Storage Concepts**

- **Advanced Networking Concepts**

- **Building a Xen Cluster**

- **XenVM Migration**

- **XenVM Backup and Recovery Solutions**

- **Full Virtualization in Xen**

☑ **Summary**

☑ **Solutions Fast Track**

☑ **Frequently Asked Questions**

Introduction

Xen is an advanced virtualization solution that encapsulates three layers of virtualization: devices, memory, and CPU. Due to these types of virtualization, which are sophisticated and difficult to implement, you can achieve very good performance results with Xen.

In this chapter, we will discuss advanced Xen concepts like storage and networking, live migration, clustering, and backup solutions. Various solutions exist in these areas, and we will discuss the pros and cons of some of them.

The Virtual Split Devices Model

In Xen, I/O is performed by virtual split devices, which have a frontend layer and a backend layer. The idea behind this is safe and efficient hardware isolation. The backend layer is part of domain 0 (dom0). It is the only layer that has direct access to the hardware devices in a default Xen installation. Note that it is possible to configure domUs with hardware access, too—something called "driver domains." Also note that work is done to enable domUs to access hardware devices (such as infiniband) without usage of driver domains—for example, there is ongoing research about VMM-bypass for I/O access using infiniband for VM environments (see http://nowlab.cse.ohio-state.edu/publications/conf-papers/2006/usenix06.pdf). Each unprivileged domain has a frontend layer of itself. Access from the frontend to the backend and backwards is performed by event channels and shared memory. Each domain can have up to 1024 event channels on i386 machines, and up to 4096 event channels on x86_64 machines. The frontend and backend share memory pages for communication, which is controlled by a grant tables mechanism. Figure 7.1 illustrates the Split Devices mechanism.

Figure 7.1 Split Devices Diagram

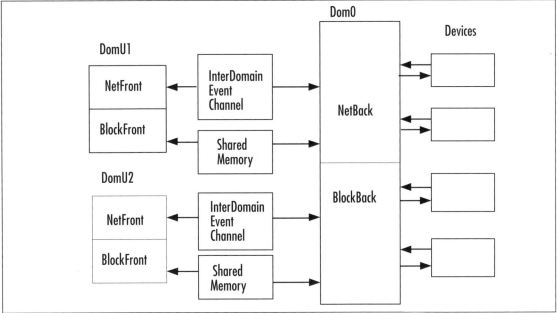

Advanced Storage Concepts

A variety of storage methods can be used in Xen. The main reason for employing the Copy-On-Write method is to save disk space. When thinking about sharing storage—a mandatory requirement in many cases—iSCSI storage is one of the available solutions. We discuss the various storage solutions in the following sections.

High-Performance Solutions for Xen

Disk access is done in Xen by a virtual block device (VBD). Any block device that can be accessed from the block backend can be exported as a VBD. These devices include Network Block Devices (NBDs), iSCSI, Logical Volume Manager (LVM) devices, Global Network Block Devices (GNBDs), and more. The disk = […] entry in the domain configuration file shows the mapping between the device node and the VBD. The VBD is a split device, (as explained earlier in this chapter), and messages that pass between the BlockFront and the BlockEnd can be of two types: READ or WRITE.

When you work with a physical device, you should have a disk = ['phy:…'] entry in the domain configuration file; and when you work with a file, you should have a disk = ['file:…'] entry in that configuration file. When working with iSCSI devices, this entry can be: disk = ['phy:...'], and if you have the block–iSCSI script installed, it can also be: ['iscsi:...']—for example, disk = ['iscsi: iqn.2001–04.com.example:diskarrays-sn-a8675309', hda, w']. More details on this option later in the chapter.

In certain cases, you should have some type of shared file system or clustered file system—for example, when performing live migration, or when you have a Xen-based cluster. Live migration only handles the transfer of memory pages; file systems are not transferred. As a result, a shared file system is needed, so an application that performs I/O will be able to continue to run as before. When working in a cluster, multiple clients can access shared storage. In such cases, you should not use an ordinary file system because of the risk of data corruption. Thus, you must use a cluster file system, which has a locking mechanism to avoid data corruption. Also, in some cases, you may want to use a Copy-on-Write image, because it needs less disk capacity.

iSCSI Integration with Xen

iSCSI is a transport protocol that works on top of TCP (see RFC 3720). You do not have to buy expensive equipment to use it and it is quite simple to deploy. In Red Hat Fedora Core, the storage is called "iscsi-target" and the client is termed "iscsi-initiator." In SUSE, the storage is named "iscsi-server," and the client is termed "iscsi-client." The iSCSI storage can have one or more logical units that process client commands. Logical units are assigned identifying numbers called logical unit numbers (LUNs). iSCSI is a block-level protocol that encapsulates SCSI commands into TCP/IP frames. After an iSCSI client logs in to an iSCSI server, a session is held between them. The iSCSI target can be configured to require authentication for login. The iSCSI session is in layer 5 (session layer) of the OSI seven-layer model. In most cases, the performance of iSCSI is worse than Fibre Channel due to the overhead added by using the TCP/IP protocol. However, employing technologies that become more and more popular, like Gigabit and 10Gb/s network cards or network cards with TCP Offload Engine (TOE), may reduce this overhead. An iSCSI initiator can be a software initiator or a hardware-based iSCSI initiator (host bus adapter, HBA). HBA is in fact an extended network interface card. In addition to performing all regular network card functions, it also processes iSCSI protocol commands and iSCSI TCP commands, thus freeing the system CPU from doing iSCSI processing.

TIP

You can download an open-source implementation of iSCSI from SourceForge.net. To build an iSCSI target, download the iSCSI Enterprise Target (iET) at http://iscsitarget.sf.net. You can also download and install an iSCSI initiator supported on Linux from www.open-iscsi.org (see Figure 7.2).

Figure 7.2 iSCSI Initiators and an iSCSI Target

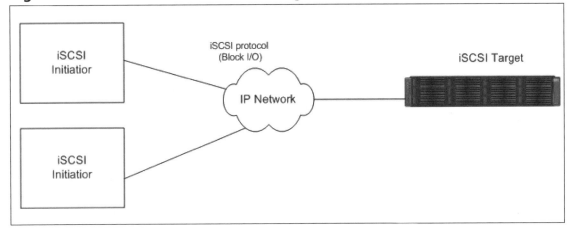

Configuring & Implementing...

Setting Up an iSCSI Initiator

In order to set up an iSCSI initiator on your Xen host to access iSCSI-based storage, you must configure the initiator using user space tools. Here is an example of a three-step process.

Continued

1. First, send a SendTargets message from the initiator to get a list of available iSCSI targets using the following command:

```
iscsiadm -m discovery —type sendtargets -p 192.168.0.190:3260
```

2. Then, in order to show discovered targets, perform the following:

```
iscsiadm -m node
(192.168.0.190:3260,1 iqn.2001-04.com.example:storage.disk2.sys1.xyz
```

3. To log in to that target, use

```
iscsiadm -m node -T iqn.2001-04.com.example:storage.disk2.sys1.xyz -p
192.168.0.190 -l
```

4. You can log out from a target by using

```
iscsiadm -m node -T iqn.2001-04.com.example:storage.disk2.sys1.xyz -p
192.168.0.190 -u)
```

The target replies to the *SendTargets* command by returning a list of all iSCSI nodes it knows about.

We should mention here that you may also encounter queries to an Internet Storage Name Server (iSNS). This server allows iSCSI targets to register with a central point.

You can see by tail /var/log/messages which device was assigned to the target (sda, sdb, and so on). /var/log/messages is the kernel log file. Alternatively, you can use fdisk –l to detect new, added devices or use a utility called lsscsi to view your SCSI devices and detect which device was added. You can download lsscsi from http://sg.torque.net/scsi/lsscsi.html.

Next, you can add the device in the domU configuration file by either setting the *disk = ['phy: …]* entry to point to that device or by using a script to accomplish the same.

TIP

If you want to implement a script to facilitate iSCSI storage for Xen, the block-iscsi script created by Kurt Garloff from SUSE R&D is a great example to follow. You can download Kurt's script at: www.suse.de/~garloff/linux/xen/scripts/block-iscsi.

To modify the script to meet your needs, adjust the disk entry as follows, where the iqn is the node you discovered and want to use.

```
    disk = [ 'iscsi: iqn.2001-04.com.example:diskarrays-sn-a8675309', hda,
w' ]
```

Using iSCSI storage this way does not require anything special to configure in domU; the disadvantage of using iSCSI storage in this manner is its slowness. A better way is to use iSCSI storage directly from domU: perform the login to iSCSI targets from domU and mount them from domU. This requires some configuration on domU (for example, for automatic iSCSI log in to the iSCSI targets).

NOTE

Every initiator and target node must have a single name defined for it. This name is used as part of all sessions between iSCSI targets and initiators. iSCSI names are of two types.

iqn stands for iSCSI qualified name. iSCSI devices, or nodes, must be allocated unique names. The iqn is the preferred standard. Its format is "iqn" plus a date field plus the reverse DNS name with unique qualifiers. For example: iqn.2001-04.com.example:diskarrays-sn-a8675309.

The other type is Enterprise Unique Identifier (*eui*). Its format is "eui" plus 16 hex digits. For example,
eui.02004567A425678D.

Copy-on-Write

Copy-on-Write (CoW) is an optimization technique for storage. The premise is that when multiple clients want to modify their copy of the resource, the operating system hands all of the clients' pointers to the same resource. When a client wants to modify its copy of the resource, a true copy is created to prevent making changes to that copy, which is owned by the other clients.

A variety of CoW solutions can be used for Xen, including the following:

- Blktap
- DmUserspace
- UnionFS

Blktap is a user space toolkit that provides user level disk I/O. It consists of a kernel module and some user space libraries. It uses the asynchronous calls of Linux libaio. It is already included as part of the Xen project. You can create a qcow disk using a utility called qcow-create, which is a utility that is part of Xen blktap tools. qcow is one of the formats supported by the QEMU processor emulator open-source project, which Xen uses. It represents a fixed-size block device in a file. Since a qcow image has an asynchronous backend, the performance when working with blktap with qcow images is good. It also supports AES encryption and transparent decompression. You can use it in domU by using the tap:qcow option for a QCOW image in the configuration file of the guest domain, such as in the following sample:

```
disk = [ 'tap:qcow:/server/qcow.img,xvda,w' ]
```

NOTE

Blktap has utilities for qcow conversion. *img2qcow* converts a raw disk or file system DomU image into a qcow image, and *qcow2raw* converts a qcow image into a raw file system or disk image.

DmUserspace

DmUserspace provides Copy-on-Write behavior by user space control over the device mapper. It exists as a patch to Xen and as a standalone module with user space tools. It is in the process of being integrated into the Linux kernel device mapper. Its use is simple. If you use the patch version, you just need to adjust the disk entry in the domU configuration file. For example, instead of:

```
disk = [ 'phy:/dev/vols/os,hda1,w' ]
```

It should be something like:

```
disk = [ 'dmu:dscow:/work/os.dscow: /dev/vols/os,hda1,w' ]
```

When the domain starts, all changes made to the disk will be stored in /work/os.dscow; the base image /dev/vols/os will not change.

If you don't use the patched version, you will need to first create a Copy-on-Write dscow image with the *dscow_tool* by running the following command:

```
dscow_tool -c /tmp/mydom.dscow /tmp/base.img
```

Then, start cowd, the user space daemon, to create a pseudo device called myblockdev as follows:

```
cowd -p dscow myblockdev /tmp/mydom.dscow
```

This will create a device named /dev/mapper/myblockdev, which will behave as a block device and will have Copy-on-Write semantics. All writes will be saved in /tmp/mydom.dscow. The base image, /tmp/base.img, will not change. DmUserspace also includes qcow support.

> **NOTE**
>
> DmUserspace was written by Dan Smith of the IBM Linux Technology Center. For more information, see http://static.danplanet.com/dm-userspace.

UnionFS

UnionFS is a stackable file system that enables you to manage a set of directories as a single unified view. Each directory is called a branch and has a priority and can be either read-only or read-write. When the highest priority branch is read-write, UnionFS provides you with copy-on-write semantics for read-only branches. You can use UnionFS in Xen by initrd—for example, see http://wiki.xensource.com/xenwiki/GinoUnionCOW. It can be done also without initrd (for example, see http://wiki.xensource.com/xenwiki/InstructionsFromMichaelLang). UnionFS is currently not part of the Linux kernel, but it is in Andrew Morton's mm tree and is in the process of being integrated into the Linux kernel. For more information about UnionFS, see: http://www.fsl.cs.sunysb.edu/project-unionfs.html.

> **NOTE**
>
> UnionFS is used in LiveCD projects like Knoppix, SLAX, Clusterix, and more. For more information, visit www.am-utils.org/project-unionfs.html.

Advanced Networking Concepts

Xen has two primary networking architecture options: bridging and routing. The default is bridging. In order to change it to routing, change the network-script entry in /etc/xen/xend-config.sxp from network-bridge to network-route, and the vif-script entry from vif-bridge to vif-route. Whenever working with bridging, when xend starts it runs the /etc/xen/scripts/network-bridge script. First, it renames the eth0 interface to peth0. Than it creates a bridge named xenbr0, and two interfaces are added to this bridge: peth0 and vif0.0. You can attach other interfaces to the bridge using brctl xenbr0 addif interfaceName. You can also see which interfaces belong to the bridge via brctl show and create new bridges in dom0 by using brctl add. The vif-bridge script is called for the unprivileged domains virtual interfaces.

Apart from the networking scripts mentioned previously, there are also scripts for configuring a NAT—and for more complex network settings, you can add scripts of your own. All of the scripts are located under /etc/xen/scripts.

Bridging VLANs

VLAN stands for virtual LAN. It is a method for creating independent networks within a LAN. It is implemented by tagging the Ethernet frame using the IEEE 802.1Q tagging protocol. Using VLAN improves overall performance, because multi-casts and broadcasts from VLANs are kept within the VLAN (broadcast domain). You can also configure VLAN for security. VLANs can be defined in software using the vconfig utility. For more information on VLAN, go to http://linux-net.osdl.org/index.php/VLAN.

Configuring & Implementing...

VLAN Creation

Suppose you want to create a VLAN from dom0 and add to it eth0 from dom0 and a virtual interface from domU. To do this, create VLANs from domain 0 using the following process:

1. Load the VLAN kernel module:

```
modprobe 8021q
```

Continued

2. Run the following commands, which add eth0 to a VLAN that has a VID of 45 (the number was chosen arbitrarily):

```
vconfig add eth0 45
ifconfig eth0.45 up 192.168.0.1 netmask 255.255.255.0
```

Verify the configuration by running ifconfig –a in dom0. This should show you that eth0.45 is among the other interfaces of this domain.

In order to configure an interface to be in a VLAN in domU, do the following:

1. Create the file: /etc/sysconfig/network-scripts/ifcfg-eth0:45. In this file, add the following lines:

```
DEVICE=eth0:45
BOOTPROTO=static
IPADDR=192.168.0.2
NETMASK=255.255.255.0
ONBOOT=YES
TYPE=Ethernet
VLAN=yes
```

2. Bring up the interface.

WARNING

Do not try to use the NetworkManager utility when working with bridging in Xen. It won't work properly, and other network control programs may not work correctly either.

Creating Interface Bonds for High Availability and Link Aggregation

Bonding is a Linux driver for aggregating multiple network interfaces into a single logical interface. By doing this, you can achieve high availability. The bonding module detects link failures and reroutes the traffic to a different interface. With bonding, you can assign two or more network cards the same IP address.

Configuring & Implementing…

Bonding Example

Suppose you have three network cards: eth0, eth1, and eth2, and you want to create a bond between eth1 and eth2 in dom0. The following are the steps you must take to accomplish this:

1. In /etc/modprobe.conf, add the following lines:

```
alias bond0 bonding

options bond0 miimon=100 mode=0
```

Then, we will create the following configuration file: /etc/sysconfig/network-scripts/ifcfg-bond0.

It will have the following data:

```
DEVICE=bond0

BOOTPROTO=none

ONBOOT=no
```

2. Change the entries in two files under the /etc/sysconfig/network-scripts directory so both eth1 and eth2 will work with bonding. This can be done by using the following code:

```
/etc/sysconfig/network-scripts/ifcfg-eth1 will be:

DEVICE=eth1

BOOTPROTO=none

ONBOOT=no

MASTER=bond0

SLAVE=yes


/etc/sysconfig/network-scripts/ifcfg-eth2 will be:

DEVICE=eth2

BOOTPROTO=none

ONBOOT=no

MASTER=bond0

SLAVE=yes
```

3. Restart the interfaces by using

Continued

```
        service network restart
```

   4. **Create a bridge in dom0, named xenBondBridge, by running the following:**

```
brctl addbr xenBondBridge
```

   5. **Disable arp and multicast as follows:**

```
ip link set xenBondBridge arp off
ip link set xenBondBridge multicast off
ip link set xenBondBridge up
ip link set xenBondBridge address fe:ff:ff:ff:ff:ff
ip link set xenBondBridge arp off
ip link set xenBondBridge multicast off
```

   6. **Add the bond to the bridge you created and start the bond:**

```
brctl addif xenBondBridge bond0
ifup bond0
```

WARNING

Trying to add bond0 to a bridge without disabling arp and multicast will result in an error that reads "Can't add bond0 to the bridge."

Routing, Forwarding, and Other Network Tricks

When you are working with routing, starting xend will call the network-route script, which enables IP forwarding by setting /proc/sys/net/ipv4/ip_forward in dom0 to a value of 1. When a guest domain starts, the vif-route is called. It copies the address of eth0 into vif<id#>.0 (id# is the ID of domU when it starts).

TIP

You can use the ebtables filtering tool to filter traffic in the bridge (see http://ebtables.sourceforge.net). Using ebtables, you can perform packet filtering based on the Link Layer Ethernet frame fields. You can also alter MAC addresses. Ebtables is part of the Linux kernel.

Building a Xen Cluster

Xen is an ideal candidate Virtual Machine Monitor (VMM) for a high-performance computing (HPC) paravirtualization system given its performance metrics and its large-scale development efforts. Lawrence Livermore National Laboratory (LLNL) did some interesting research on the performance impact of Xen using current HPC commodity hardware. The results show that usually the Xen solution poses no statistically significant overhead over other OS configurations currently in use at LLNL for HPC clusters, except in very specific cases. (See "Paravirtualization for HPC Systems" by Rich Wolski *et al.* at www.cs.ucsb.edu/~ckrintz/papers/ISPA-XenHPC.pdf.)

Several deployments come to mind for Xen-based clusters—for example, a single computer that acts as a complete cluster, running several Xen guests. Another deployment configuration can be a cluster where each node runs some domU guests. These guests may run on every node of the cluster. Should a crash occur, this guest may start on a different node in a very short time. You can use live migration of domains for maintenance and for load balancing in such a deployment configuration. This illustrates some of the benefits of deploying a Xen-based cluster.

Possible solutions for building a Xen cluster can be Red Hat Cluster Suite (see http://sourceware.org/cluster) or Oracle Real Application Cluster (RAC) (see www.oracle.com/technology/products/database/clustering/index.html). The nodes will be Xen domUs.

When you are choosing a file system for the cluster, two options are recommended: GFS (or GFS2) and OCFS2. GFS, the Global File System from Red Hat, is a shared storage file system available for clusters. It has a distributed lock manager (dlm), which enables the secured sharing of files using a locking mechanism. GFS is part of the Linux kernel. GFS2 is an improved version of GFS and is part of version 2 of the Red Hat Cluster Suite.

OCFS2 (Oracle Cluster File System) is a cluster file system. It has many similarities to ext3 and has a distributed lock manager that is implemented differently than GFS dlm. It was integrated into the version 2.6.16 of the Linux kernel. It is posix-compliant and is a journaling file system. It supports direct I/O and asynchronous I/O. OCFS2 has its own kernel space cluster membership service and heartbeat functions. It comes with two in-memory file systems: configfs and ocfs2-dlmfs. OCFS2 uses configfs to communicate with the in-kernel heartbeat thread and the in-kernel node manager; ocfs2_dlmfs, on the other hand, is used by OCFS2 tools to communicate with the in-kernel dlm OCFS2 for releasing or taking dlm locks. OCFS2 is not compatible with OCFS1. It also uses debugfs, an in-memory file system developed by Greg Kroah-Hartman. It helps in the debugging process as it lets code in kernel space export data easily to userspace.

Fencing, or I/O Fencing, is a mechanism for removing a malfunctioning node from a cluster, thus preventing it from causing data corruption. Fencing supports two operations: removal of a node and recovery of a node. When heartbeat detects that a node fails, the cluster manager directs the fencing system to remove that node from the cluster. The most effective way to do this is known as STONITH (an acronym that stands for "Shoot The Other Node In The Head"). It forces the system on that node to power off or reboot.

When setting up an RAC, you will need shared storage for the Oracle Cluster Registry (OCR) and for Database files. Apart from this, you will need shared storage for the Xen environment, which can be for example iSCSI or block devices. You also need at least two interfaces, one for private use (cluster interconnect) and one as a public interface (intranet).

NOTE

If you want a shared GFS/OCFS2 partition, you will need to add "w!" to the physical device ID in the domain configuration file. For example, disk=['phy:/dev/vg1/xenstore, sda2,w!'].

The following example shows how to set a Xen-based cluster using the Red Hat cluster suite (see Figure 7.3). Two nodes, host1 and host2, will run dom0 Xen, in which two domUs will run. Host3 and host4 will be the nodes for storage. On each of the storage nodes, host3 and host4, you will install and run Distributed Replicated Block Device (DRBD). Heartbeat service will run between host3 and host4.

Figure 7.3 A Xen Cluster

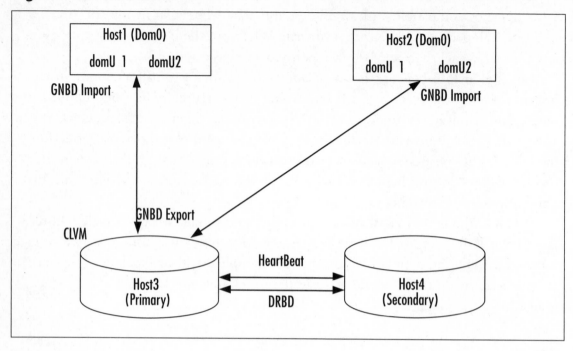

DRBD is a block device mirroring technique that is designed to build high-availability clusters. This is done by mirroring a whole block device via network TCP connection. You could think of it as a network RAID1.

First, you will install drbd-8 by performing the following actions:

```
wget http://oss.linbit.com/drbd/8.0/drbd-8.0.1.tar.gz .
tar xvzf drbd-8.0.1.tar.gz
cd drbd-8.0.1
make KDIR=/work/src/xen-3.0.4_1-src/linux-2.6.16.33-xen
make install && make tools && make install-tools
```

Then, you should configure the /etc/drbd.conf file.

An example of a drbd.conf for two nodes—node3 and node4—follows:

```
resource cluster {
protocol C;
handlers {
    pri-on-incon-degr  "echo '!DRBD! pri on incon-degr' | wall ; sleep 60; halt -
f";
    }
startup {
```

```
 degr-wfc-timeout 120;
}
disk {
 on-io-error detach;
}
net {}
syncer {
 rate 5M;
}
on node3 {
 device /dev/drbd0;
 disk /dev/vg1/cluster;
 address 192.168.0.73:7788;
 meta-disk internal;
}
on node4 {
 device /dev/drbd0;
 disk /dev/vg1/cluster;
 address 192.168.0.74:7788;
 meta-disk internal;
}
}
```

As you have probably noticed, the "disk /dev/vg1/cluster" entry refers to a storage device you have not yet created. Now you will create it. To create storage partitions, first install the lvm2-cluster; this is the cluster extensions for userspace logical volume management tools. It runs a daemon called clvmd, which distributes LVM metadata updates around a cluster. All nodes in the cluster must run the clvmd daemon. You do this by downloading the code from ftp://sources.redhat.com/pub/lvm2 and building it.

Suppose /dev/sda5 is the partition you intend to use for DRBD replication. If so, you must create logical volumes with the *same size* on all storage nodes. (By the way, when using software RAID1, there is a similar size equality constraint.)

NOTE

Protocol C in the configuration file, drbd.conf, specifies that write IO is reported as completed if it has reached both local and remote disk. Two other valid protocol specifiers exist: B and C.

Protocol A specifies that write IO is reported as completed if it has reached the local disk and local TCP send buffer, while protocol B specifies that write IO is reported as completed if it has reached the local disk and remote buffer cache.

```
pvcreate /dev/sd5a
vgcreate vg1 /dev/sda5
lvcreate -L 10G -n cluster vg1
```

pvcreate initializes PhysicalVolume for later use by the Logical Volume Manager (LVM), and *vgcreate* creates a volume group named vg1. Subsequently, *lvcreate* creates a logical volume in the volume group we created, vg1. This logical volume is 10G in size and is named "cluster."

NOTE

Without the –n (name) option, a default name of "lvol#" will be generated where # is the LVM internal number of the logical volume.

The drbdadm is the administration tool for DRBD. The first time you want to activate the nodes, run "drbdadm create-md resourceName" to initialize the meta-data storage.

The command *drbdadm up* is a shortcut for attach and connect.

Now perform the following two commands on both nodes:

```
drbdadm create-md cluster
drbdadm up all
```

Both nodes started as Secondary and Inconsistent, as you can see by running cat /proc/drbd.

Choose one host to be the primary, and on that host run

```
drbdadm — —overwrite-data-of-peer  primary all
```

NOTE

In previous versions of DRBD, setting a node to be primary is done by using

drbdadm — —do-what-I-say primary all

The —overwrite-data-of-peer flag replaced —do-what-I-say flag for more clarity.

You can create an OCFS2 file system on /dev/drbd0 by using

```
mkfs.ocfs2 -L ocfs2_cluster /dev/drbd0
```

–L dictates that the volume label for this file system will be ocfs2.

Install the Red Hat cluster suite and apply the following two patches. (See www.redhat.com/archives/cluster-devel/2006-June/msg00162.html.)

```
wget ftp://sources.redhat.com/pub/cluster/releases/cluster-1.02.00.tar.gz
tar xvzf cluster-1.02.00.tar.gz


cd cluster-1.02.00
./configure —kernel_src=/work/src/xen-3.0.4_1-src/linux-2.6.16.33-xen
make install
```

Load the gnbd module using

```
modprobe gnbd
```

Create a configuration cluster file for the cluster: /etc/cluster/cluster.conf. This is an XML file.

The following is a simple example of cluster.conf; the cluster has four nodes. host3 and host4 are the storage backend, which export a block device via gnbd. For the sake of simplicity, use empty fence tags.

```
<?xml version="1.0"?>
<cluster name="xencluster" config_version="1">


<clusternodes>
  <clusternode name="host1">
      <fence>
      </fence>
  </clusternode>
  <clusternode name="host2">
      <fence>
      </fence>
```

```
      </clusternode>
      <clusternode name="host3">
            <fence>
            </fence>
      </clusternode>
      <clusternode name="host4">
            <fence>
            </fence>
      </clusternodes>
<fencedevices>
</fencedevices>
</cluster>
```

The same cluster.conf should be on every node on the cluster.

The ccsd is a daemon that must be run on each node that wishes to join a cluster.

Start the ccsd daemon by using

```
ccsd
```

Afterward, each node should join the cluster by running

```
cman_tool join
```

When you want to leave the cluster, run

```
cman_tool leave
```

You can see the status of the cluster and the membership information of its nodes by running the *clustat* command. For example, after adding two hosts to the cluster—host3 and host4—and running *clustat*, you get

```
Member Status: Quorate

  Member Name                      ID    Status
  ___  __                          __  ___

    host3                           1 Online, Local
    host4                           2 Online
```

You need to export GNBD devices from storage backend. This is done by using

```
gnbd_serv
```

gnbd_serv will start the gnbd server daemon (gnbd_serv). Then use

```
gnbd_export -e clusterfs -d /dev/drbd0
```

(The –e specifies the gnbd export device: it will be /dev/gnbd/clusterfs.)

Import the GNBD storage device from storage backend by using

```
gnbd_import -i ipAddress
```

Install ocfs2-tools with the following:

```
wget http://oss.oracle.com/projects/ocfs2-tools/dist/files/source/v1.2/ocfs2-tools-
1.2.3.tar.gz .
tar xvfz ocfs2-tools-1.2.3.tar.gz
cd ocfs2-tools-1.2.3
./configure && make && make install
```

o2cb.init is the init script for ocfs2-tools. After installation, copy vendor/common/o2cb.init to /etc.init/o2cb. The o2cb was originally written for SLES and RHEL4, but it also supports other distributions like Fedora and others.

NOTE

The initial release of OCFS supported *only* Oracle database workloads, whereas OCFS2 provides full support as a general-purpose file system.

Prepare the configuration file /etc/ocfs2/cluster.conf. An exact copy of this file should be copied to all cluster nodes.

The following is an example of /etc/ocfs2/cluster.conf:

```
node:
        ip_port = 7777
        ip_address = 192.168.0.71
        number = 0
        name = host1
        cluster = xencluster

        ip_port = 7777
        ip_address = 192.168.0.72
        number = 1
        name = host2
        cluster = xencluster

node:
        ip_port = 7777
```

```
            ip_address = 192.168.0.73
            number = 2
            name = host3
            cluster = xencluster

node:
            ip_port = 7777
            ip_address = 192.168.0.74
            number = 3
            name = host4
            cluster = xencluster

cluster:
            node_count = 4
            name = xencluster
```

If a new node is being added to the cluster, all existing nodes must have their "cluster.conf" updated *before* mounting the ocfs2 partition from the new node. Moreover, changes to this file must be propagated to the other nodes in the cluster. Also, changes in cluster.conf require that the cluster be restarted for the changes to take effect. The node name should match the hostname of the machine.

TIP

You can perform initial setup of OCFS2 using the ocfs2console graphical tool. Using this tool you can configure OCFS2 cluster nodes, propagate configuration to other nodes, and more.

Then you can mount the ocfs2 file system by running the following commands:

```
modprobe ocfs2
```

```
/etc/init.d/o2cb load
```

/etc/init.d/o2cb configure (For setting a configuration for OCFS2)

```
/etc/init.d/o2cb online xencluster
```

```
mount -t ocfs2 /dev/gnbd/clusterfs /mnt/cluster
```

You can get info about the ocsf2 modules with `/etc/init.d/o2cb status`, and unload the modules using `/etc/init.d/o2cb unload`. You can tune OCFS2 with the tunefs.ocfs2 utility, which enables you to increase the number of node slots (to increase the number of nodes that can concurrently mount the volume), change the volume label, and increase the size of the journal file.

Every cluster node imports the GNBD device, which is exported by the storage hosts and mounts it. OCFS2 is the cluster file system used in this GNBD device.

You can use heartbeat between the cluster storage nodes as a high availability solution. First, install the heartbeat service using

```
yum install heartbeat
```

Then you should configure three files: /etc/ha.d/ha.cf, /etc/ha.d/haresources, and /etc/ha.d/authkeys. DRBD installation creates a file named /etc/ha.d/resource.d/drbddisk. Configure it according to your needs; it is called when a DRBD host becomes primary. Afterwards, start the heartbeat service on both storage hosts, host3 and host4. For more on how to configure these files and on the heartbeat high availability solution, see www.linux-ha.org.

XenVM Migration

Live Migration enables us to transfer unprivileged domains between hosts on the same subnet. When performing live migration, the downtime is very low and reaches about 50 to 300ms.

In order to minimize downtime, live migration is done in stages. First, the source domain sends a request to a destination domain. The source domain cannot be domain 0. The destination domain verifies that it has enough resources for the request. This stage is called *Reservation*. If the destination host has enough resources, proceed to the second stage, where all memory pages are copied using a TCP socket. This stage is also called *Iterative Pre-copy*. Some iterations occur in this stage when in each iteration you copy the pages dirtied while the previous iteration occurred. Then at some edge, when there is a relatively small number of dirtied pages in each iteration, you stop the source domain and copy the remaining pages. This stage is called *Stop and Copy*. When this stage finishes, resume the VM on the destination host. This stage is called *Activation*.

To enable live migration, first edit the /etc/xen/config.sxp file and uncomment the following two lines:

```
#(xend-relocation-port 8002)
```

```
#(xend-relocation-address '')
```

The first line is for setting Xen to listen on TCP port 8002 for incoming migration requests. The second line permits connections from any host.

Run live migration from dom0 by using the following command:

```
xm migrate —live sourceDomain destinationDomain
```

You can view which domains are running on each machine by running xm list.

Figures 7.4 and 7.5 demonstrate live migration of domU4 from Host A to Host B:

Figure 7.4 Live Migration Stage A (Before Migration Started)

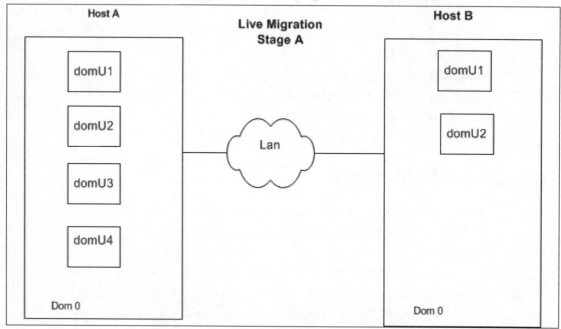

There is another type of migration, non-live migration, that pauses the source domain, copies the memory pages to the host, and resumes its operation on the host. The downtime when using non-live migration naturally is much longer. Non-live migration is done by issuing the same *xm migrate* command but omitting the —*live* flag.

Figure 7.5 Live Migration Stage B (after domU4 Was Transferred from Host A to Host B)

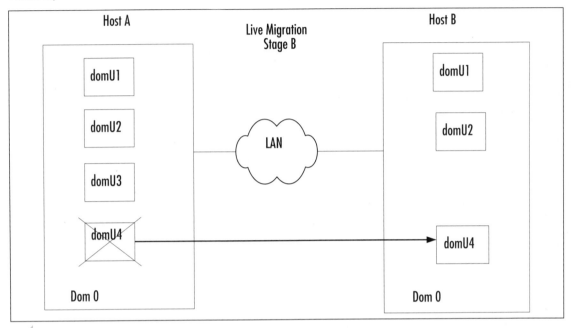

> **NOTE**
>
> It is important to notice that live migration does not transfer the file system from the source to the destination. It is assumed that both domains, source and destination, share the same file system, by means of a Fibre-Channel or iSCSI SAN or NFS, for example, or any other shared storage method.

You can use live migration as a solution for load balancing or a disaster recovery plan, or for taking down physical machines for maintenance without stopping the VM running on them, or for managing a pool of VMs running on a cluster.

Another method of migration is called "self migration." In self migration, the unprivileged domain being migrated handles the migration itself. For more on live migration and self migration, visit www.cl.cam.ac.uk/research/srg/netos/papers/2005-migration-nsdi-pre.pdf.

Currently migration of Windows-based domUs is not supported in Xen. Supposedly, in near-future releases of Xen, live migration of Hardware Virtual Machine (HVM) domains will be supported.

XenVM Backup and Recovery Solutions

One of the most important tasks of system administrators is preparing a backup and recovery solution. With that in mind, we will next discuss some solutions for the backup and recovery of Xen guests.

Options for Backing Up Your XenVM

In a configuration where all block devices in domUs are provided by LVM, you can use lvm-snapshots. You can mount a snapshot in dom0 and then use a backup tool, such as *rsnapshot* or *rdiff-backup* or *duplicity*, to perform a backup. *rsnapshot* is a backup utility based on rsync. For more information, see www.rsnapshot.org.

If you don't have LVM, you can shut down domU and then back it up using some backup utility.

If you have domUs inside a DMZ and you don't have backup agents on them, you can do the following:

1. Make LVM snapshots of these domUs from dom0.

2. Block attach these snapshots to a backup server.

3. The backup server mounts the snapshots and backs them up the same way it backs up a local file system.

4. The backup server unmounts the snapshots.

5. The snapshots are block-detached.

6. The snapshots are discarded.

Block-attach and block-detach are subcommands of the *xm* command. They allow you to hotplug/unplug a block device to a domU. Block-list shows the list of block devices attached to a domain. An example for the preceding series of actions could be:

```
lvcreate -L1G -s -n mydomU sata/mydomU-snapshots
xm block-attach amandaserver phy:sata/mydomU-snapshots
blkid=$(xm block-list amandaserver| tail -n 1| awk '{ print $1; }')
xm block-detach amandaserver $blkid
lvremove -f sata1/mydomU-snap
```

Making Xen Part of Your Disaster Recovery Plan

You can install Xen with Software RAID1, or disk mirroring. The following example demonstrates the installation of Xen on /dev/md0, which uses a RAID set comprised of sda2 and sdb2. All writes are performed to both disks. Should the Xen host experience a disk failure, the other disk can replace it. See www.freax.be/wiki/index.php/Installing_Xen_with_RAID_1_on_a_Fedora_Core_4_x86_64_SMP_machine for more information.

A different strategy for disaster recovery could consist of the following: suppose you want a disaster recovery for a Xen-based server. If the server does not contain data, like a Web server (apache for example), you can perform "xm save" once a week or once a month, copy the saved image to a disaster recovery server, and then perform "xm restore" on the Web server since "xm save" stops the domain. If some disaster occurs (a motherboard or hardware failure, for example), run "xm restore" on the recovery disaster server, fix the fault on the problematic server, and migrate that domU back to the server. If the server is a database server, however, you should also back up the file system using common backup methods like LVM snapshot.

Full Virtualization in Xen

On x86 processors, when running in protected mode, there are four privilege levels. The operating system kernel executes in privilege level 0 (also called "supervisor mode") while applications execute in privilege level 3. Privilege levels 1 and 2 were not used, except in rare cases (for example, in OS/2). Certain special instructions to the processor are only allowed in privilege level 0 since they affect the whole systems behavior. When the processor detects such an instruction at a level other than privilege level 0, it generates a general-protection violation.

There are two general approaches to virtualization: full virtualization and paravirtualization. Paravirtualization is based on a principle of making some sections of the operating system aware that it's running on top of a virtual machine monitor, actually known as the hypervisor. The hypervisor will manage the different virtual machines (also known as guests)—for example, letting each guest run for a certain amount of time and then the next guest for another set amount of time, thus allowing the guests to appear to run simultaneously (similar to the way the operating system deals with multiple applications). Part of the modification to the operating system is to shift all privilege level 0 code into privilege level 1, which means the code will occasionally cause a general protection fault that ends up inside the hypervisor, which helps the hypervisor track and control what the guest is doing.

The New Processors with Virtual Extensions (VT-x and AMD-V)

Full virtualization (a.k.a., unmodified guests) is based on no changes to the operating system source-code, and is very difficult to achieve without hardware extensions in the processor. Hardware manufacturers like Intel and AMD have begun to recently (starting in 2005) develop processors with built-in virtualization extensions. With these new processors, you can run an unmodified guest operating system.

Naturally, many will prefer a situation where the guest operating system code need not be modified, especially in the case of a closed-source operating system like Windows or operating systems with a small user-base that makes the effort of modifying the operating system source-code prohibitively expensive.

Intel has developed the VT-x technology for the x86 processor. This technology provides hardware virtualization extensions. With Intel's VT-x, the VMM runs in "VMX root operation mode" while the guests (which are unmodified OSes) run in "VMX non-root operation mode." While running in this mode, the guests are more restricted, and some instructions, like RDMSR, WRMSR, and CPUID, will cause a "VM exit" to the VMM. VM exit is a transition from non-root operation to root operation. Some instructions and exceptions will cause a "VM exit" when the configured conditions are met. Xen handles the VM exit in a manner that is specific to the particular exception.

To implement this hardware virtualization, Intel added a new structure called VMCS (Virtual Machine Control Structure), which handles much of the virtualization management functionality. This structure contains the exit reason in the case of a VM exit. Also, ten new instruction opcodes were added in VT-x.

These new opcodes manage the VT-x virtualization behavior. For example, the VMXON instruction starts VMX operation, while the VMREAD instruction reads specified fields from the VMCS, and the VMWRITE instruction writes specified fields to the VMCS. When a processor operates in VMX root operation mode, its behavior is much like when it operates in normal operating mode. However, in normal operating mode, these 10 new opcodes are not available.

Intel also published its VT-d (Intel(r) Virtualization Technology for Directed I/O). VT-d enables I/O devices to be directly assigned to virtual machines. It also defines DMA remapping logic that can be configured for an individual device. There is also a cache called an IOTLB which improves performance. For more details on VT-d, see Intel's documentation at http://download.intel.com/technology/computing/vptech/Intel(r)_VT_for_Direct_IO.pdf.

In AMD-V—a.k.a., SVM (Secure Virtual Machine)—there is something quite similar, but the terminology is a bit different: You have Host Mode and Guest Mode. The VMM runs in Host Mode and the guests run in Guest Mode. In Guest Mode, some instructions cause VM EXIT, which is handled in a manner that is specific to the way Guest Mode is entered.

AMD added a new structure called the VMCB (Virtual Machine Control Block), which handles much of the virtualization management functionality. The VMCB includes an exit reason field which is read when a VM EXIT occurs. AMD added eight new instruction opcodes to support SVM. For example, the VMRUN instruction starts the operation of a guest OS, the VMLOAD instruction loads the processor state from the VMCB, and the VMSAVE instruction saves the processor state to the VMCB. The VMCB contains a set of bits to indicate to the processor which particular instructions are to cause a VMEXIT and which can flow freely in the guest.

For more details, see the *AMD64 Architecture Programmer's Manual*, Volume 2: System Programming, Chapter 15, titled "Secure Virtual Machine," which is available at www.amd.com/usen/assets/content_type/white_papers_and_tech_docs/24593.pdf.

AMD also had published its I/O virtualization technology specification (IOMMU).

The AMD IOMMU technology intercepts devices' access to memory. It finds out to which guest a particular device is assigned, and decides whether access is permitted and whether the actual address is available in system memory (page protection and address translation). You can think of AMD IOMMU as providing two facilities for AMD processors: the Graphics Aperture Remapping Table (GART) and the Device Exclusion Vector (DEV). In the AMD IOMMU, there is optional support for IOTLBs. For more details, see AMD I/O virtualization technology (IOMMU) specification Rev 1.00 at www.amd.com/usen/assets/content_type/white_papers_and_tech_docs/34434.pdf.

Since AMD and Intel are similar in many ways, a common API called HVM (Hardware Virtual Machine) was developed. For example, HVM defines a table called hvm_function_table, which is a structure containing functions common to both Intel VT-x and AMD SVM. These methods are implemented differently in the VT-x and AMD SVM trees.

With Xen running in paravirtualized mode, there is a device model based on Backend/Frontend virtual drivers (also called "split drivers"). See the introduction to this chapter. The Backend is in domain 0, while the Frontend is in the unprivileged domains. They communicate via an interdomain event channel and a shared memory area (using the sharing mechanism of grant tables).

Only domain 0 has access to the hardware through the unmodified Linux drivers. When running on VT-x or SVM, you cannot use this IO model because the guests run unmodified Linux kernels. So both VT-x and SVM use the emulated device sub-system of QEMU for their I/O. QEMU runs in Xen as a userspace process. Using QEMU has a performance cost, so, in the future, it is possible that QEMU will be replaced by a better performing solution. It is, however, important to understand that an IOMMU layer, even one built according to the new AMD or Intel specs, cannot in itself be a replacement for QEMU, because the same device may need to be shared between multiple domains.

It is possible for an unmodified guest to use paravirtual (frontend) drivers in the same way as paravirtualized mode, but drivers must be developed for the particular OS being used as a guest.

As mentioned earlier, Intel VT-x and AMD SVM have much in common (like usage of QEMU and the common API which HVM abstracts). However, some differences do arise—for example:

- The AMD SVM uses a tagged TLB; this means they use an ASID (Address Space Identifier) to distinguish between host-space entries from guest-space entries. By using this identifier, you don't have to perform a TLB flush when there is a context switch between guest and host. This significantly reduces the number of TLB flushes. A TLB flush slows the system because after a TLB flush occurs, subsequent accesses to memory will require a full page table lookup.

- Intel's VTX doesn't support real-mode. In order to boot an Intel VT-x machine, you need a special piece of code called VMXassist, which uses VM86-mode to simulate real-mode. Using a Linux loader to load a guest OS starts in real mode. AMD SVM, on the other hand, supports real-mode for guests, so it does not need the VM86 mode of the VMXassist.

Next-generation processors with virtualization extensions from both AMD and Intel will probably have new, exiting features that improve performance and functionality; one new feature will probably be IOMMU support, which was discussed briefly earlier. Another feature is multilevel translation in hardware; this feature will improve the process of the domU virtual addresses translation process. There is already some support for this feature in the unstable version of Xen—it is called hap (hardware assisted paging). (In AMD processors, this feature is called "nested paging.")

In conclusion, we can see many similarities between Intel VT-x and AMD SVM when running Xen, sometimes the terms are even similar (like VM Entry/VM Exit). In addition, performance slowdown due to QEMU is common to both. Moreover, next generation processors will probably also have some similar features.

For more information about the new processors with virtualization extensions from AMD and Intel, see http://wiki.xensource.com/xenwiki/XenIntro.

Summary

Xen provides support in several advanced areas, like storage and networking. You can integrate Xen with advanced storage methods like iSCSI or various CoW solutions. You can also apply various networking solutions like using VLANs, bonding, routing, and more. You have seen that Xen can be integrated easily into a cluster in various deployment configurations—for example, in the Red Hat cluster suite or Oracle Real Application Cluster (RAC). Overall, Xen is an interesting virtualization project that evolves dynamically and seems to support many highly advanced features in various areas.

Solutions Fast Track

The Virtual Split Devices Model

☑ Xen uses virtual split device drivers for virtual I/O with frontend and backend layers. The frontend drivers are used in unprivileged guests, domUs, while backend drivers are used in dom0.

☑ It is possible to create additional domains, domUs, with unmodified drivers for the underlying I/O devices. These domains are referred to as "driver domains."

☑ The frontend and backend use shared memory pages for communication. Access is controlled through the use of grant tables.

Advanced Storage Concepts

☑ All devices exported via iSCSI will be presented as SCSI disks, regardless of their type.

☑ CoW (Copy-on-Write) is an optimization technique for storage.

☑ For Xen, there is a variety of CoW solutions: blktap, DmUserspace, UnionFS, and more.

☑ iSCSI is a transport protocol that works on top of TCP.

Advanced Networking Concepts

- ☑ Xen has two primary networking architecture options: bridging and routing.

- ☑ By default, Xen starts with bridging.

- ☑ You can define VLANs in software using the vconfig utility.

- ☑ Bonding is a Linux driver for aggregating multiple network interfaces into a single logical interface.

- ☑ VLAN is a method for creating independent networks within a LAN.

Building a Xen Cluster

- ☑ Two file systems that are candidates for clusters are GFS and OCFS2.

- ☑ Both are included in the Linux Kernel.

- ☑ domUs are the nodes of the cluster.

- ☑ DRBD are used for network block-device mirroring.

XenVM Migration

- ☑ Live migration is the transfer of unprivileged domains between hosts on the same subnet.

- ☑ Live migration is performed using xm migrate –live sourceDomain destinationDomain.

- ☑ Live migration does not transfer the file system of the source to the destination.

- ☑ The downtime when using nonlive migration is much longer than the downtime when using live migration.

XenVM Backup and Recovery Solutions

- ☑ "xm save" stores an image of the domain; it can be used for recovery upon disaster.

- ☑ "xm restore" starts a domain from a saved image.

- ☑ Block-list shows the list of domains attached to a domain.

☑ Block-attach and block-detach allow you to hotplug/unplug a block device to a domU.

Full Virtualization in Xen

☑ There are two general approaches to virtualization: full virtualization and paravirtualization.

☑ New processors with virtualization extensions were developed to support running unmodified operating systems as guests. Intel had developed the VT-x and AMD had developed the AMD–V (a.k.a., SVM).

☑ A common API called HVM (Hardware Virtual Machine) was developed in Xen to support common functionality of the new processors with virtualization extensions.

☑ Some instructions and exceptions will cause a "VM exit" that will be handled in Xen in a manner specific to the particular exception.

Frequently Asked Questions

The following Frequently Asked Questions, answered by the authors of this book, are designed to both measure your understanding of the concepts presented in this chapter and to assist you with real-life implementation of these concepts. To have your questions about this chapter answered by the author, browse to **www.syngress.com/solutions** and click on the **"Ask the Author"** form.

Q: What is the maximum number of interfaces I can add in domU?

A: The maximum number of interfaces is restricted to three.

Q: I need to set a MAC address for a domain instead of a random address.

A: In the domain configuration file, use mac= … in the vif directive.

Q: How can I see which bridges are in dom0 and what they consist of?

A: Run *brctl show* from dom0.

Q: I see "STP disabled" when I run *brctl show*. What does "STP" stand for?

A: STP stands for Spanning Tree Protocol, a networking protocol for finding shortest paths and avoiding loops.

Q: How can I change the bridge name from xenbr0 to mybr0?

A: In xend-config.sxp, set the network-script to be (network-script 'network-bridge bridge=   mybr0).

Q: What is fencing?

A: Fencing is a mechanism for removing a malfunctioning node from a cluster.

Q: I want to install a Xen-based cluster. Which open-source file systems are available for me?

A: You can use GFS from Red Hat or OCFS2 from Oracle.

Q: Why other file systems are not suitable for such a cluster?

A: You need a locking mechanism against simultaneous writes from different clients.

Q: I saw that in some domU configuration files, the disk = […] entry includes the "ioemu" directive. What is it for?

A: When using full virtualization, you can use the "ioemu" directive, it tells Xen to use its patched QEMU driver for the device.

Q: What does GNBD stand for?

A: Global Network Block Device.

Q: What does the exclamation mark in the "disk" entry of the domU configuration file denote?

A: The exclamation mark notes that the storage device may be shared.

Q: What does DRBD stand for?

A: Distributed Replicated Block Device.

Q: And what does DRBD do?

A: It provides mirroring for block devices over a network TCP connection.

Q: What does STONITH stand for?

A: Shoot The Other Node In The Head.

Q: What does HVM stand for?

A: HVM is the acronym for hardware virtual machine. This is the common API for the new processors in Xen.

Q: What is the main benefit of full virtualization when compared with paravirtualization?

A: You can run an unmodified operating system with full virtualization, whereas when working with paravirtualization you must work with modified operating systems.

Q: What is the difference between full virtualization and paravirtualization in regards to the device driver model?

A: When working with paravirtualization, you use the split devices model. When working with full virtualization, you use the emulated device subsystem of QEMU for I/O.

## Chapter 8

The Future of Virtualization

Solutions in this chapter:

- **The Unofficial Xen Road Map**
- **Virtual Infrastructure in Tomorrow's Data Center**
- **The Magic Recipe: Other Hardware and Software Virtualization Trends**

☑ **Summary**

☑ **Solutions Fast Track**

☑ **Frequently Asked Questions**

Introduction

Virtualization… virtualization… virtualization. You have likely heard lots about virtualization in the past, and have probably reached your saturation point thanks to all of the chapters in this book. By now, you have either become excited about the possibilities and are sold on the concept as realized by products such as Xen, or you are still skeptical about what true value it could have for you or your company. Though all we have talked about is exciting indeed, we have only begun to tap into the potential of what virtualization can really do for enterprises. The promise of a reformed view of data center and infrastructure management will be the focus of many new technologies over the next few years. As server virtualization increases in popularity and becomes more commonplace, companies will look for other synergies within their own infrastructures to accomplish similar goals: simplification, cost containment, if not reduction, and consolidation.

In this final chapter, we will discuss the road map, including its various aspects as officially published by XenSource, along with various generalizations observed in the Xen development life cycle based on customer needs. Next, we will illustrate how Xen fits into a virtual infrastructure, combining it with other virtualization products. We will also invoke some forward thinking as we present some visionary plans from different virtualization companies on where virtualization technology can take your organization in the future.

The Unofficial Xen Road Map

While Xen continues to gain ground and market share among the popular virtualization technologies available, it must also evolve as an enterprise-ready platform that continues to add increased value to companies of all sizes. It will not be enough for the Xen community to provide maintenance releases that address and fix defects or provide support for updated hardware. The demonstration of innovation is what has brought Xen to where it is today. New features and new ways of doing things, as well as the same innovative attitude, will be needed to keep Xen a viable option in the future.

Recognizing this, XenSource is collaborating with the Xen development community in a call for those new features and tools, so as to not just maintain the existing binaries. The main focus for the past few years has been on stability, ensuring that the product survived its infancy without any catastrophic issues. Now, in its adolescence, Xen has an eye fixed on VMware, Microsoft, and others, all with mature products. For

Xen to wear the crown as the victor in this race, it must not only meet the needs of its users today, but anticipate what they will need in the future and develop a platform that is extensible and flexible enough to adapt to those changing needs.

Though it would be difficult to list all the activities in which the Xen team is currently engaged or is planning, we can summarize those development activities into focus areas. This informal and unofficial road map for Xen discusses four of those focus areas:

- Performance and scalability

- Operating system support

- Beyond the x86 CPU architecture

- Architecture enhancements

TIP

If you want the inside scoop on what the minds at XenSource are considering for upcoming versions of Xen, check out the Official Xen road map at http://wiki.xensource.com/xenwiki/XenRoadMap. If you'd also like to see what the various developers are working on, you can reference the following site: http://wiki.xensource.com/xenwiki/WhosDoingWhat.

Performance and Scalability

Virtual machines are rapidly taking the place of their dedicated hardware counterparts. Though this pattern continued to accelerate in their push toward lower costs, improved flexibility and speed of provisioning, and maximizing the return on investment in IT infrastructure, acceptance of virtualization has been hampered in production environment concerns with performance and scalability. Development, testing, and less-critical computer systems seem obvious targets for virtualizations, but many companies still struggle with migrating their more business-critical systems with heavy computing needs to those virtual machines that have been granted a fraction of the underlying hardware resources. In addition to performance and scalability, companies are also concerned about stability and true problem isolation.

As virtual machine monitors progress, the focus on maintaining the quality of raw business value of the hosting guest operating systems and applications will be important. Though reduced infrastructure complexity can be obtained through server consolidation, the ability to process and execute transactions within the time that the business requires cannot be sacrificed. Future versions of Xen will focus on squeezing the most from server subsystems since greater intelligence is built into its hypervisor. Of interest will be improving CPU, memory, and I/O performance.

NUMA-Aware Architecture

Highly parallel computing can take advantage of powerful hardware architectures. Complex systems have been designed with performance optimizing and maximizing components and technologies. In addition, operating systems have been developed to exploit the hardware architecture upon which they run, unlocking their performance-enhancing abilities. However, it would be a shame to migrate those operating systems to virtual machines and lose their potential for high returns and performance, even when running on the same performance-optimized hardware platform.

This can be seen in systems that have been designed with Non-Uniform Memory Architecture (NUMA). NUMA is based on the concept that a CPU can access local memory quicker than it can non-local, or remote, memory. NUMA architectures support scaling in CPUs in symmetric multiprocessing (SMP) architectures since each CPU maintains its own local memory and memory controller logic. Figure 8.1 illustrates memory access in a common NUMA system, along with the three memory paths a processor can take to access data. The most efficient and highest performance (#1) is found when the CPU access data is stored in its cache. This is often done at the same speed as CPU frequency. If a cache miss occurs, the CPU can either access memory in its local bank using its dedicated memory controller (#2) or interface the memory controller of another processor to access data in non-local memory (#3). The last path results in the slowest data access path due to the increased latency and hops.

NUMA addresses the problem of memory access caused by the overwhelming effects of high-speed CPU cache, which is incapable of satisfying the needs of operating systems and the applications that run on them. In some cases, multiprocessor systems can be impacted highly by constant "cache misses" due to memory constraints, thus resorting to seeks on lower-speed memory buses. For example, the 64-bit Intel Xeon MP Processor has on die L2 and L3 cache, the latter as high as 8MB. While the CPU cache is accessible at processor speeds of up to 3.33GHz, a cache miss will resort to a search in the machine's system memory across the 667MHz front-side bus. That is five times slower! Machine memory access is further impacted by the fact that all processors share the same memory bus and controller, making environments with high memory activity, such as some virtualization platforms, prone to even poorer memory performance.

Figure 8.1 NUMA Data Access Paths

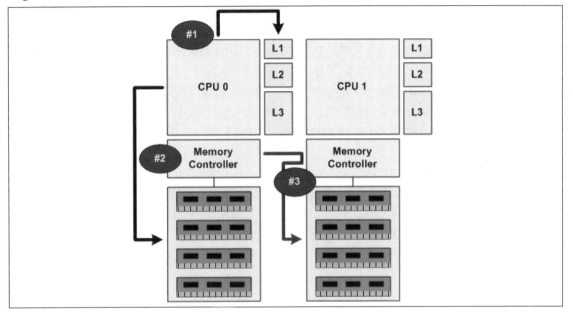

On the flip-side, NUMA gives each CPU a fast bus to its own bank of memory, reducing the occurrence of non-local memory hits and improving memory access by a factor that is roughly the number of processors. However, even with this unique memory architecture, not all of the data that a processor requires end up in its local bank, requiring access from the memory banks of other processors. As this has the effect of slowing down processors, the overall realized speed of the NUMA system depends on the nature of tasks at any given time.

Supporting NUMA-aware memory virtualization will be important since both AMD's Opteron processor and Intel's Itanium processor utilize NUMA even on smaller two-way systems. Taking this into consideration, the Xen team is challenged with optimizing the memory virtualization supported by the hypervisor to keep memory operations spread across the appropriate memory banks of the scheduled processors. A guest with its virtual memory mapped to physical machine memory addresses in the banks of the processors executing its instructions will perform well. This can be an intelligent, NUMA-aware function of the hypervisor and guest working together since, unlike full virtualization platforms, the guest is aware of the physical memory addresses it uses.

Multicore Processors

RISC platforms have long enjoyed the benefits of processors with more than one execution core, taking advantage of high-performance, multithread execution. Although Intel introduced Hyper-Threading with the later Pentium 4 and same-generation Xeon processors, they did not achieve the same level of concurrency with thread execution as having two identically capable processing cores. This kept the x86 and early x64 platforms at a serious performance disadvantage, barely keeping up with single-server workloads, much less the combined workloads of multiple virtual machines executing on a single server. Enter dual-core processors.

With the introduction of dual-core processors, the future began to look bright for x86 and x64 platforms. The charge was led by AMD with its Opteron offering, which provides greater performance than earlier single-core Opterons, and gives a supporting boost of greater hyper-transport link bandwidth. This was quickly followed by two generations of dual-core processors from Intel, a later release by AMD with an updated Opteron, as well as dual-core offerings in the desktop space with the Core 2 Duo and AMD64 X2 processors.

As 2006 drew to a close, Intel again upped the ante with quad-core processing (two of their dual-core processors on the same chip) with twice the cache size (up to 8MB of L2) for both their server and desktop line. AMD is bound to follow up with their 4 x 4 architecture, and both companies have plans for true quad-core releases in the future. But what will follow that? Eight- and 16-core solutions?

This is an important factor for the Xen team to consider as CPU schedulers will become increasingly critical. The majority of Xen implementations are, and will be, on two-way and some four-way servers. These servers present a strong value proposition for virtualization since there is no reason to "scale up" versus "scaling out." Unlike large workload servers, such as beefy database servers, virtualization veterans agree that workloads should be spread out across a greater number of servers to achieve a more linear increase in resources with each incremental server unit added to the pool. The increased cost for servers that are eight-way and more is exponentially greater two-way and four-way servers, but performance per CPU actually tends to roll off in a diminishing-returns fashion. Even though Xen supports up to 32-way architectures, it is not unreasonable to think that most of the development efforts to optimize the scheduler sEDF and Credit schedulers currently found in Xen were made with the common two-way server with four execution cores in mind. As two-way systems morph into platforms with 8, 16, and 32 execution cores, software developers will have to code wisely to avoid the law of diminishing returns, as experienced with large n-way systems in the early x86 days.

We will discuss multicore processors later in this chapter. First, we present an overview of Xen's direction on the PowerPC, one of the original multicore CPU architectures in the popular midrange market. We will also discuss the realm of possibilities with Sun Microsystems' UltraSPARC T1. Then we will focus on the multicore road map for both Intel and AMD.

Smart I/O

Users of Xen will acknowledge that CPU and memory performance is so close to native that you almost forget that guests are virtualized—that is, until those same guests need to achieve high-levels of I/O utilization. Although Xen's paravirtualization architecture allows both modified and unmodified guests with good I/O performance, the demands are also ever-increasing, a fact that is bound to tax the existing hypervisor design in many situations, the same way as with a typical physical platform.

Acknowledging the need for improving I/O performance without placing additional overhead on the guest operating system and consuming more of its resources, hardware manufacturers have developed new I/O device architectures that promise to give a server's I/O an injection of nitrous oxide. Notably, Remote Direct Memory Access (RDMA), TCP/IP Offload Engines (TOEs), and new bus technologies such as PCI-Express (PCIe) and InfiniBand enable raw I/O performance at unprecedented levels. However, even these new promising technologies offer challenges to operating systems vendors today. How much more of a challenge will they pose to Xen's architecture then?

Technology Highlight…

Smart I/O Devices: RDMA and InfiniBand

Remote Direct Memory Access (RDMA) is a network interface card feature that lets one computer directly place information into the memory of another computer. The technology reduces latency by minimizing demands on bandwidth and processing overhead.

Continued

Conventional hardware architecture (along with the supporting software in the operating system and device drivers) imposes a significant CPU and memory load on a server. Bottlenecks are commonly developed, though to various degrees depending on the system in question, due to the data that must be copied between the kernel and application. Memory bottlenecks can cause a more severe condition as connection speeds exceed the processing power and memory bandwidth of servers, such as in servers with multiple gigabit or even 10Gb interfaces.

RDMA addresses this by implementing a reliable transport protocol in hardware on the NIC and by supporting zero-copy networking with kernel bypass. Zero-copy networking lets the NIC transfer data directly to or from application memory, eliminating the need to copy data between application memory and the kernel. A concept known as *kernel bypass* lets applications issue commands to the NIC without having to execute a kernel call. The RDMA request is issued from user mode to the local NIC and over the network to the remote NIC without requiring any kernel involvement. This reduces the number of context switches between kernel mode and user mode while handling network traffic. This promises to substantially reduce the work performed by Xen's I/O virtualization model.

In comparison, the InfiniBand Architecture (IBA) is an industry standard that defines a new high-speed switched fabric subsystem designed to connect processor nodes and I/O nodes to form a system area network (the next substantial meaning for the acronym SAN). This new interconnect method moves away from the local transaction-based I/O model across busses to a remote message-passing model across channels. The architecture is independent of the host operating system (OS) and the processor platform.

IBA provides both reliable and unreliable transport mechanisms in which messages are queued for delivery between end systems. Hardware transport protocols are defined that support reliable and unreliable messaging (send/receive), and memory manipulation semantics (RDMA read/write) without software intervention in the data transfer path.

The InfiniBand specification primarily defines the hardware electrical, mechanical, link-level, and management aspects of an InfiniBand fabric, but does not define the lowest layers of the operating system stack needed to communicate over an InfiniBand fabric. The remainder of the operating system stack to support storage, networking, IPC, and systems management is left to the operating system vendor for definition. It will be interesting to see how the Xen project's adoption and implementation of InfiniBand evolves over time as this technology becomes more widespread and commonplace.

In response to these types of smart I/O devices, the Xen team will need to enhance or replace the current split device architecture with its frontend and backend drivers. Device channels will need to be optimized in order to not introduce any unnecessary latency to the I/O process. Software-based IOMMUs will need to be retrofitted to work closer and to more tightly integrate with provided hardware IOMMUs, or be eliminated all together. Of course, as software is replaced by hardware, access-control, the mechanism for maintaining safety and isolation, will need to transform and adapt to such conditions as well.

Operating System Support

The operating systems…need we say more? The foundation of any server instance is the operating system upon which the business value applications execute. The hope that one day everyone will run the same operating system or that all operating systems will, in turn, be mutually compatible is a wish in vain. In fact, as Xen's popularity expands with a more diverse selection of customers, the need to support a more diverse selection of operating systems will exist. While this may seem trivial to the open-source community (one that laughs in the face of a challenge), the commercial side of Xen may hit some critical challenges.

Of the greatest importance, XenSource will need to raise the bar a couple of notches with its XenServer product family to meet its ubiquitous goals. While the 3.2 release takes the commercial VMM a step further in that direction, the pace will need to pick up to help Xen compete with other commercial VMM offerings.

Support in Linux Distributions

And while XenSource is up for the challenge, it appears that others are standing in line next to it as well. It reminds me of a scene at the end of a movie when the underdog gains unwavering courage in the face of the opposition—before you know it, he's not alone but finds himself in the company of many others. Playing on that "strength in numbers" idea, Xen is being rewarded for its commitment to open-source Linux. In fact, all of the major Linux distributions have chosen to adopt the VMM as their virtualization technology of choice rather than reinvent the wheel. This accomplishes several things for Xen. First, it gives greater exposure for the VMM since it is distributed with the operating system. Second, it improves the installation and integration experience. No longer will users have to compile the kernel and modules, modify their boot loader, or hack around with dom0 driver integration.

Leading the charge is Novell, which was an early adopter of Xen in its commercial SUSE offering, followed by Red Hat with Fedora Core 6 and RHEL 5, and Sun with an updated release to Solaris 10. It is inevitable that all other distributions will follow suit, although competing technologies such as KVM and UML are fighting for the limelight in the open-source world of Linux. Also, Xen is bound to make a large landing with Mac OS users since they have not been provided satisfactory offerings from Microsoft and others that come close to Xen's feature set.

What the Xen team does need to do, however, is make sure consistency is maintained. Recently, Xen issued a public notice stating that companies redistributing their hypervisor should not call it "Xen." Maybe this was done to not associate the tightly quality-controlled release with the derivatives that will grace the distributions, bound to deviate from the stable code based in one form or another. And walking both the "free" world and commercial market, how will Xen continue to maintain demand for its XenServer offering with built-in implementations already lurking in the distributions around the globe?

Furthermore, getting Xen up and running is one thing, but improving the move to modified domUs has proven to be slow as well. To really hit the home run, Xen will need to work with each of the Linux distributions to facilitate a new type of offering… the domU offering. Imagine it: you go to Red Hat's Fedora project page and download the CD/DVD of the latest release of Fedora Core (FC) to install, or download the Xen domU of FC. Finally, as virtual appliances continue to be accepted, the Xen team should work with open-source developers to ensure a Xen appliance is an available download, whether for production or evaluation, allowing Xen customers to further achieve value with the VMM.

Xen and Microsoft

By now, you may have heard about the agreement between Microsoft and XenSource on July 18, 2006. XenSource had announced prior to this agreement that it was going to provide support in its hypervisor for Windows-based guests, using Intel and AMD hardware virtualization technologies in their latest processor offerings. However, the formal agreement signed between Microsoft and XenSource goes much further than just the ability to run Windows in a domU. In fact, it is the very discussion of hypervisor technology that lies at the base of their agreement.

The two companies have begun to collaborate in the development of virtualization technology that will enable interoperability between XenSource's hypervisor and Microsoft's Windows Server virtualization, an offering that will be available within 180 days of the release of the next Windows server operating system, codenamed "Longhorn Server." The interoperability will allow Xen-enabled guests, or rather modified, paravirtualized guests, to run on Microsoft's upcoming hypervisor.

Two things become important, then, in this new and brave world. First, Microsoft will begin to offer official support for operating systems other than Windows, although the extent of their support is still to be announced. It is expected they will have to support core functionality as it relates to CPU and memory management, networking, and storage. Officially, this new technology will not be a free offering, but will be made available through commercial licensing channels, either from Microsoft, XenSource, or from both. This interoperability between XenEnterprise and Longhorn will create an interesting proposition to IT enterprises.

So maybe the future of operating system interoperability is not that far-fetched. Who would have ever guessed that Microsoft Windows server would also be running RHEL, SLES, BSD derivatives, or even Solaris? But all of this will be possible if the XenSource-Microsoft technology works as planned.

Other HVM Guests

In a similar move to the XenSource-Microsoft agreement, the future looks bright for other operating systems not easily supported in Xen currently. With the first generation of HVM from Intel and AMD proving just how the CPU can assist in virtualization tasks, second- and third-generation HVM processors will undoubtedly allow even more integration and assistance with VMMs for even more guest operating system compatibility. The dreams of many involve the ability to run Novell Netware, Sun Solaris (not just the OpenSolaris flavor), Apple Mac OS, and a wider range of Windows operating systems, such as Vista and Longhorn, on top of the Xen hypervisor. And why not? With Smart I/O and improved CPU and memory virtualization through hardware, just about any x86/x64 compatible operating system should be a candidate for its own domU real estate.

Beyond the x86 CPU Architecture

With efforts led by developers at IBM and Intel, Xen is bound to make an explosion on the fronts of other CPU architectures in full-fashion soon. While reasonable performance has been observed, there is still a lot of work to be done to bring the VMM up to the same level as it exists today on x86. In this section, we will review the Xen team's development efforts for popular RISC platform offerings. We will discuss Xen's current capabilities on the road map, if one exists, for the following architectures:

- Intel IA-64 (Itanium and Itanium 2)

- IBM PowerPC

- Sun Microsystems UltraSPARC

IA-64 Feature Sync with x86

IA-64 is the oldest non-x86 port of the Xen VMM. Performance is excellent with very low overhead. Although Windows guest VMs are not in the support model yet, multiple SMP Linux domUs are supported. With the age of this port and the evolution of its feature set, Xen for IA-64 has nearly the same functionalities as its x86-based sibling, including

- Virtual block devices use the standard frontend/backend virtual split device model.

- The standard set of control tools and commands are available to manage the Xen environment.

- HVM guests are supported with the Intel-VT capabilities available in the latest generation of Itanium 2 processor.

With most of the hard work accomplished already, the IA-64 port can look forward to development focus on VM life-cycle features, such as save/restore, live migration, and additional functionality since it evolves in the x86 port as well (snapshots, storage management, and so on). Efforts will be placed on stabilizing this platform even further, with emphasis on virtual physical address space for each guest and support for driver domains to enhance performance under heavy I/O workloads.

With the release of Microsoft Windows Server "Longhorn" on the horizon, we can expect that the new relationship with Microsoft will also extend to IA-64 virtualization as well. This may also fuel additional efforts to provide unmodified Windows guest virtualization through existing HVM capabilities up through and including Windows Server Data Center Edition for greater than eight-way Windows guests.

Porting to PowerPC

IBM developers are heavily working on the Xen port for the PowerPC 970 processor. Leading the charge at IBM are Hollis Blanchard and Jimi Xenidis (no pun intended). Based on the POWER4 architecture used in the IBM System p series of midrange servers, the PowerPC 970 was introduced in 2002 to cover the huge gap left by Intel between 32-bit x86 Pentium and Xeon, and Intel's sole 64-bit offering, the IA-64, and today the 970 comes in both single-core and dual-core versions. Although practically abandoned by Apple in favor of Intel's Core 2 Duo, the PowerPC 970FX, 970MP, and 970GX are still extensively used by other IBM partners as well as in IBM's PowerPC-based blade servers, the JS20 and JS21.

NOTE

IBM's PowerPC 970 and 970FX lacked the virtualization feature that has made the POWER architecture so popular. Consequently, it was not possible to run multiple operating systems on a single JS20 blade, for example. Xen brings the ability to virtualize such systems for Linux use, and promises to enhance the virtualization capabilities of the PowerPC 970MP and 970GX even more.

Also note that since Xen requires that guest operating systems be modified, the focus has been to port the hypervisor to stably run Linux for PowerPC in dom0 and domU. Though it is theoretically possible to support other guests as well, there are no plans at the moment to support Windows, AIX, or other operating systems in Xen for PowerPC.

Currently, the port has accomplished the majority of the core functions, including most dom0 functionality and tool compatibility and, most importantly, SMP and virtual I/O device support. Though lacking the save/restore features and live migration available in x86 versions, Linux for PowerPC domUs are a reality.

The future of the PowerPC port, however, should be focused on the upcoming 2007 release of the POWER6 architecture and the far-away release of POWER7. With IBM moving towards standardizing all of their non-x86 systems on the POWER6 platform, sufficient virtualization may allow AIX and i5/OS to be run inside of a Xen domU, though this may not make much sense given IBM's native capacity to virtualize those platforms already. Although IBM's current ability to micro-partition CPU resources and even build redundant I/O virtualization, called Virtual I/O Servers in IBM's Advanced Virtualization Technology, such functionality is provided at a high cost of resource utilization. What would make sense, however, is to integrate some of the user mode management tool functionality into the Hardware Management Console (HMC) and other IBM virtualization toolsets, making their Advanced POWER Virtualization Xen-aware and compatible.

Porting to the UltraSPARC Architecture

While x64 is gaining popularity among the Sun crowd as a platform for the Solaris operating system, the UltraSPARC processor is still alive and well. It may not make much sense, however, to reach beyond existing x64 support to look at the traditional UltraSPARC IV and IV+ architectures. Though they are capable of large workloads, in the case of virtualizing smaller workloads to aggregate on a single server, even Sun has recognized the potential of x64 with their line of AMD Opteron-based systems.

However, with the introduction in late 2005 of the UltraSPARC T1, or Niagara, processor, Sun leads the entry-level and midrange server market in multicore and multithreaded processors, by count as least. From a core-count perspective, a single T1 processor can contain as many as eight cores. As a multithreaded processor, each core can execute four threads concurrently. The multithreaded nature of the T1 processor helps it overcome the impact of cache misses by moving delayed threads off of the execution queue until data has been fetched and placed into the cache while the remaining threads continue to execute. Even with a small cache size (3MB of L2), the 1.2GHz T1 beats a two-way, quad-core 1.9GHz POWER5 and a four-way, dual-core Intel "Paxville" Xeon MP on several industry benchmarks. With a T1-based system running as many as 32 threads at the same time, one would think that this would be an ideal platform for virtualization.

Ironically, one challenge that may have delayed the acceptance of the T1 processor for virtualization uses is the architecture itself. The T1 was designed to be implemented in a single-processor, or uniprocessor, system. Also, all of the cores share the same floating point unit (FPU). While these may be acceptable limitations for some uses, such as mid-tier application servers and high-traffic Web servers, it may prove to be a hindrance for virtual workloads.

Recognizing these limitations, Sun is preparing the Niagara 2 architecture to run heavier workloads by releasing the T2 processor. It will improve on its sibling by doubling the multithread performance with eight threads per core, increasing the size of its L2 cache, supporting SMP, and providing a dedicated FPU for each core. Later iterations, currently known as Niagara 3, will further increase thread concurrency and cache size, while boosting core count per processor and memory bandwidth. Just imagine a four-way server supporting 128 concurrent threads with the latest in memory and I/O bus technologies; overkill for some applications, yes, but it sounds enticing as a platform for virtual infrastructure. If the Xen team could take advantage of this architecture with a port of the hypervisor, it could end up being one of the most popular platforms for Xen. In fact, Xen could be the saving grace for Sun's processor architecture since Sun has fallen short in its promise to deliver next-generation computing and virtualization functionality with its latest "container" approach in the Solaris 10 release.

Architecture Enhancements

Evolving Xen for improved performance and scalability, guest support, and additional hardware platforms is bound to be a focus for the development team over the next few years. However, there are some key architectural enhancements they are working on now or will be looking at in the near future, even if in parallel with other key development priorities. Focusing on the hypervisor itself, there is work to be done in the storage arena as well as with resource management and virtual devices.

Control Tools

The team has elaborate plans to greatly improve the control tool stack for Xen. Most of the emphasis will be placed on standardizing the management interfaces and structure of Xen, as well as giving administrators greater insight and control of their Xen infrastructure like never before. While a lot of functionality exists in both native and third-party control tools, Xen needs improved administration and deployment tools as well, specifically in the area of centralized management and storage management.

One of the major initiatives will be to implement standards-based management in Xen, the foundation of which has been defined by the Distributed Management Task Force (DMTF). Included in the plans are the development of a Common Information Model (CIM) object to support life-cycle management of Xen guests as well as certain aspects of Xen hosts, and Web-Based Enterprise Management (WBEM) to provide a simple query/result set mechanism to retrieve management data. It's possible Xen may even become compatible with Carmine, Microsoft's up-and-coming Virtual Server management application. Including such standards for management will allow administrators to utilize their existing enterprise systems' management tools used to manage other components in their infrastructure, such as IBM Tivoli and CA Unicenter, to gain insight into their Xen virtual infrastructure as well.

Much effort will also be made to improve the management of the virtual machine life-cycle. Although Xen currently has *save* and *restore* features, it lacks the more sophisticated functionality needed to compete with other hypervisor products and technologies. The Xen tools are expected to eventually provide snapshot functionality, improved backup/restore integration with guests, storage management (such as disk provisioning and on-demand disk growth), and improved cloning and provisioning capabilities.

Finally, much work has been done with remote administration, utilizing XML over RPC, or XML-RPC. XenSource has already made great strides with this for their XenSource XenServer Administrator Console application; however, developing a more robust API and exposing it for easier interaction with custom developed code will be important. Rather than utilizing a thick client with TCP socket bindings to the API on the servers, Xen may have a Web service that can be consumed and thus expose a rich set of objects to manage the host and guests. Also replacing the Administrator Console will be a Web-based GUI with similar functionality that supports "anywhere, anytime" management.

Virtual Hard Disk Images and XenFS

Many Xen implementations today take advantage of raw volumes dedicated to a single domU. This configuration is popular because of the performance gains as well as the lower administrative overhead of tracking disks-to-VM. However, the popularity of file-based encapsulation of virtual machines will continue to develop, especially when factoring in the benefits of guest portability and self-containment.

In order for Xen users to shift to this model, the Xen team will have to deliver a more robust and higher-performance solution. The team can choose two paths for the road map: develop a new file-backed model unique to Xen, or incorporate existing virtual hard disk (VHD) technology that is already mature and stable. It is foreseeable that the latter path will be chosen, focusing VHD efforts on VMware's VMDK format, Microsoft's, or some other player, such as QEMU QCOW. QEMU QCOW seems to be the winner, according to XenSource resources, because of its existence as GPL code already, and the closed, or semi-closed, nature of the other two formats. Doing so, however, means dumping the existing *loop* driver and expanding on the *blktap* approach that can already be found in Xen in limited form.

> **NOTE**
>
> QEMU Copy-on-Write (QCOW) has some great advantages. Like other Copy-on-Write systems, actual disk consumption can be substantially lowered with disk image sharing across guests. For example, all guests can boot from the same boot volume but have individual data volumes. QCOW also limits the disk space consumed to what is actually being used. So if you create a 500GB disk for a guest that only has 20GB of data stored, the actual space used on

the physical mass storage is 20GB. The adoption of QCOW may help accelerate the implementation of features such as overlay images, which can be used to enable virtual machine snapshots.

Virtual Device Enhancements

As Xen grows in popularity among a more diverse selection of users, the demand for additional virtual device support will continue to put pressure on the Xen development team to extend the functionality further. This is especially true in the area of Xen desktop virtualization, where users will want access to a wider array of devices not commonly found in the data center.

USB will need a large focus from the team. Two factors will drive the development effort. First, USB has become commonplace as a connection interface to computer systems. Though basic support existed in earlier versions of Xen, this functionality has been limited in the current 3.x release to USB host controller ownership assignment to a dedicated guest. And with the advent of USB-over-IP, there are new possibilities for implementing USB support now.

In addition to enhanced USB functionality, the following device enhancements are being considered:

- **Remote console support** Currently, Xen only supports a virtual serial console to interact with guests without network support, as may be the case while configuring a newly deployed domU. This is suitable for Linux and Windows 2003 (using the Special Administration Console, or SAC), but presents a challenge for guests such as the now-supported Windows 2000 family and Windows XP. Novice Linux users running distribution with X Server may not be familiar with configuring the operating system via a serial console, preferring the Gnome or KDE GUI tools for such tasks. Currently, the only way to gain access to a graphic console is through VNC, RDP, or another protocol, but therein lies the problem for guests without network support. The solution currently being discussed is to implement an in-kernel *fbdev* paravirtual frame buffer driver, which uses a shared memory device channel to make the frame buffer available to domain 0, where it can either be rendered locally, or converted to a network frame buffer protocol. This is already the case for HVM guests today, so this will help bring a consistent look and feel for all guests, HVM-based or not. Another benefit of having the PV frame buffer as a kernel *fbdev* is that it can emulate text mode and display messages during the boot sequence (not just when the operating system is fully booted), providing close-to-native user experience.

- **Advanced graphics** To support graphic remote consoles and achieve satisfactory performance for two-dimensional graphics, a more complex backend driver for the frame buffer, with copy and fill region commands and a separate hardware cursor, will be required. In HVM guests, video card emulation is used to accomplish this already. However, in the case of paravirtualized guests, the kernel fbdev interface is not rich enough to supply this data, requiring the Xen team to modify X Server to achieve decent graphics performance. Achieving satisfactory performance for three-dimensional graphics requires a substantially higher-level interface than that for two dimensions. With both the X Server and Microsoft window systems moving in the direction of using three-dimensional rendering even for desktop graphics as well as games and CAD/CAM, the Xen team will need to develop frontend drivers that encapsulate and transport OpenGL and Direct3D commands into backend domains where they can be rendered by the actual high-end graphics cards.

- **Smart I/O** Although we have discussed this already in this chapter, smart I/O device support will be ongoing in upcoming Xen releases. InfiniBand and RDMA technology has basic support in Xen today, as long as they are supported in the dom0 operating system. However, the hypervisor has not been optimized for those devices or other hardware-acceleration devices. The challenge for the Xen team will be to establish a framework for frontend/backend driver architecture that will allow rapid acceptance and support of new hardware technologies in Xen. Rather than waiting for two to three releases to get support, the new framework will allow optimized use of those technologies in domUs by the next release, if not the current one. Even better, wouldn't it be great to have hardware manufacturers provide their own PV drivers?

Virtual Infrastructure in Tomorrow's Data Center

Server virtualization has been driven by the need of IT organizations to reduce their server footprint and reclaim space in their at-capacity data centers. Consolidation efforts have, for the most part, been very successful, proving that virtualization is a real and viable solution to the "server sprawl" problem. However, it is not enough to just consolidate; you must optimize the infrastructure as well. Accomplishing this requires more than just replacing physical servers with their virtual equivalents. Infrastructure optimization must look at all data center components as a whole, and will vary depending on the size of the company. We will look at future trends that will drive the possibilities of virtualization, and also examine possible solutions for both the small and medium-sized business (SMB), as well as large enterprises.

Technology Trends Driving Improvements in Virtualization

While the benefits are easy to realize in SMB-sized companies, larger enterprises are often the greatest beneficiaries of virtualization. While the debate concerning larger companies has been over "scale-out" or "scale-up" strategies for enterprise-class server systems, those companies must now compound that issue with another one: physical or virtual. Xen is well poised to play an important role in enterprise data centers, and will continue to fortify that position with enhancements and additions to future releases along its road map. To make an educated choice, enterprises must consider the relationship between:

- Xen
- The underlying hardware
- The corporate strategy for application and infrastructure deployment

Hardware Economies of Scale

Virtualization's introduction to larger corporate entities was often in support of development and test initiatives, and was rarely considered for production use. This was understandable since the CPU architecture with the most growth, x86, had a fairly low performance ceiling. Even with the introduction of hyper-threaded technology (not to be confused with multithreaded), a conventional two-way or four-way server could host only a handful of virtual machines, each with some degree of performance loss. At the same time, midrange server offerings provided hardware-level partitioning, such as IBM's LPAR technologies found in the Unix and mainframe offerings, but the costs were astronomical compared to x86. So the question became one of choosing between larger yet more expensive midrange servers that could scale up, and smaller commodity servers implemented in a scaled-out fashion but with a lower price tag overall. Companies rapidly converted to x86 for both Windows and Linux, migrating their business applications to take advantage of lower total cost of owner-ship (TCO) and better returns on investment (ROIs).

The economy of scale is being achieved now with new dual-core and quad-core servers with extensions for hardware-virtualization assistance. The current release of Xen enables modified and unmodified guests to perform at near-native levels. The trend is not transforming from "scale-out" to "scale-out and virtualize." A rack of two-way servers working together as a virtual host farm can account for dozens of virtualized server instances, and an unprecedented level of density. The high-density accomplishments that companies are achieving are helping reduce infrastructure complexity. At the same time, overcrowded data centers are reclaiming precious square footage thanks to consolidation efforts and the lowered cost of environmental issues, such as power and cooling.

Multicore and Multithreaded Computing

CPU manufacturers have pushed their processor architectures to their limits over the past few years. As clock speeds have increased, thermal envelope limitations and the need to do more with less has led their engineers to devise creative ways to develop high-performing processors to satisfy future needs while maintaining backwards compatibility.

The most common way to extract more from the CPU is to layer more than one core on the processor die. Dual-core processors have existed in the IBM PowerPC and Sun UltraSPARC line for some time, but such technology was only recently made available on the x86 platform. Both Intel and AMD have played rounds of leapfrog with their releases of dual-core processors. As both companies have shifted their focus on delivering quad-core options to their customers, neither has delivered a true die with four distinct cores—yet. While the race is on to reach true quad-core status, they are setting their sites on what lies beyond quad-core. Table 8.1 lists the 2007 and 2008 road map for both Intel and AMD.

Table 8.1 The CPU Road Map for 2007/2008

	Platform	Codename	Feature	Release Date
Intel	Desktops	Ridgefield	45-nm version of the Core 2 Duo based on the Penryn architecture	Second half, 2007
		Yorkfield	45-nm quad-core, still on two dies	First half, 2008
		Bloomsfield	45-nm quad-core, on single die	2008
	Servers	Tigerton	65-nm Core 2–based quad-core chip update to the Intel Xeon MP with new front-side bus	Second half, 2007
		Dunnington	45-nm, up to eight-core processor for two-way systems	2008
		Harpertown	Updated version of Dunnington eight-core only, with 12MB of L2 cache	2008
		Gainestown	Up to eight-core, based on new Nahalem architecture, including integrated memory controller, support for DDR3 RAM, and integrated graphics	2008

Continued

Table 8.1 continued The CPU Road Map for 2007/2008

	Platform	Codename	Feature	Release Date
		Beckton	Intel Xeon MP version of the Gainestown; may feature larger cache as well	2008
AMD	Desktops	Altair	65-nm quad-core on a single die based on the Griffin architecture	Second half, 2007
		Antares	65-nm dual-core based on Barcelona	Second half, 2007
		Fusion	Similar to Antares, except with integrated graphics (ATI-based)	Second half, 2007
	Servers	Deerhound	65-nm quad-core on a single die; introduction of L3 cache and HyperTransport 3.0	Second half, 2007
		Shanghai	45-nm up to quad-core with Direct Connect Architecture 2.0, PCI-express 2.0, DDR3 support, larger cache, and 10Gb NIC	First half, 2008

Even more important to Xen, the 2008 processor releases from Intel and AMD will include improved CPU and memory virtualization (version 2.0). They will also introduce native hardware-based I/O virtualization as well as improved TCP offload for improved network throughput, in preparation for the shift to 10Gb Ethernet as the data center connectivity standard.

Historically, the typical enterprise application life cycle includes a major release every three to four years. So it can be expected that the load and demand placed on the hardware by application workloads will not see a major jump upwards for some time. At this point, it appears that the raw processing power of computer hardware will more than stay ahead of the application loads that will run on top of them, increasing the amount of underutilization of resources. This will further drive the adoption of virtualization technologies, such as Xen, as the primary and preferred platform for all but the most intensive workloads.

While x86 CPU manufacturers continue to drive additional cores into their offerings, other Xen platforms are doing the same, as well as allowing each core to execute more than one thread concurrently. This multithreaded approach, though not as efficient as with core count increases, still allows the underlying server platform to satisfy a higher degree of concurrent scheduling for Xen guests. And the more instructions that Xen can schedule, the higher the load it can support and the better performing the guests will run.

Multithreaded processors will appear to the Ring-0 software as individual processors, one for each potentially executing thread, and thus will be queued for execution in the same manner that single-threaded execution cores are. For example, a single-core processor that supports two concurrent threads will appear to Xen as two distinct processors, allowing Xen to schedule two instructions from its guests simultaneously. A key difference, however, with multithreading is that each thread is handled by a "logical processor" rather than a physical one, as is the case with multi-core architecture. Executing in the same physical environment, each thread will share CPU cache, memory, and I/O bandwidth, and, in some cases, the CPU-allocated FPU and memory controller, causing the per-thread increase to be less efficient in gain than a per-core increase.

As hardware manufacturers continue to introduce features that assist in, or directly perform, virtualization tasks, the lines between full virtualization and paravirtualization will change. The combination of multiple cores executing multiple threads concurrently while providing offloading assistance of I/O and virtualization overhead make "100 percent virtualization" achievable, even in large enterprises. Operating systems will become virtualization-aware, containing hypervisor-like logic that will take advantage of hardware VT feature sets. Even more, the need for complexly developed code to serve as an intermediary between the operating system and hardware will diminish over time as the hypervisor and operating system become one.

Solutions for Small and Medium-Sized Businesses

Virtualization has been a boon in the SMB arena. Companies without the budget for large and lavish data centers can easily sustain the servers needed to run their business applications on a small footprint of infrastructure. They are capable of truly realizing the benefits of virtualization because the typical workload per application (messaging, CRM, finance, and so on) is smaller than that of a larger enterprise. Placing Xen at the heart of the virtual infrastructure will help SMB-sized companies accelerate their return on technology investments, even with the flagship product.

While consolidation may not be that important for the typical SMB, cost-effective and optimized infrastructure is. Creative solutions based on Xen can help businesses contain costs while meeting business needs and addressing real business problems. Two such solutions demonstrate how virtualization can really change the paradigm of servers: integrated computing and the data center in a box.

Integrated Computing

Integrated computing is a term for tightly coupled services that form the framework for business activities. Tied to business processes, each service is a software-based technology that can be leveraged by SMBs to run their business effectively. Consider the example shown in Figure 8.2.

Figure 8.2 Integrated Computing Representation

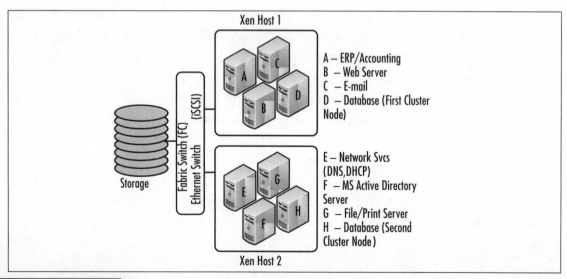

In this configuration, the SMB has two physical hosts, Xen Host 1 and Xen Host 2, which are connected to low-cost, SAN-based storage, either fibre-connected or iSCSI. Each physical host is running Xen, open-source or the commercial product, and hosts four guests. Xen Host 1 has guests A thru D, while Xen Host 2 is hosting guests E thru H. Also notice that the database servers on each (Guests D and H) form a cluster, a high-availability requirement for the SMB's business-critical application. Not shown in the figure are the network connections, two per host, requiring four gigabit Ethernet ports. Although small, this configuration demonstrates just how virtualization can simplify a potentially complex infrastructure of systems and connectivity.

Data Center in a Box

No scenario is too small for virtualization. In the future, virtualization technologies like Xen will be commonplace and will be the norm rather than the exception. Except for extreme cases of resource requirements, the typical installation of an operating system will be in a virtual machine instead of on a physical server. Such cases will be rare in the SMB space, where virtual machines are capable of serving just about every workload presented by the business. When this becomes the standard, the paradigm of what data center infrastructures look like and their bite into the selling, general, and administrative (SG&A) expenses budget will change. As long as you need at least two servers, Xen can help you simplify and reduce costs. Another practical example of how virtualization can change what you think about systems architecture, we will take a look at an extreme approach to data center consolidation—the data center in a box, as illustrated in Figure 8.3.

In this example, all the IT services that support an SMB's operation run on a single physical server with plenty of hardware resources running XenSource's XenExpress. Using Xen's virtualization technology, several servers are being hosted on this single server. What makes this different than other scenarios is the combination of services being hosted. They make up an entire data center ecosystem, including software-based firewalls and routers forming a perimeter DMZ, the Web server, internal applications, the database, e-mail, and file/print servers. Behind the scenes, a single privileged domain, dom0, contains the backend drivers for all the underlying hardware devices, while several domUs host a variety of Linux and Windows guests and their respective applications.

Figure 8.3 Data Center in a Box

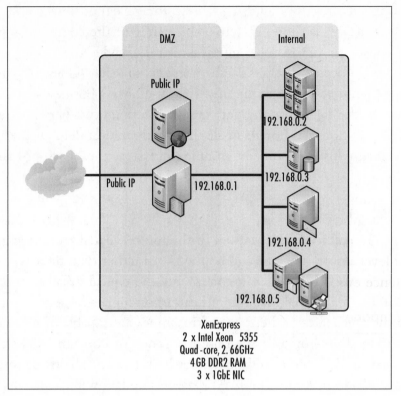

Large Enterprises

Large enterprises have the opportunity to benefit most from server virtualization. Relief is needed as floor space, power, and cooling have reached an all-time high, bringing many data centers to their maximum capacity. Add to that the increasing requirements for reliability, availability, security, and compliance, and the need for a change becomes clear. We will next discuss how virtualization addresses these problems.

Reliability and Availability

Reliability and availability are inseparable. For that reason, the points we discuss here apply to both. Although reliability is not the only factor that can impact application availability, it is key to running a consistent and predictable business operation. Applications that enable core business processes thus become the weak link in the chain, crippling the business with unexpected outages and lost revenues. The call for increased reliability, and availability as we will discuss shortly, has led to heavy investments in redundant hardware and software. In many cases, less critical applications are not implemented with high levels of redundancy or tend to be run in less reliable environments, creating pockets of risk throughout the organization.

Virtualization addresses reliability through three key areas: fault containment, simple recovery, and built-in failover capabilities. Focusing on Xen, fault containment is achieved through the use of unprivileged domains, or domUs, that isolate and ensure the safety of each guest operating system from faults in other running guests. The lack of fault propagation gives Xen guests the same degree of reliability as the underlying hardware. Since fewer servers must be deployed, enterprises can allocate funding in their budget to build up their host hardware to a substantially more robust level. Figure 8.4 provides an example of the level of fault tolerance that can be accomplished at the hardware layer. Every guest hosted on that hardware benefits from the same level of hardware reliability, regardless of criticality or tolerance for outages. In essence every server is highly reliable and highly available.

Figure 8.4 Components of a Highly Available Xen Host

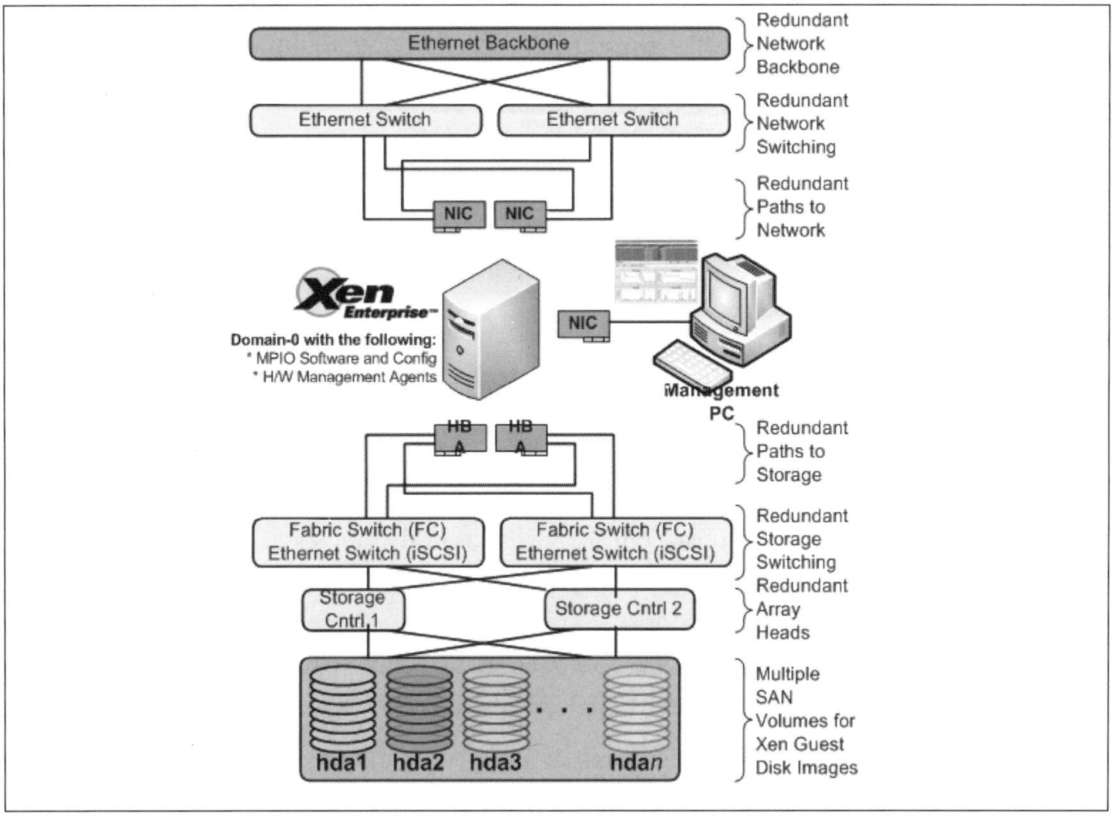

Security

Security is another frontier where virtualization will help large enterprises. Conventional security implementations factor in layers of protection, ranging from firewalls and intrusion detection systems (IDSes) at the network layer to access control lists (ACLs) to antivirus/antispyware software to protect the running kernel from malicious code. In fact, all of these areas have a basic component in common: privilege. The risk would be substantially mitigated if it was limited to user-space access, but most IT security risks exist because they take advantage of direct or indirect vulnerabilities to access through privileged operations. On a traditional server or desktop system, this is difficult to stop because it is not possible to police Ring-0 operations without integration into the kernel of the operating system, often requiring expensive third-party hardware and software. But, theoretically, this is not a problem for the virtual infrastructure.

Since guests run their kernel operations in a privileged ring other than Ring-0, it is possible to develop code in the VMM to analyze and assess the safety and viability of all privileged calls being made by guests. Virtualization provides strong isolation while allowing organizations to encourage best security practices and even undo any changes made. Let's take a look at the future of the VMM, or hypervisor, and the role it may play in securing the IT landscape with the following:

- Embedded IDS

- Network interposition

- Attack-resistant virtual hardware

- VM (guest) recovery

With an embedded IDS, the VMM can be used to inspect network traffic going to, or coming from, virtual machines. This is particularly effective in split device driver models, such as that found in Xen, but may be tricky in models providing more direct access in guests. However, an embedded IDS in the VMM would benefit from centralized management and consistent rules and policies across all hosted VMs. As multicore processor designs continue to develop, the VMM IDS can be given a dedicated CPU core (or fraction of one) to guarantee sufficient compute resources to carry out its task. With the potential cost savings from not having to purchase elaborate hardware-based IDSes or host IDSes, embedded IDSes will further enhance the business case for virtualization.

Another future security enhancement of the VMM is the interposition to enhance security. The goal of VMM network interposition is to only allow safe and correction communication. It is becoming increasingly difficult to identify network traffic caused by malicious users or processes. However, most organizations should be able to profile the expected traffic patterns for their applications in a manner similar to configuring access in a firewall. This "good traffic" profile can even be learned over time, dynamically generating a set of policies that can be used to discern good from bad traffic. If network communication is attempted that does not fit the correct profile as defined by the policy, those packets are dropped or contained for further analysis.

One of the pros of virtualization is the use of a consistent hardware set across all virtual machines, regardless of the operating systems running inside the VM. In all cases, software and code logic is used to present the hardware environment to the guest operating systems. This code either lives inside the VMM itself or is part of the hardware-assist virtualization technologies. Future developments in the virtual hardware should include modifications that can be used to prevent attacks.

Technology Highlight...

The Collective: A Virtual Appliance Computing Infrastructure

Computers today run billions of operations per second, dazzle us with video and sound, store libraries of data, and quickly exchange data with millions of other computers. Yet, computers and software are still difficult to deploy and maintain. Applications and user data are tied to individual computers, making it harder to deal with hardware failures. When users move around, they must remember to bring their computers with them. And, keeping software up-to-date on each computer is a challenge; too many computers suffer security compromises because people fail to apply available updates or correctly configure protections.

Research is being performed at Stanford University to create a new system architecture, called the Collective, that will address those issues. Based on VMM technology hosted on the x86 architecture (to support both Windows and Linux), the Collective attempts are focused on user compute environments, but can easily be adapted to meet the needs of enterprise server landscapes. In the Collective system architecture, virtual appliances, and their updated versions, are deposited in repositories. Individual computers run a

Continued

universal appliance receiver that retrieves the latest copies of virtual machines from repositories upon request. In other words, the computers operate as a cache of appliances. The system uses a number of optimizations to minimize the cost of the storage and transfer of appliances. This approach allows a small number of professional staff to create fully tested, integrated environments that are made available quickly to all users anywhere on the network.

As part of their research, the researchers have made several major findings, including the following:

- **Efficient migration of appliances** X86 appliances, complete with operating systems, application programs, and possibly user data, can be very large. It has been found that the storage and transfer of appliances can be effectively optimized using the techniques of caching, demand paging, memory ballooning to reduce the memory state, and Copy-on-Write disks to capture changes. The time to transfer an appliance on a DSL link (384 kbps) is typically less than 20 minutes.

- **Virtual appliance networks** Generalizing the concept of virtual appliances to include a virtual network enables the encapsulation of network management knowledge and sets of related services.

- **The Collective Virtual-Appliance Language (CVL)** Researchers have developed a language for describing the composition of virtual appliances to create virtual networks of appliances. The language uses the concept of inheritance to allow appliances to be individually configured and customized while retaining the ability to be upgraded automatically.

- **Livewire: An intrusion detection system for virtual machines** Through the Livewire prototype, the researchers demonstrated that virtual machine technology can be used to build an intrusion detection system (IDS) that is both difficult to evade and difficult to attack. Like a host-based IDS, it has excellent visibility since it can access all the states of the computer being watched. Like a network-based IDS, it is not vulnerable to being disabled by the attacker.

- **Terra: A virtual machine-based platform for trusted computing** The researchers have developed a flexible architecture for trusted computing, called Terra. Terra allows applications to run in an "open box" VM with the semantics of a modern open platform, or in a "closed box" VM with those of dedicated, tamper-resistant hardware. They have developed attestation primitives to cryptographically identify the contents of closed-box VMs to remote parties and showed how to implement them efficiently.

Continued

- **Remote timing attacks** The researchers demonstrated the first remote timing attack where a private key can be extracted from a Web server. Patches to eliminate such a vulnerability were developed and applied to the OpenSSL library. Our paper on the topic won the best paper award at the 2003 Usenix Security conference.

- **C Range Error Detector (CRED): A dynamic buffer overrun detector** The researchers have developed a practical detector that finds all buffer overrun attacks as it directly checks for the bounds of memory accesses. Unlike the original referent object–based bounds-checking technique, CRED does not break existing code because it uses a novel solution to support program manipulation of out-of-bounds addresses. Finally, by restricting the bounds checks to strings in a program, CRED's overhead is greatly reduced without sacrificing protection in the experiments they performed. CRED is implemented as an extension of the GNU C compiler version 3.3.1, and has been tested on over 20 open-source programs, comprising over 1.2 million lines of C code. The software is publicly available at http://sourceforge.net/projects/boundschecking.

The most intriguing aspect of future VMM–enhanced security will be virtual machine recovery. Future VMMs will be able to record the various executions inside a VM, similar to how a digital video recorder (DVR) such as TiVo or Microsoft's Media Center continually record television programs. This record/playback capability further enhances the snapshot ability found in many VMMs today, and is useful for various areas such as development and testing cycles, as well as debugging or troubleshooting production applications. However, it is particularly useful in security incident management. Using rollback and replay of virtual machine execution, it then becomes possible to perform deep and accurate forensics to identify the techniques used in an attack, as well as recover from attacks by removing intrusion damage and backdoors from the virtual machine.

Compliance

Compliance is a very impactful area that challenges corporate enterprises' policies and processes today. The list of acronyms that account for the several millions of dollar spent each year continues to grow, and includes Sarbanes–Oxley (SOX), Gramm-Leach-Bliley (GLB), SAS70, PCI, and HIPAA, just to name a few of the U.S. domestic challenges. Couple those with international compliance laws such as Australia's APRA, the Data Protection Act (DPA), and Freedom of Information Act 2000 (FIA2000) in the UK, compliance can become a nightmare for global enterprises.

One way that virtualization can assist large enterprises with the compliance struggles extends beyond the data center to the desktop. Virtual desktop solutions have actually existed for some time with solutions based on Microsoft's Terminal Server and Citrix Presentation Server for server-hosted desktop user environments. However, using virtualization to carve up a robust server into multiple isolated desktop environments is more appealing under the scope of compliance. These solutions are maturing steadily and will soon be the standard for the typical corporate PC; however, the future of virtual desktops will solve many of the compliance problems encountered by large enterprises, including the following:

- Resolving issues with insufficient controls for change management.

- Resolving issues with abnormal transactions not being identified in a timely manner and/or the violation of security policies within the network.

- Handling centrally managed security patch processes or removal of the need to patch as a whole because of VMM security layers.

- Moving sensitive data normally stored on a PC into the data center.

- Securing desktop environments with the same level of protection and policies as in the corporate office, even for remote or offshore users, since the desktop never actually leaves the data center.

The Magic Recipe: Other Hardware and Software Virtualization Trends

While we have discussed server virtualization in general to a great degree in this book, and how you can achieve the benefits of virtualization through the use of the Xen VMM, server virtualization alone will not allow you to realize the maximum potential of the virtual infrastructure. Many of the same issues that exist within the server landscape also exist in other critical areas as well, such as underutilization (or wasted) resources, too much hardware, difficulty managing disparate hardware sets within the infrastructure, and so on.

This section discusses how to further consolidate, centralize, and optimize the hardware infrastructure on which virtual machines will run. We will briefly discuss increasing server densities with blade servers, virtual storage presentation, and application virtualization.

Increasing Density Further with Blade Servers

Although server virtualization allows IT organizations to achieve higher densities (in other words, servers per rack) than possible before, server density can be increased even further by deploying blade servers. All of the major hardware manufacturers offer an x86-based blade infrastructure that promises to accomplish the same goals of infrastructure consolidation and centralization, although their approach varies. In all cases, though, blade servers accomplish higher densities for both physical and virtual hosts.

If we compare the standard 42U server rack, the highest density that can be achieved using typical rack-mounted servers is 42 servers (using 1U servers). However, supporting this density can require a substantial cost penalty in infrastructure, factoring in the cabling, power, and core and edge switch port connections (network and SAN) to support that quantity of servers. In comparison, the same rack can accommodate up to four blade server chassis for up to 64 servers, more than a 50-percent increase in density. At the same time, the supporting infrastructure is substantially reduced through the use of integrated chassis switching for Ethernet networking and SAN connectivity. Since only uplinks to the core data center infrastructure are needed, cabling is substantially reduced, as well as the port count consumed on core enterprise switches, further reducing costs.

Blade servers are not perfect for all scenarios, though, since they are limited in expansion options. Each brand of blade servers has a specific set of I/O expansion that is available, and adoption of newer technologies tend to be available for blade servers long after the release of their standard PCI equivalents for the typical non-blade server. For most implementations, especially for deployments of VMMs such as Xen, blade servers can be an ideal hardware platform.

Storage Virtualization

The prominent gains from operating a virtualized server infrastructure include rapid provisioning, transparent and consistent hardware presentation, and the pooling of resources to maximize utilization without waste. However, many companies are not able to fully realize these benefits without also doing something about their physical storage and network. Storage and network virtualization is subsequently growing in popularity as a means to truly virtualize the entire IT infrastructure landscape.

Storage virtualization refers to the process of abstracting logical storage from physical storage. The presentation of the storage to virtual hosts, such as XenEnterprise hosts, is comprised of a location-independent address space. This is accomplished using controller logic that remaps the presented address to the actual physical address. This remapping allows for new storage configurations that help optimize the utilization and placement of data that is stored in a SAN. For example, a volume presented to a Xen host can exist across multiple physical arrays, optimizing I/O performance and spindle count. At the same time, the storage controller provisioning the virtualized storage to the hosts can analyze and trend I/O patterns and migrate volumes from one tier (Fibre-Channel storage) to another (SATA storage) without any interruption of service and without the knowledge of the host itself. Storage virtualization can also be used to make data storage more robust and resilient by using techniques such as replication and pooling.

Network Virtualization

Network virtualization is a method of combining the available resources in a network by splitting up the available bandwidth into channels, each of which is independent from the others, and each of which can be assigned (or reassigned) to a particular server or device in real time. Each channel is independently secured, and every subscriber has shared access to all the resources on the network from a single computer.

Network management can be a tedious and time-consuming business for a human administrator. Thus, network virtualization is intended to improve the productivity, efficiency, and job satisfaction of the administrator by performing many of these tasks automatically, thereby disguising the true complexity of the network. Files, images, programs, and folders can be centrally managed from a single physical site. Storage media such as hard drives and tape drives can be easily added or reassigned. Storage space can be shared or reallocated among the servers. Network virtualization is also intended to optimize network speed, reliability, flexibility, scalability, and security. Network virtualization is said to be especially effective in networks that experience sudden, large, and unforeseen surges in usage. By tackling these issues and providing increased flexibility, network virtualization can further increase Xen's (and other VMMs') value proposition to both small and large enterprises.

Summary

Virtualization is still at "buzz word" status today. As a technical concept that is helping organizations improve efficiency and substantially reduce infrastructure costs, it is gaining in popularity with IT organizations of all sizes. With the current offerings of virtualization technologies, such as XenSource's XenServer product family, and hardware assists available in current multicore processors, the popularity of virtual infrastructures is growing as companies acknowledge and desire the benefits they promise.

In the future, though, virtualization will play a more prominent role in the data center. Fueled and supported by HVM improvements and development efforts of hardware manufacturers, enhancements within the VMMs themselves, and the inclusion of other infrastructure components in the overall virtual landscape, virtual will prove to be better than "real." Xen is well poised to play an instrumental role, but will need to expand on an already impressive feature set with a road map that delivers on the true potential of virtualization.

Both small to medium-sized businesses and larger enterprises will base a large portion, if not all, of their future technology investments on products that will propel the "virtual first" methodology for infrastructure management and delivery.

Solutions Fast Track

The Unofficial Xen Road Map

- ☑ The performance and scalability of Xen guests will improve as the hypervisor takes advantage of CPU and memory virtualization in NUMA-aware architectures with multicore processors

- ☑ I/O virtualization will improve and Xen will shift I/O management even more back to the guests, further reducing the overhead on the hypervisor with direct smart I/O devices such as RDMA NICs and InfiniBand.

- ☑ Xen will continue to support additional x86-compatible operating systems through guest modification, as well as a wider range of HVM-based guest platforms.

- ☑ Although primarily targeted to run on the x86 architecture, Xen is currently being ported to the IBM PowerPC and Intel IA-64 architectures. These platforms will align with the feature set and functionality currently available on x86. There is also potential for ports to other platforms, such as Sun's UltraSPARC T1/T2.

☑ Along with growing support for new hardware technologies, the Xen hypervisor itself will grow with rich features, such as improved control tools, an open file system to support virtual hard disk images and QCOW, and virtual device enhancements.

Virtual Infrastructure in Tomorrow's Data Center

☑ Hardware economies of scale are driving improvements in virtualization. In particular, multicore and multithreaded processors promise to break the boundaries that currently limit guest performance and viability.

☑ Small and medium-sized business will benefit from virtualization due to integrating computing and a substantially reduced infrastructure, requiring a minimal investment in hardware to deploy a wide range of business applications.

☑ Larger enterprises will be turning to virtualization to improve reliability and availability, security, and compliance through improved demonstrable controls and audit trails.

The Magic Recipe: Other Hardware and Software Virtualization Trends

☑ Blade servers can help further increase the density achieved in virtual and physical server deployments. They also help lower infrastructure costs by centralizing and reducing the cabling and switch ports needed for both Ethernet networking and SAN connectivity.

☑ Storage virtualization, the abstraction of logic storage from physical storage, supports server virtualization by reducing the management overhead and increasing utilization of storage devices in a manner transparent to VMMs.

☑ Network virtualization can help further secure and improve the performance of network traffic within a virtual infrastructure by providing independently secured and isolated channels as a backbone for virtual machine communication with the rest of the public and private network.

Frequently Asked Questions

The following Frequently Asked Questions, answered by the authors of this book, are designed to both measure your understanding of the concepts presented in this chapter and to assist you with real-life implementation of these concepts. To have your questions about this chapter answered by the author, browse to **www.syngress.com/solutions** and click on the **"Ask the Author"** form.

Q: What processor architecture does Xen support today?

A: The current release of the Xen hypervisor, release 3.0.4, supports all available x86 processor architectures in the 686 (P6) family, up to and including the latest multicore offerings from Intel and AMD. Experimentally, Xen has also been ported with limited functionality to the IBM PowerPC 970 (not the POWER4/4+ or POWER5) and the Intel IA-64 (Itanium and Itanium 2) architectures. The Xen hypervisor is also future-ready to support upcoming quad-core and eight-core offerings.

Q: Which processor is recommended for Xen implementations?

A: The base premise for virtualization is to reduce the physical infrastructure by hosting the maximum number of guests on a single physical server without adversely impacting application performance and response. Based on this, it is recommended you host your Xen VMM on either Intel's Core 2 multicore architecture (Intel Core 2 Duo E, Q, X, and QX 6000-series for desktops, and Intel Xeon 5100 and 5300 series for servers) or AMD's dual-core offerings (AMD64 X2 for desktops and AMD Opteron Rev F for servers).

Q: Who is responsible for the direction and road map of the Xen VMM?

A: XenSource Inc. is responsible for setting the direction of the VMM's development efforts. While providing the majority of resources to the project, development efforts are supplemented by the open-source community, as well as IBM, Intel, HP, and others. Ian Pratt, the recognized father of Xen, in particular, maintains the official road map, as well as the "who's working on what" pages on the Xen Wiki, available at http://wiki.xensource.com/xenwiki/.

Q: Does the development of future virtualization technologies pose a threat to computer hardware manufacturers?

A: Although at face value, virtualization can pose a threat to reduced sales of hardware units, there are opportunities for hardware manufacturers to provide value-added solutions, products, and services to support virtualization. This is particularly important since software-based VMMs rely on partnerships with such companies to help develop and support their products.

Q: What is the future vision of the data center?

A: In an ideal situation, server, storage, and network hardware resources will be pooled together and centrally managed to provision, support, and monitor virtual machine instances. Knowing which physical server is running a particular guest or which array contains its data will be irrelevant. Guests will migrate as needed based on policies defined by administrators, maximizing and optimizing the use of pooled compute resources.

Q: What other companies are important to the development and growth of Xen?

A: Due to the x86-inherent nature, both Intel and AMD partnerships and code contributions to the hypervisor project are important to Xen's future. Also, IBM has played a substantial role, exclusively developing many features and components found in Xen today. However, the relationship with the various Linux distributions (such as Red Hat and Novell) will be important, and the recently forged relationship with Microsoft will prove key to the hypervisor's growth and acceptance in the IT community.

Glossary of Terms

The following virtualization terms are found in this book or are commonly used in the art of virtualization. These terms relate to Xen or to the virtual infrastructure as a whole.

A

Application Program Any computer program designed to perform a specific function directly for the user or for another application program. Compare with *Operating System*.

Application-Level Partitioning See *Operating System Partitioning*.

Autonomic Computing A self-managing computing model that controls the functioning of computer applications and systems without input from administrators, hiding the system's complexity while maintaining efficiency and availability.

B

Backend One-half of a communication endpoint. Interdomain communication is implemented using a frontend and backend device model interacting via event channels. See also *Frontend*.

Bare Metal Environment Installing a virtualization hypervisor as the first layer of software on a system before any operating system. Compare with *Hosted Environment*.

Binary Translation (BT) Technique used by virtualization software to translate instruction sets that the guest operating systems send to the virtual hardware. This is an alternative approach to paravirtualization.

Blade See *Server Blade* and *Blade Chassis*.

Blade Chassis A rack-mounted chassis that houses multiple blade servers and shared infrastructure components, such as network and storage switches, KVM switches, power, and, in some cases, cooling, resulting in the highest server density in racks commercially available today. A blade chassis can also provide centralized management for all the blade server and I/O devices hosted in the chassis. Also see *Server Blade*.

Borrowed Virtual Time The CPU scheduler commonly used in the Xen hypervisor that is used to give proportional fair shares of the CPU to guest domains. Compare with *Simple Earliest Deadline First*.

Business Continuity The requirement that a service must be available at all times or business operations will be impacted. Includes high availability and disaster recovery.

BVT See *Borrowed Virtual Time*.

C

Capacity Planning   Determining the resource requirements of a given set of business services to ensure that sufficient resources are made available before the services are implemented.

Central Processing Unit   The logic circuitry that executes the command instructions that drive a computer.

Clustering   Employing multiple computers, storage devices, and redundant interconnections to form what appears to data consumers as a single highly available system for load balancing and business continuity.

CPU   See *Central Processing Unit*.

D

Disaster Recovery   Ensuring the availability of business services at a remote location in the event that the infrastructure becomes completely unavailable at the primary location.

Domain   Within the context of Xen, a running virtual machine within which a guest operating system executes.

Domain-0   Within the context of Xen, the first domain automatically started at boot time. Domain-0 has permission to control all hardware on the system, and it is used to manage the hypervisor and the other domains.

Domain-U   Subordinate domains that are managed and controlled by the first domain, Domain-0 or dom0. Domain-Us are less privileged domains that have partial access to the underlying physical resources. In particular, they can interact with the memory subsystem in an unprivileged read-only manner. However, when they need to perform a privileged system call, they rely on those instructions being trapped and handled by the drivers in Domain-0 or the hypervisor itself.

dom0   See *Domain-0*.

domU   See *Domain-U*.

E

Emulation Presenting a facsimile of a resource that is not present to a consumer so that the consumer is not aware of the resource's absence, allowing the consumer to exist in an environment other than the one for which the consumer's system was designed.

Encapsulated A property of virtualization that refers to the way that the virtual machine's storage is contained in a single file on a storage system, greatly simplifying provision, replication, and backup.

F

Five Nines An expression used in the IT industry wherein the system is available 99.999% of the time. This is equivalent to 5.39 minutes of total downtime in a given year. See also *High Availability*.

Frontend The device as presented to the guest. The other half of the communication endpoint. Special device drivers are used to expose the device to the guest operating system. These drivers interact with backend drivers via an event channel mechanism and I/O device rings. See also *Backend*.

Full Virtualization A virtual machine monitor exports a virtual machine abstraction identical to a physical machine so that standard operating systems can run just as they would on physical hardware with no modifications. Compare with *Paravirtualization*.

G

Grid Computing Presenting a group of similar computers to job submitters as a single computer image to allow either asynchronous scheduled execution of jobs on the first available system in the group or to support execution of individual jobs across multiple physical computers.

Guest Operating System In a hosted environment, the operating system running in a virtual machine created on top of the host operating system and supported by the virtualization software. Compare with *Host Operating System*.

H

HA   See *High Availability*.

Hard Partitioning   A type of system partitioning that provides electrical isolation between partitions of a single system, while allowing them to divide the resources on the system, such as I/O devices. The separation is physical and allows multiple operating systems to run by creating multiple physical layers.

Hardware Independence   Virtualizing the underlying hardware that an operating system interacts with and ensuring that the proper virtual machine monitor and hypervisor are used to enable the operating system and its applications to be moved to any hardware platform without modification.

Hardware-Level Virtualization   See *Full Virtualization*.

Hardware Virtual Machine   The full-virtualization mode supported by Xen. This mode requires hardware support, such as Intel's Virtualization Technology (VT) and AMD's Pacifica technology.

High Availability   The requirement that a business service be continuously operational for a desirably long length of time.

High-Level Language Virtual Machine   Virtualization implemented as an application program on top of an operating system. The application exports a virtual machine that can run programs written and compiled for the specific virtual machine definition.

Host Operating System   The operating system first installed on a computer that can run virtualization software to host one or more virtual machines. Compare with *Guest Operating System*.

Hosted Environment   Installing virtualization software on top of an existing standard operating system to provide services for one or more virtual machines. The host operating system provides the virtual machines the services to interface with the underlying hardware. Compare with *Bare Metal Environment*.

HVM   See *Hardware Virtual Machine*.

Hyperthreading   See *Simultaneous Multithreading*.

Hypervisor   The first layer of software installed on a computer system in a bare metal environment, but below other virtualization services (e.g., a virtual machine monitor). It allows multiple, possibly heterogeneous operating systems to share a single hardware platform.

I

I/O Virtualization Presenting storage and networking resources to virtual machines through an emulated layer to provide hardware independence and portability.

Industry Standard Architecture See *x86 Architecture*.

Infrastructure The computing resources that support business processes.

Intel Architecture See *x86 Architecture*.

Isolated A property of virtualization that refers to the inability of a virtual machine to affect any other virtual machine even though they both are running on the same hardware.

L

Live Backup Copying an encapsulated virtual machine, while powered on, from outside of the context of the virtual machine, for archiving purposes.

Live Migration Moving a virtual machine, while powered on, from one physical system to another without interruption of the service it provides.

Load Balancing Shifting workloads among available processors and systems to increase efficiency.

Logical Processor A hyperthreading CPU presents itself as multiple logical CPUs to the operating system so that the OS will schedule threads on all the logical CPUs simultaneously as though they were independent processors.

M

Management Console A software package located externally to one or more related packages for the purpose of monitoring and administering those packages from a single location.

Multitasking See *Preemptive Multitasking*.

Multithreading The ability of an operating system or program to spawn multiple simultaneous execution paths (in addition to its main thread of execution) to more efficiently process parallel operations Compare with *Preemptive Multitasking*.

N

Network Virtualization   See *Virtual Local Area Network*.

Native Operating System   Refers to the typical operating system that is not optimized for the virtual machine environment and must run in full-virtualization mode. It cannot run in paravirtual mode. This type of operating system is also called shrink-wrapped, out-of-the-box, unmodified, or fully virtualized guest.

O

On-Demand Computing   Providing computing resources to meet business demands on an as-needed basis.

Operating System   The program that, after being initially loaded into the computer by a boot program, manages all the other programs in a computer and their interactions with the hardware. Compare with *Application Program*.

Operating System Partitioning   A feature of a standard operating system wherein isolated instances of the same host OS are created to eliminate application-level conflicts and facilitate resource management. The partitions have independent characteristics, such as hostname and IP address, but often share the same kernel with the global OS.

OS   See *Operating System*.

P

P2V   See *Physical-to-Virtual*.

Pacifica, AMD   See *Virtualization Hardware Assist*.

PAE   See *Physical Addressing Extensions*.

Paravirtualization   Supporting multiple, possibly heterogeneous operating systems on the same hardware platform by modifying the operating systems to make them "virtualization aware." This process reduces hypervisor overhead and increases performance by eliminating the need for full hardware virtualization, but it often prevents virtual-to-physical migrations. Compare with *Full Virtualization*.

Partition   An isolated new instance of the host OS, lying on it, and featuring autonomous characteristics like host name, network settings, and installed applications. Partitions are managed by a partitioning solution or component.

Pervasive Computing   The ability to perform computing tasks from any location using a variety of devices, being brought about by the convergence of miniaturized electronics, and particularly wireless technologies and the Internet.

Physical Addressing Extensions   A technique created by Intel for 32-bit x86 architecture machines to address up to 64 GB of physical memory.

Physical Layer   This is the physical machine supporting the Virtual Machine Monitor. It constitutes all the hardware resources that are available to it.

Physical-to-Virtual   Migrating an operating system and its installed applications from a physical computer to a virtual machine (or a partition) without modification. Compare with *Virtual-to-Physical*.

Policy-Based Automation   Policies automate resource management based on business-defined conditions, such as time of day, trouble alarms, and capacity or availability issues, by triggering reconfigurations without impacting running applications.

Preemptive Multitasking   The execution of more than one program at a time on the same CPU with time sharing strictly controlled by a scheduler.

Processor   See *Central Processing Unit*.

Provisioning   Making available the resources, hardware and/or software, to satisfy a business need.

S

SAN   See *Storage Area Network*.

Scalability   The ability to continue to function well when changed in size or volume either directly or when moved to a new context

SEDF   See *Simple Earliest Deadline First*.

Self-Healing   Any hardware or software system that can detect its own faults and inefficiencies and make the necessary adjustments to restore itself to normal operation.

Server Blade   A computer system contained on a single pluggable board. Most server blades consist of CPUs and memory, whereas some also contain the I/O components. High efficiency is achieved by removing power, cooling, and network and storage interconnects from the server blades themselves and using a high-bandwidth midplane or backplane for I/O traffic.

Server Consolidation Reducing existing infrastructure server sprawl by eliminating unnecessary services and hosting the remaining services on fewer physical servers, often through the use of server virtualization, to achieve fewer points of management and lower operating costs.

Server Containment An IT strategy to minimize server sprawl by provisioning new services on virtual machines hosted on a virtual infrastructure leading to better infrastructure unification.

Server Rationalization Executing server consolidation with a concentration on reducing management complexity, often by consolidating to a smaller number of more homogeneous computers.

Server Sprawl The irrational proliferation of servers in the corporate infrastructure due to the policy of one application/one server.

Server Virtualization Decoupling server hardware from the operating systems and applications that run on it, either by partitioning the hardware into multiple virtual machines or aggregating it into a single larger server image.

Service Level Agreement Parameters dictated by a business unit to a service provider with regard to performance, availability, and resiliency.

Shadow Page Table A shadow version of a guest operating system's page table. Useful for numerous things, such as tracking dirty pages during live migration.

Simple Earliest Deadline First Another CPU scheduler available in the Xen hypervisor to provide weighted CPU sharing in an intuitive way to guest domains. It uses real-time algorithms to ensure time guarantees. Compare with *Borrowed Virtual Time*.

Simultaneous Multithreading Similar to time-slice multithreading, or superthreading, except that the multiple threads introduced into the pipelines on a given clock cycle can be from any available process, not all from the same process. This type of CPU often presents multiple logical processors to the OS. Compare with *Time-Slice Multithreading*.

SLA See *Service Level Agreement*.

SMP See *Symmetric Multiprocessing*.

SPT See *Shadow Page Table*.

Storage Area Network A collection of storage resources connected to computers through a high-speed network to facilitate storage provisioning and increase overall utilization.

Storage Virtualization The pooling of physical storage on a storage area network into what appears to be a single storage device that is managed and provisioned from a central console. See also *Storage Area Network*.

Superthreading See *Time-Slice Multithreading*.

Symmetric Multiprocessing Employing more than one CPU to simultaneously execute more than one program or thread with equal probability.

T

Time-Slice Multithreading The capability of a CPU to issue more than one thread of the same process into multiple pipelines on the same clock cycle. That is, more than one thread can enter the pipelines at once, but they must all be from the same process. This capability increases processing efficiency by allowing the execution of available threads when other threads have stalled, such as waiting on memory. It requires thread-level parallelism within a process. Compare with *Simultaneous Multithreading*.

U

Ubiquitous Computing See *Pervasive Computing*.

Utility Computing A service provisioning model in which a service provider makes computing resources and infrastructure management available to the customer as needed, or on-demand computing, and charges them based on metered usage rather than a flat rate.

V

V2P See *Virtual-to-Physical*.

V2V See *Virtual-to-Virtual*.

VBD See *Virtual Block Device*.

VIF See *Virtual Interface*.

Virtual Block Device   The name of the storage-based backend device connected by an event channel to a storage-based frontend on the guest.

Virtual Infrastructure   Creating a layer of abstraction between computing, storage, and networking hardware, and the operating systems running on it, resulting in a pool of homogeneous resources across the data center on which business services can be quickly and reliably provisioned and managed.

Virtual Interface   The name of the network backend device connected by an event channel to a network frontend on the guest. Compare with *Virtual Block Device.*

Virtual Local Area Network   Partitioning available network resources into independent groups to insulate related traffic and reduce management complexity.

Virtual Machine   A partitioned, isolated, and encapsulated abstraction of physical hardware to present a consistent, logical image of hardware resources (processor, memory, disk, network) to a hosted operating system to enable server virtualization.

Virtual Machine Monitor   A virtualization software layer managing hardware requests from a virtual machine, passing them to a hypervisor, and simulating answers from real hardware.

Virtual Symmetric Multiprocessing   Providing two or more virtual processors to a single virtual machine or partition.

Virtual-to-Physical   Migrating an operating system and its applications from a virtual machine or partition to a physical computer without modification. Compare with *Physical-to-Virtual.*

Virtual-to-Virtual   Migrating an operating system and its applications from a virtual machine or partition hosted in one virtual infrastructure to a virtual machine or partition hosted in a different virtual infrastructure, without modification.

Virtualization   The decoupling of a resource or request for a service from the underlying physical delivery of that service such that the consumer needs no knowledge of the characteristics of the delivery system.

Virtualization Hardware Assist   Moving aspects of virtualization from a software hypervisor to CPU-level hardware to increase speed and efficiency. Intel is implementing as VT; AMD as Pacifica.

Virtualization Layer   The software layer provided by a Virtual Machine Manager that supports one or more virtual machines.

VLAN   See *Virtual Local Area Network*.

VMM   See *Virtual Machine Monitor*.

VSMP   See *Virtual Symmetric Multiprocessing*.

VT, Intel   See *Virtualization Hardware Assist*.

W

Workload Management   Ensuring the existence of sufficient resources to meet business service demands or ensuring the ability to quickly provision them on the infrastructure.

X

x86 Architecture   A computer hardware platform based on the Intel family architecture begun with the 8086 and continuing to the Pentium and later families. Includes compatible chipsets manufactured by companies such as AMD. Best known for being the primary platform for the Microsoft Windows and Linux operating systems.

Other Virtualization Technologies and How They Compare with Xen

This book has provided the readers with an in-depth account of the Xen virtual machine monitor as well as the history of, theory behind, and an outlook forecast of virtualization technologies as a whole. We have discussed the different components of the virtual infrastructure, including hardware, software hypervisors, and other infrastructure layers, such as storage and networking.

In this appendix, we will take a more agnostic look at the different types of server virtualization and other virtual machine software available. We will also note how these products compare with Xen.

Hardware Virtualization Software

Virtualization software that presents a virtual set of hardware to a guest operating system makes up the majority of server virtualization products available. These virtualization products provide a VMM that either partially or fully virtualizes the underlying hardware, allowing both modified and unmodified guests to run in a safe and isolated fashion.

The most popular of these products, especially for the enterprise, are VMware, Microsoft, and Xen, in order of commercial market share. VMware and Xen are the most mature of the group, offering the richest set of features, such as live migration and bare-metal installation and execution of the hypervisor, as well as the widest array of supported guest operating systems.

Operating System-Level Virtualization Software

Operating system-level virtualization software is either included as part of an operating system, such as Solaris containers, or is installed on top of an operating system, such as Virtuozzo and OpenVZ. These products present an operating system environment that is fully or partially isolated from the host operating system, allowing for safe application execution at native speeds.

> **NOTE**
>
> The key differentiator with operating system-level virtualization software is that, unlike hardware virtualization software, no virtual hardware environment is presented to guests.

In a few ways, operating system-level virtualization software products provide some advantages over hardware virtualization software. First, they can usually run the same operating system that the host is running without having to duplicate every layer and subsystem. This is possible because some of the lower-level functions are shared with the host, thus eliminating the overhead that duplication would cause. Second, it is possible to offer a patch-once approach, allowing administrators to patch the host operating system, which in turn patches subordinate guests. Finally, these products tend to offer the widest array of hardware compatibility, because practically any device that can be used in the host operating system can be used in the guest virtual environments as well.

Software Comparison Matrix

In Tables B.1 through B.4, we present you with a comparison of various hardware and operating system-level virtualization software products. These tables are not an exhaustive list of all virtualization software offerings available, but rather a comprehensive comparison of many of the popular products is use today. Both the open-source Xen hypervisor and the commercial XenServer product family from XenSource have also been included in the list.

Table B.1 List of Hardware Virtualization Software

Name	Creator/Founder	Host CPU	Guest CPU	Host OS	Guest OS (Officially Supported)
Bochs	Kevin Lawton	x86, SPARC, PowerPC, Alpha, MIPS	x86	AIX, BeOS, IRIX, Linux, OS X, Windows	BSD, Linux, Windows
CoLinux	Dan Aloni	x86	x86	Linux, Windows	Linux
Denali	University of Washington	x86	x86	Denali	Ilwaco, NetBSD
KVM	KVM Project	x86	x86	Linux	Linux, Windows
Logical Domains	Sun	UltraSPARC T1	SPARC	Solaris	FreeBSD, Linux, Solaris
Parallels Workstation	Parallels, Inc.	x86	x86	Linux, Windows	FreeBSD, Linux OS/2, Solaris, Windows
QEMU	Fabrice Bellard	x86, IA-64, SPARC, PowerPC, S/390, ARM, M68k	x86, SPARC, PowerPC, MIPS	BeOS, BSD, Linux, OS X, Solaris, Linux	BSD, Linux, Windows
UML	Jeff Dike	x86	x86	Linux	Linux

Continued

Table B.1 continued List of Hardware Virtualization Software

Name	Creator/Founder	Host CPU	Guest CPU	Host OS	Guest OS (Officially Supported)
Virtual Iron	Virtual Iron Software, Inc.	x86	x86	none; bare-metal	BSD, Linux, OS/2, Windows
Virtual PC	Microsoft	x86, PowerPC	x86	OS X, Windows	Linux, OS/2, Windows
Virtual Server	Microsoft	x86	x86	Windows	Linux, Windows
VMware Workstation	VMware	x86	x86	Linux, Windows	FreeBSD, Linux, Netware, Solaris, Windows
VMware Server	VMware	x86	x86	Linux, Windows	FreeBSD, Linux, Netware, Solaris, Windows
VMware ESX Server	VMware	x86	x86	None; bare-metal	FreeBSD, Linux, Netware, Solaris, Windows
Xen	University of Cambridge	x86, IA-64, PowerPC	x86	NetBSD, Linux, Solaris	xBSD, Linux, Solaris, Windows

Continued

Table B.1 continued List of Hardware Virtualization Software

Name	Creator/Founder	Host CPU	Guest CPU	Host OS	Guest OS (Officially Supported)
XenServer Family	XenSource	x86	x86	None; bare-metal	Linux, Windows
z/VM	IBM	z/Arch.	z/Arch.	None; z/VM runs directly inside LPAR	Linux for System z, z/OS, z/TPF, z/VSE, z/VM

Table B.2 Continued List of Hardware Virtualization Software

Name	SMP	Type of Virtualization	License Type	Typical Use	Relative speed	Commercial Support Available?
Bochs	Yes	Emulation	LGPL	Developer, hobbyist	Very slow	No
CoLinux	No	Porting	GPL	Developer, hobbyist	Native	No
Denali	No	Paravirtualization, porting	N/A	Research	Slow	No
KVM	No	In-kernel virtualization	GPL	Developer, hobbyist, server consolidation	Near-native	No
Logical Domains	Yes	Paravirtualization	Free CDDL	Web hosting, server consolidation	Near-native	Yes
Parallels Workstation	No	Full virtualization	Retail	Developer, hobbyist, tester, business workstation	Near-native	Yes
QEMU	Yes	Full virtualization	GPL, LGPL	Developer, hobbyist, server consolidation	Near-native	No
UML	No	Porting	GPL	Developer, hobbyist	Slow	No

Continued

Table B.2 Continued List of Hardware Virtualization Software

Name	SMP	Type of Virtualization	License Type	Typical Use	Relative speed	Commercial Support Available?
Virtual Iron	Yes	Native virtualization	Retail	Developer, tester, server consolidation	Near-native	Yes
Virtual PC	No	Full virtualization	Free Retail	Developer, tester, training	Near-native with VM additions	Yes
Virtual Server	No	Full virtualization	Free Retail	Developer, tester, training, enterprise server consolidation	Near-native with VM additions	Yes
VMware Workstation	Yes	Full virtualization	Retail	Developer, tester, training	Near-native with VM tools	Yes
VMware Server	Yes	Full virtualization	Free Retail	Developer, tester, training, server consolidation	Near-native with VM tools	Yes
VMware ESX Server	Yes	Full virtualization	Retail	Developer, tester, training, enterprise server consolidation	Near-native with VM tools	Yes

Continued

Table B.2 Continued List of Hardware Virtualization Software

Name	SMP	Type of Virtualization	License Type	Typical Use	Relative speed	Commercial Support Available?
Xen	Yes	Paravirtualization with porting, native virtualization	GPL	Developer, tester, training, server consolidation	Near-native	No
XenServer Family	Yes	Paravirtualization with porting, native virtualization	Retail	Developer, tester, training, enterprise server consolidation	Near-native	Yes
z/VM	Yes	Paravirtualization	Retail	Enterprise servers	Native	Native Yes

Table B.3 List of Operating System-Level Virtualization Software

Name	Creator	Host CPU	Guest CPU	Host OS	Guest OS (Officially Supported)
Jails	FreeBSD	x86	x86	FreeBSD	FreeBSD
OpenVZ	SWsoft	x86, IA-64, PowerPC, SPARC	x86, IA-64, PowerPC, SPARC	Linux	Linux
Solaris Containers	Sun	x86, SPARC	x86, SPARC	Solaris	Linux, Solaris
Virtuozzo	SWsoft	x86, IA-64	x86, IA-64	Linux, Windows	Linux, Windows
VServer	Open-source project	x86, IA-64, Alpha, PowerPC, SPARC, ARM, S/390, MIPS	same as host	Linux	Linux

Table B.4 Continued List of Operating System-Level Virtualization Software

Name	SMP	License	Typical Use	Relative Speed	Commercial Support Available?
Jails	Yes	FreeBSD	Web hosting, server consolidation	Native	No
OpenVZ	Yes	GPL	Server consolidation	Native	No
Solaris Containers	Yes	Free CDDL	Developer, tester, enterprise server consolidation, Web hosting	Native	Yes
Virtuozzo	Yes	Retail	Developer, tester, server consolidation	Native	Yes
VServer	Yes	GPL	Developer, Web hosting, server consolidation	Native	No

Products are listed in alphabetical order, and present the following information for each product:

- **Creator/founder** The products can be placed in two categories: commercial or open source. This column lists either the founder of the open-source project, the project itself, or the commercial (for-profit) company that developed the product.

- **Host CPU** The CPU architectures upon which the product can run. Note that not all features are available on all architectures.

- **Guest CPU** Lists the CPU architecture that virtual machines created with the product will see. The most popular architecture is x86.

- **Host OS** The operating system required to install the virtualization software. Note that some products are bare-metal, meaning that they are distributed and installed from media directly on an empty server.

- **Guest OS (officially supported)** This is the list of operating systems that can be run inside virtual machines, as indicated by the project's current documentation or by the commercial developer. Although it may be possible to run additional operating systems, such configurations are not supported and not recommended.

- **SMP** This column indicates whether virtual machines running on the virtualization software support multiple processing (SMP) or not. Note that this is not whether the software supports multiple processors, as all of the products in the list do.

- **Type of virtualization (hardware virtualization only)** This column indicates the virtualization technique used by the software. Primarily, each product can be broken down into four types: emulation, porting, paravirtualization, full virtualization, and native virtualization. For more information about these types, see Chapter 1.

- **License type** This column indicates the type of license agreement for the use of the product.

- **Typical use** The common use for the product, although the product can be used for many other uses.

- **Relative speed** The operating speed of the typical virtual machine as compared with bare metal performance.

- **Commercial support** Whether paid commercial support is available for the product. In most cases, if support is available, it is through the creator of the product.

Index